Casebook Series

GENERAL EDITOR: A. E. Dyson

IN PREPARATION

Shakespeare
Julius Caesar

A CASEBOOK

EDITED BY

PETER URE

Aurora Publishers Incorporated
NASHVILLE/LONDON

FIRST PUBLISHED 1969 BY
MACMILLAN AND COMPANY LIMITED
LONDON, ENGLAND

COPYRIGHT © 1970 BY
AURORA PUBLISHERS INCORPORATED
NASHVILLE, TENNESSEE 37219
LIBRARY OF CONGRESS CATALOG CARD NUMBER: 76-127581
STANDARD BOOK NUMBER: 87695-049-7
MANUFACTURED IN THE UNITED STATES OF AMERICA

CONTENTS

ACKNOWLEDGEMENTS

Extract from *Shaw on Shakespeare*, ed. Edwin Wilson (1962) (The Public Trustee and the Society of Authors); W. Warde Fowler, *Roman Essays and Interpretations* (The Clarendon Press); C. H. Herford, *Ben Jonson* (The Clarendon Press); G. Wilson Knight, 'The Eroticism of *Julius Caesar*', from *The Imperial Theme* (Methuen & Co. Ltd); J. E. Phillips, *The State in Shakespeare's Greek and Roman Plays* (Columbia University Press); Professor S. Musgrove, lecture on *Julius Caesar* to the Australian English Association, 1941; E. M. Forster, *Two Cheers for Democracy* (Edward Arnold (Publishers) Ltd and Harcourt, Brace & World Inc.); Willard Farnham, *Shakespeare's Tragic Frontier* (University of California Press); John Houseman, 'Filming *Julius Caesar*', from *Sight and Sound*, July–September 1953; Herbert Blau, 'Language and Structure in Poetic Drama', from *Modern Language Quarterly*, XVIII (1957); R. A. G. Carson, 'The Ides of March', from *History Today*, March 1957; M. M. Mahood, *Shakespeare's Wordplay* (Methuen & Co. Ltd); Anne Righter, *Shakespeare and the Idea of the Play* (Chatto & Windus Ltd); Roland Mushat Frye, 'The fault, dear Brutus . . .', from *Shakespeare and Christian Doctrine* (Princeton University Press; © Roland Mushat Frye 1963); Geoffrey Bullough, *Narrative and Dramatic Sources of Shakespeare*, V (Routledge & Kegan Paul Ltd and Columbia University Press); Professor Norman Rabkin, 'Structure, Convention and Meaning in *Julius Caesar*', from *Journal of English and Germanic Philology*, LXIII (1964); J. I. M. Stewart, *Character and Motive in Shakespeare* (Longmans, Green & Co. Ltd); L. C. Knights, 'Personality and Politics in *Julius Caesar*', from *Further Explorations* (Chatto & Windus Ltd and Stanford University Press); Leo Kirschbaum, 'Shakespeare's Stage Blood and its

Critical Significance', from *Publications of the Modern Language Association of America*, LXIV (1949); Brents Stirling, 'Or Else This Were a Savage Spectacle', from *Unity in Shakespearian Tragedy* (Columbia University Press); Virgil K. Whitaker, *Shakespeare's Use of Learning* (Henry E. Huntington Library and Art Gallery); Ernest Schanzer, *Shakespeare's Problem Plays* (Routledge & Kegan Paul Ltd and Schocken Books Inc.); Sir Mark Hunter, 'Politics and Characters in Shakespeare's *Julius Caesar*', from *Royal Society of Literature Essays by Divers Hands*, X (1931); John Anson, '*Julius Caesar*: Politics of the Hardened Heart', from *Shakespeare Studies*, II (1966); John Palmer, *Political Characters of Shakespeare* (the Executors of the Estate of John Palmer); Harley Granville-Barker, *Prefaces to King Lear, Cymbeline and Julius Caesar* (B. T. Batsford Ltd and Princeton University Press; © 1963); John Dover Wilson, 'Ben Jonson and *Julius Caesar*', from *Shakespeare Survey* 2 (Cambridge University Press).

GENERAL EDITOR'S PREFACE

EACH of this series of Casebooks concerns either one well-known and influential work of literature or two or three closely linked works. The main section consists of critical readings, mostly modern, brought together from journals and books. A selection of reviews and comments by the author's contemporaries is also included, and sometimes comments from the author himself. The Editor's Introduction charts the reputation of the work from its first appearance until the present time.

What is the purpose of such a collection? Chiefly, to assist reading. Our first response to literature may be, or seem to be, 'personal'. Certain qualities of vigour, profundity, beauty or 'truth to experience' strike us, and the work gains a foothold in our mind. Later, an isolated phrase or passage may return to haunt or illuminate. Where did we hear that? we wonder – it could scarcely be better put.

In these and similar ways appreciation begins, but major literature prompts to very much more. There are certain facts we need to know if we are to understand properly. Who were the author's original readers, and what assumptions did he share with them? What was his theory of literature? Was he committed to a particular historical situation, or to a set of beliefs? We need historians as well as critics to help us with this. But there are also more purely literary factors to take account of: the work's structure and rhetoric; its symbols and archetypes; its tone, genre and texture; its use of language; the words on the page. In all these matters critics can inform and enrich our individual responses by offering imaginative recreations of their own.

For the life of a book is not, after all, merely 'personal'; it is more like a tripartite dialogue, between a writer living 'then', a reader living 'now', and whatever forces of survival and honour link the two. Criticism is the public manifestation of this dialogue, a witness to the continuing power of literature to arouse and excite. It illuminates the possibilities and rewards of the dialogue, pushing 'interpretation' as far forward as it can go.

And here, indeed, is the rub: how far can it go? Where does 'interpretation' end and nonsense begin? Why is one interpretation superior to another, and why does each age need to interpret for itself? The critic knows that his insights have value only in so far as they serve the text, and that he must take account of views differing sharply from his own. He knows that his own writing will be judged as well as the work he writes about, so that he cannot simply assert inner illumination or a differing taste.

The critical forum is a place of vigorous conflict and disagreement, but there is nothing in this to cause dismay. What is attested is the complexity of human experience and the richness of literature, not any chaos or relativity of taste. A critic is better seen, no doubt, as an explorer than as an 'authority', but explorers ought to be, and usually are, well equipped. The effect of good criticism is to convince us of what C. S. Lewis called 'the enormous extension of our being which we owe to authors'. A Casebook will be justified only if it helps to promote the same end.

A single volume can represent no more than a small selection of critical opinions. Some critics have been excluded for reasons of space, and it is hoped that readers will follow up the further suggestions in the Select Bibliography. Other contributions have been severed from their original context, to which some readers may wish to return. Indeed, if they take a hint from the critics represented here, they certainly will.

A. E. DYSON

INTRODUCTION

I

ON 21 September 1599, a Swiss doctor travelling in England, who was much taken with the London playhouses and their elegant entertainments, went across the river at about two o'clock in the afternoon to the 'house with the thatched roof' in order to see a play about Julius Caesar. He recorded afterwards in his journal that it was very well acted by about fifteen persons, and that there was a dance at the end. What he had seen was almost certainly a performance of Shakespeare's play during its first run at any theatre. It is rare for us to be able to date a performance at an Elizabethan public playhouse so exactly; the interest on this occasion is enormously increased because the theatre concerned was to be the most famous in modern Europe – the first Globe (1599–1613) of Shakespeare's company, the King's or Lord Chamberlain's Men, which had just that autumn opened its doors. It seems probable that in the death of the mighty Caesar, the 'first Emperor', Shakespeare and his fellows carefully selected a subject which would match up to the conscious splendours of the occasion. There in the fine building with its gleaming roof, with the smell of fresh wood and cloth, and with its imitation marble glowing with new lustre, there was to be celebrated not some Italian baudery or vain and wanton toy of love but the excellent tragedy of the famous ruler of the most high and palmy state of Rome. In the play Cassius says:

> How many ages hence
> Shall this our lofty scene be acted over,
> In states unborn, and accents yet unknown!

Isolated from their subtle context, the lines beat with a pulse of pride. It must have been with such a proud sense of occasion that the Lord Chamberlain's Men played out their lofty scene.

The Tragedie of Julius Caesar, as it is entitled in the First Folio of 1623 (which is the only source of our text of this play), has not generally wanted for an audience since. The subject itself is still a famous one; Prince Edward in *Richard III*, schoolboy as he was, knew that

> Death makes no conquest of this conqueror;
> For now he lives in fame, though not in life.

Long after its first performances in 1599 the play remained in the repertoire of Shakespeare's company and was several times performed at Court, even up to nearly forty years later. Its theatrical life was vigorous throughout the history of the seventeenth- and eighteenth-century theatre. There was a break in the middle of the next century, but an elaborate revival by Sir Herbert Beerbohm Tree in 1898 brought the play back, and it has held its position on both stage and cinema screen since then. The Hollywood film version (with Sir John Gielgud as Cassius) remains the only really decent American film of a Shakespeare play; Marlon Brando's performance as Antony, which was very controversial at the time, has in fact proved unforgettable. Disappointingly enough, from all this theatrical life (which includes three operas based on the play) there have survived few really vivid written records.

If there is a reason for this, it may be connected with the fact that until the twentieth century there was a tendency for criticism to take the play for granted. Its 'high Roman' austerity, which is certainly an important element in it, may still endear it to some; but what Granville-Barker called 'noble Romans, flinging their togas gracefully about them' are not any longer much relished. Even Dr Johnson thought the play 'somewhat cold and unaffecting': the natural vigour of Shakespeare's genius had been obstructed by the need to adhere to 'Roman manners'. It is easy to mistake the patrician behaviours for frigidity, nor is M. W. MacCallum's vision of Brutus as a character cast 'very much in the form of a cultured and high-souled English nobleman' extremely congenial. MacCallum, though, was a sound critic of the Roman plays, and in case his view should seem typically

Victorian we might remember that years earlier Edward Dowden, another Victorian, if an Anglo-Irish one, was much sharper about Shakespeare's critical detachment from a Brutus whom he did not admire as much as Plutarch did. Like it or not, though, the play is full of *romanitas*, of an imaginative awareness of the unique greatness of Roman power, even in crisis, and of what it must have been like to be at the vortex of that power and to help to exercise it. As a playwright Shakespeare communicates some of this to us by dramatising Roman government and manners – the city and the camp, tribunes, consuls, soothsayers and even togas: Caesar's robe, on more than one occasion, plays a salient role. If we agree with Dr Johnson, and with Mark Van Doren, that Shakespeare wrote as if he were '*too* conscious of a remote Roman grandeur' (in Van Doren's words), that robe, ghastlily plucked off to reveal a naked corpse, may make us think again about remote and graceful togas.

Yet there is no need to deny that Shakespeare often requires effects of Roman grandeur. His audience, as they packed themselves into the new Globe, held, with Prince Edward's naive confidence, that 'that Julius Caesar was a famous man'. In the dearer, threepenny seats, which the Swiss visitor tells us about, there were persons of moderate ostentation who were interested in the more inward difficulties of *imperium* and were capable of reflecting upon the ways in which political causes interlock with the strengths and weaknesses of living men. It is these latter elements that modern criticism of the play has specially attended to. But Shakespeare doubtless calculated that even the graver sort would have an appetite for the antique Roman glories about which they had learnt when they were young.

This second essay in the Roman mode (his first was *Titus Andronicus*) is not one of Shakespeare's very greatest plays, but it has the *comprehensive* character of a masterpiece. It is theatrical and driven by sustained poetical energy, without any lapses into the threadbare writing that occurs in the English history plays that precede it; and yet it is analytic and profound. When he wrote it Shakespeare did not take the famousness of his history for granted but made it his business, as Henry James thought the

novelist should, to 'dramatise! dramatise!' all the time. Other
Elizabethans – and there were many – who wrote about Caesar
were in danger of supposing that the name of Caesar would do
their work for them. *Julius Caesar* has much of the quality of
Hamlet, the next play, in being largely actor-proof. Antony's
scene in the Forum (III ii), which reads less well than it plays,
maintains its miraculous internal energies and forward drive
even when the actor is incompetent and understands nothing of
the skills of Elizabethan dramatic speech.

Van Doren has complained that there is 'more rhetoric than
poetry' in the play. The distinction is a bad one, for poetry is in
many ways best regarded as a branch of what the Elizabethans
called rhetoric. It is especially misleading in the case of this
play to think of them as opposed to each other. Antony's Forum
speech is a great act of oratory. Elsewhere, the play has much
'speechifying'; but we normally use that word to imply that we
are being got at and have become bored or irritated in consequence; Antony's speechifying, and that of Brutus and Cassius
and the rest, is directed not at us but at each other. The speeches
are deeds done, in a society which is shown as moving and being
moved primarily by the power of words, or, rather, by the arts
of the orator, words accompanied by the proper and revealing
gestures. (Shakespeare shockingly manipulates this for dramatic
effect when at the point of the assassination Casca says '*Speak,
hands, for me!*': only gesture remains – a gesture brutally remote
from the discipline of the schools of rhetoric, although words
soon resume their sway.) Because the speechifying is, in this
sense, action, it becomes fully theatrical. In the theatre, words,
whether we call them poetry or rhetoric (and both these terms
are more useful, perhaps, to describe words as they can be ordered
in places *other* than the theatre), can only be dull unless they have
been transmuted in this way. *Julius Caesar* is comprehensive
partly because its mutations of words are remarkably rich and
varied: Caesar cheers himself up, or swells himself up, Brutus
agonises with his soul in private or wrestles with Cassius's
infiltration of it, politicians soothe or inflame the people, with
words men strike through each others' armour and at each others'

wills; words are everybody's profession. This may have been Shakespeare's idea about politicians, or about great Rome itself, the Rome of Cicero and Quintilian, the original fountains of Renaissance rhetoric. *Julius Caesar* is comprehensive because its wordiness and its theatricality exquisitely minister to each other. And when this interdependence, this living by words, breaks down, there remain the sword and the knife: Shakespeare also makes his dramatic occasions out of the link between volubility and deadly silence.

II

No marked tradition of comment about the play established itself much before the middle of the last century. The few great writers who made judgements – Ben Jonson, Dryden, Dr Johnson, Coleridge – did so unsystematically, being mainly concerned with details that happened to interest them. As we might expect, Coleridge pitched on an interpretative problem of major size (Brutus's soliloquy, II i 10–34) but quite failed to solve it. Dryden, starting from some thoughts about this play, went on to attempt a reasonably comprehensive comparison of Shakespeare and Ben Jonson; in it he contrives to present Shakespeare as both an artless peasant and a master of design, and, unable as usual to reconcile his admiration with his principles, hardly seems to be aware that Shakespeare cannot have been both. There is evidence from the first two centuries of comment that the quarrel scene between Brutus and Cassius (IV ii) was a special focus of interest: Fletcher the dramatist may have taken ideas from it as early as *The Maid's Tragedy* (1610) and *Valentinian* (1614). This is because it shows two heroic noble friends at odds – a favourite subject for heroic tragedy for at least a century. Towards the end of the seventeenth century, the archivist and critic Thomas Rymer (d. 1713), a celebrated populariser of French formalist ideas about literature, made Shakespeare the chief target of his polemics against English barbarism. He is at his most carping and least cogent in the pages which he gives to *Julius Caesar* at the end of *A Short View of Tragedy* (1693):

'*Caesar* and *Brutus* were above his conversation: To put them in Fools Coats, and make them Jack-puddens in the *Shakespear* dress, is a *Sacriledge....*'* He thought the play full of irrelevance, and is horribly shocked by the way in which the stately Brutus is turned into a 'son of the Shambles' because he urges the conspirators to bathe 'up to the elbows' in the Dictator's blood. Though one often suspects that Rymer was blind to Shakespeare's genius because he *wouldn't* see it, there is something refreshing about him: *he* didn't think that Shakespeare's Romans were too cold and classical – for his taste they were nothing like high-minded enough; and in the bathing-in-blood episode he points to an element in the play which must be explained and not ignored. More than two centuries were to elapse before a real attempt was made to understand Rymer's 'Shambles' by such modern writers as Brents Stirling and the late Leo Kirschbaum.

Dr Johnson's brief comments, already quoted, may reflect educated opinion in the eighteenth century. If so, it shows how impossible it is to give coherence to the history of opinion about the play in his time. Although he was an immeasurably greater critic than Rymer, both men owed general allegiance to the same set of ideas about literature: yet the one thought the play cold and constrained, the other thought it villainous and low. It is partly no doubt the difference between extremism and common sense. The story of Voltaire's entanglement with the play has been related in T. R. Lounsbury's *Shakespeare and Voltaire* (1902). His reactions were compounded of unsurprised contempt for the brutal Anglo-Saxon absurdity of it all (Rymer all over again) and an admission that the piece moved and held him from the first scene:

... there is much that is natural: that naturalness is often low, vulgar, and barbarous. These are no Romans who are talking; they are peasants of a past age conspiring in a wine-shop; and Caesar, who invites them to drink a bottle with him, does not in the least resemble Julius Caesar. The absurdity is outlandish,

* *Critical Works*, ed. Curt A. Zimansky (New Haven, Conn., 1956) p. 165.

but there is no weakness. From time to time sublime points glitter and shine forth like diamonds scattered in the mire. I must admit that I like this monstrous spectacle more than long confidences of a cold love, or political discussions yet more cold.*

Others as late as the nineteenth century were to be shocked at Shakespeare's disrespectful handling of persons of such consequence as Julius Caesar; one wonders whether they would have supported the proposition that Caesar *never* invited his friends to drink a bottle with him. Such commentators often assume that their own view that Caesar was not only the greatest of politicians and national heroes but also a man of unruffled personal decorum at all times is universally accepted. It was a mistaken assumption; the recent work of Geoffrey Bullough and others has shown that the character and status of Caesar have nearly always been matters of fierce dispute, like those of Brutus. But the imaginary consensus was used to justify some strong feelings about Shakespeare's departure from the rules of classical composition and classical composure.

In the nineteenth century criticism became more systematic, especially in the hands of foreign commentators (at this time it was still considered ungentlemanly at English universities for the English to study their own literature). The important areas of discussion – and they are still the ones which every student of the play has to think about sooner or later – were, firstly, the construction, and, secondly, the characterisation of Brutus, Caesar and Cassius. At first sight, it seems queer to have the titular hero murdered half-way through; some would accept this if only the title were 'Marcus Brutus': others argue that the play is just ill-made; the wind goes out of its sails a good deal after the death of Caesar, 'the third and fourth acts are ill connected' (as Henry Hallam said), and the play has two peaks with a sag in the middle. The plot of the play can easily be described so as to make it look as though the story was badly managed. Shakespeare

* Quoted from the Furness Variorum edition (Philadelphia, 1913) p. 421.

knew, as Polonius did, that the famous thing about Caesar was that he was 'killed at the Capitol' and that that is basically what people would come to see at the Globe; they might even get bored if the actual killing were too long delayed and mutter ''Twere well it were done quickly' – in *Macbeth*, too, the big killing comes early. Shakespeare, in satisfying this demand, was at pains to see that no sag occurred, and therefore the whole of the third Act, after Caesar dies seventy-six lines from its beginning, is a most sustained and glorious piece of writing, and, in performance, enthralling. The way in which Antony, hitherto a fairly obscure personage, grips the action is a paradigm for the way in which his inventor ensures, by screwing everything up to intensest pitch, that we shall not feel that because Caesar is dead the show is over. Indeed, the new note of passion, almost the new political style – so well brought out in the Brando performance – in much of the writing for Antony (as in his speech 'O pardon me, thou bleeding piece of earth . . .', III i 254–75) makes us realise how relatively dawdling, in accord with the hesitancy of Brutus, are the first two Acts. So unbroken is the movement of the third that in a modern production we usually have to wait until it is over before we have the interval. This may make the last two Acts seem somewhat self-contained, or even ill-connected in Hallam's sense; but interest in the fortunes of Brutus and Cassius sustains us to the end, if at a somewhat lower level of engagement than during the marvellous third Act.

Problems of construction and characterisation mingle, as they usually do, when we come to the controversy about who is the real hero of the play. It has been argued that Caesar has a structure-sustaining role to play even after he is dead: his *spirit* walks abroad, and the play is more than the story of Caesar's life (which does come to an end half-way through) – it is the working-out of what Dowden calls the 'Caesar-myth'. In this reading, Caesar and his after-image are the monstrous and heroic Feature visible from every place. In its exaggerated forms, this view may somewhat rewrite the play as a Celtic or otherworldly legend of the Emperor and his Severed Head – like the old cults about speaking heads which avenge their own murders and saints whose posthumous lives are so much richer than their earthly ones.

But, of course, there is in the play an element of 'Caesar's revenge', though there does not seem much reason for identifying Caesar as its sole hero. Adrien Bonjour in his book *The Structure of Julius Caesar* (1958) shows us that picking *any* hero does not much help us to understand the interrelation of structure and characterisation. By making us look first at the victimisation of Caesar and then at the long drawn-out expiation by Brutus, Shakespeare has struck a balance of our sympathies; in the end there is a bleeding body in either scale, and the last victim is Caesar's Brutus as the first was Brutus's Caesar. In Bonjour's words:

Julius Caesar is the story of a political murder and a posthumous revenge. A dramatic story where the victim of the murderer turns into the soul of the revenge, and the murderer himself into the avenger's victim ... our sympathies are made to oscillate from one hero, and one party, to the other, according to the side of the Roman medal we are shown, obverse and then reverse, until the swing of the pendulum eventually ceases ... and then the sympathies are perfectly divided between the victim of the crime and the victim of the punishment.*

Although metaphors of balance are appropriate to the play as a whole, they should not, of course, prevent us from exploring the inward nature of Caesar or Brutus or from analysing the political issues exposed by the play and reverberating outside it. If we do this, we should take L. C. Knight's advice and remember that 'Shakespeare offers little comfort to those who like to consider historical conflicts in terms of a simple black and white'.†
Some critics – Mark Hunter is an example – have so utterly lost patience with what they regard as the murderous idealism of Brutus as to condemn him too ragingly; they have forgotten, perhaps, that the play depicts Rome as being in a constitutional

---

* A. Bonjour, *The Structure of 'Julius Caesar'* (Liverpool, 1958) p. 24.
    † L. C. Knights, 'Personality and Politics in *Julius Caesar*', in *Further Explorations* (1965) p. 52.

crisis so perilous that if Brutus had done nothing it would have
had as decisive an effect as what he did. J. Dover Wilson, on the
other hand, in the New Cambridge edition (1949), sees Caesar
as an 'oriental monarch', führer or generalissimo, going down
infatuated to destruction: yet Caesar in the play is really an oddly
appealing mixture of weakness and strength; he is a man who
continually tries to live up to the Caesar role with the effortful
inconsistency that Cassius so despises – a colossus, but all the
same, like Nathaniel in *Love's Labour's Lost* 'for Alisander –
alas! you see how 'tis – a little o'erparted'. There must be a
correlation between our feelings about Brutus and Caesar and
our responses to the moral and political substance. The politics is
a matter about which recent criticism has shown what may be
some fresh insights.

III

These insights may originate from the interest which our century
especially has shown in imagery and its functions, as also in
iconography and 'stage-picture'. And this is true in spite of the
fact that the 'image-count' in this play is supposed to be low.
Those who, with Dr Johnson, feel the play to be cold and unaffecting and find its imaginative resources limited will discover
an answer in Wilson Knight's essays on the tragedy, for they
have greatly contributed to a general realisation that *Julius
Caesar* has its soft, warm and emotional side as well as a severe
and restrained beauty. It seems strange now that this should ever
have been overlooked. One reason may be that, since seventeenth-
century heroic drama died, we have inhibited our capacity to
understand those aspects of the play that crystallise out in the
quarrel scene (IV ii). This depicts what is really a lovers' quarrel
and reconciliation between the two noble friends, though the
true lover is Cassius and not Brutus. Its counterpart are the
passionate words and gestures in the play at large, which so
often focus on the human body. We are always being reminded
of our weak bodies and the feeble flesh, which is, in John
Webster's words, 'a little cruded milke, phantasticall puff-paste'.

Offering one's stripped and undefended body to one's own sword
or someone else's is always the *ultima ratio* of these noble Romans:
if there could be a single icon for the play, it would be a blade
piercing the naked flesh. Casca tells how Caesar 'pluck'd me ope
his doublet and offer'd [the common herd] his throat to cut'.
Cassius, 'unbraced', bares his bosom to the thunder-stone;
Antony exposes his body to the conspirators, no doubt unbracing
as he speaks:

> I do beseech you, if you bear me hard,
> Now whilst your purpled hands do reek and smoke
> Fulfil your pleasure.

Portia, wounding herself in the thigh, in the same way uses her
body to prove something. And in the quarrel-scene itself Cassius
bursts out:

> O, I could weep
> My spirit from mine eyes! There is my dagger,
> And here my naked breast; within, a heart
> Dearer than Pluto's mine, richer than gold:
> If that thou be'st a Roman, take it forth.

'Being a Roman' is not like being a nice, white, marble statue in
a museum, and such a passage predicts the emblematic use of the
lover's bleeding heart in John Ford's *'Tis Pity She's a Whore*
as well as the soft, eloquent emotionalism of *The Maid's Tragedy*
and all its progeny. It is far off from vulgar bloodthirstiness
(this is what Rymer and Voltaire couldn't see); Cassius proposes
a ceremony, a murder and a kind of *liebestod* all at once, and the
proposition and its style are expressive of his highly charged
emotional state. Similarly, Brutus has earlier suggested (as Brents
Stirling has argued) that Caesar's murder should be made cere-
monious by the washing in his blood. It is Brutus's way of trying
to make the murder express what he believes to be the deep but
pure resolve of the conspirators.

   The body also thrusts itself into men's counsels by taking sick.
As Wilson Knight has observed, everybody in *Julius Caesar*,
except Antony, is ill or seems threatened with illness: even

Cassius's sight is 'thick'; Caesar suffers from deafness and epilepsy; Caius Ligarius has the fever; Portia's nerves give way and she faints; Calpurnia is barren; Brutus by pretending to be ill helps to reinforce the theme by drawing down Portia's worried reproaches ('Is Brutus sick . . .', ii i 261–7). There is a great deal else in the play to support Wilson Knight's view that it is 'vividly and pictorially alive in point of bodily visualization'.

If real sickness, such as that of Ligarius, enacts a body-reference, then an assassination, a lynching, and a trio of suicides yet more forcibly act out the recurrent imagery of the body. And on Caesar's body in particular, of course, words and stage-pictures are richly lavished, when it is sick and alive and when it is dead and terrible, or when it has become Antony's chief exhibit:

> Kind souls, what weep you when you but behold
> Our Caesar's vesture wounded? Look you here!
> Here is himself, marr'd, as you see, with traitors.

With a short break, Caesar's corpse is visible on the stage for more than five hundred continuous lines: this is a play whose centre is most exactly a murdered human body.

It is this thing, its fearfulness and its meaning, which is in the consciousness of Brutus for so much of the time, and which he tries in vain to cover up or walk away from. Perhaps the chief result of all these different kinds of allusions to and enactments of the body is to make us acutely aware that men and causes are interlocked and that political beliefs and ideologies are not disembodied spirits, though our manner of talk often suggests that we think they are.

In L. C. Knights's view, it is the subtle working out, in the language and gestures of which the dramatic artefact is composed, of a thoroughly obvious, if sufficiently radical and neglected, principle such as this which animates the characters and explains the construction. If we attend to this working out, we may acquire what wisdom about political life the play tenders to us; and from it we must conclude that

Brutus was not, in any ordinary sense of the word, a villain; he was simply an upright man who made a tragic mistake . . . [he]

was a man who thought that an abstract 'common good' could be achieved without due regard for the complexities of the actual; a man who tried to divorce political thinking and his political action from what he knew, and what he was, as a full human person.*

Ernest Schanzer, another modern commentator who has written with great authority on this play, agrees that the main moral issue arises from 'the rival claims of personal relations and the *res publica*'.† Brutus says:

> We all stand up against the spirit of Caesar,
> And in the spirit of men there is no blood.
> O, that we then could come by Caesar's spirit,
> And not dismember Caesar! But, alas,
> Caesar must bleed for it. (II i 166–71)

This is Brutus's dilemma, and, though both may agree that he gave the wrong answer to it, it is perhaps not so clear to Schanzer as it is to Knights that he *could* have given a right, or at least a more correct, answer, or that there was such an answer to give. Knights underrates the gravity of the constitutional crisis depicted in the play – the working of the 'spirit of Caesar' – which is forcing Brutus's hand: inaction would have been a mistake, too, if of another sort.

It is not easy, either, to regard as Shakespearian one conclusion that seems to emerge from a reading of Knights's essay: that Cassius, who is always more deeply conscious than anyone else of the '*man* in the name' is, if anyone is, the exemplary figure. Plainly, as Knights himself stresses, Cassius is too stirred by personal feeling to be a successful politician, conspirator or general officer. He always prefers his friend and hates his enemy. He therefore never suffers from Brutus's painful awareness that a man may be a friend and at the same time embody a detested principle. Political principles are not disembodied spirits; but they are incarnate ones. In *Julius Caesar* this is represented as an irreducible fact of Brutus's situation, not least by means of the

* *Further Explorations*, p. 51.
† *Shakespeare's Problem Plays* (1963) p. 65.

double vision, third and first person, that we have of Caesar himself. Knights's position seems to come close to denying the Caesarism of Caesar, which is yet strongly written into the play; when 'spirit' and 'blood' mingle, as they always do, then, if we accept Knights's position, it may be that there is never any road out to political action. But, given that the Caesarism is really there, the decision that Brutus makes to kill Caesar is the same as the decision made, for example, by the modern citizen-soldier in war. How *far* may the politician or citizen alike go when called upon to act when things are desperately on the slide? As Schanzer suggests, the play may have been designed only to animate and not to answer this question.

In the light especially of the modern critical discussions represented in this collection, *Julius Caesar* can no longer be content with one sort of reputation. The gravity of its demeanour is not simplicity; and its sustained compositional energy ingeniously coexists with a warm, passionate eloquence that sometimes melts almost into hysteria. If we substitute Caesar's name for Christ's, Yeats's lines about the 'odour of blood' making all discipline and tolerance vain might serve as the epilogue for this as for so many political tragedies.

PETER URE

PART ONE
Earlier Comments

THOMAS PLATTER

DEN 21 Septembris nach dem Imbissessen, etwan umb zwey vhren, bin ich mitt meiner geselschaft v̈ber daz wasser gefahren, haben in dem streüwinen Dachhaus die Tragedy vom ersten Keyser Julio Cæsare mitt ohngefahr 15 personen sehen gar artlich agieren; zu endt der Comedien dantzeten sie ihrem gebraucht nach gar v̈berausz zierlich, ye zwen in mannes vndt 2 in weiber kleideren angethan, wunderbahrlich mitt einanderen.

After lunch on 21 September, at about two o'clock, I and my party crossed the river, and there in the house with the thatched roof we saw an excellent performance of the tragedy of the first Emperor Julius Caesar with about fifteen characters; after the play, according to their custom they did a most elegant and curious dance, two dressed in men's clothes, and two in women's.*
(from an account by Thomas Platter of his visit to England in 1599)

BEN JONSON

I remember, the Players have often mentioned it as an honour to *Shakespeare*, that in his writing, (whatsoever he penn'd) hee never blotted out line. My answer hath beene, Would he had blotted a thousand. Which they thought a malevolent speech. I had not told posterity this, but for their ignorance, who choose that circumstance to commend their friend by, wherein he most faulted. And to justifie mine owne candor, (for I lov'd the man, and doe honour his memory (on this side Idolatry) as much as any.) Hee was (indeed) honest, and of an open, and free nature: had an excellent *Phantsie*; brave notions, and gentle expressions: wherein hee flow'd with that facility, that sometime it was neces-sary he should be stop'd: *Sufflaminandus erat*; as *Augustus* said of *Haterius*. His wit was in his owne power; would the rule of it had been so too. Many times hee fell into those things, could

*Translation by T. S. Dorsch, New Arden edition, 1955. P.U.

not escape laughter: As when hee said in the person of *Caesar*,
one speaking to him; *Caesar, thou dost me wrong*. Hee replyed:
Caesar did never wrong, but with just cause: and such like; which
were ridiculous. But hee redeemed his vices, with his vertues.
There was ever more in him to be praysed, then to be pardoned.

(from *Timber: or, Discoveries; Made upon Men and Matter,*
before 1635)

LEONARD DIGGES

I doe not wonder when you* offer at
Blacke-Friers, that you suffer: tis the fate
Of richer veines, prime judgements that have far'd
The worse, with this deceased man compar'd.
So have I seene, when Cesar would appeare,
And on the Stage at halfe-sword Parley were,
Brutus and *Cassius*: oh how the Audience,
Were ravish'd, with what wonder they went thence,
When some new day they would not brooke a line,
Of tedious (though well laboured) *Catilines*.

(from commendatory verses to Shakespeare's *Poems*, 1640)

JOHN DRYDEN

In Country Beauties as we often see,
Something that takes in their simplicity;
Yet while they charm, they know not they are fair,
And take without the spreading of the snare;
Such Artless beauty lies in *Shakespears* wit,
'Twas well in spight of him what ere he writ.
His Excellencies came and were not sought,
His words like casual Atoms made a thought:
Drew up themselves in Rank and File, and writ,
He wondring how the Devil it was such wit.
Thus like the drunken Tinker, in his Play,
He grew a Prince, and never knew which way.

* i.e. writers inferior to Shakespeare. P.U.

He did not know what trope or Figure meant,
But to perswade is to be eloquent,
So in this *Cæsar* which to day you see,
Tully ne'r spoke as he makes *Anthony*.
Those then that tax his Learning are to blame,
He knew the thing, but did not know the Name:
Great *Iohnson* did that Ignorance adore,
And though he envi'd much, admir'd him more;
The faultless *Iohnson* equally writ well,
Shakespear made faults; but then did more excel.
One close at Guard like some old Fencer lay,
T'other more open, but he shew'd more play.
In Imitation *Iohnsons* wit was shown,
Heaven made his men; but *Shakespear* made his own.
Wise *Iohnson's* talent in observing lay,
But others follies still made up his play.
He drew the life in each elaborate line,
But *Shakespear* like a Master did design.
Iohnson with skill dissected humane kind,
And show'd their faults that they their faults might find:
But then as all Anatomists must do,
He to the meanest of mankind did go,
And took from Gibbets such as he would show.
Both are so great that he must boldly dare,
Who both of 'em does judge and both compare.
If amongst Poets one more bold there be,
The man that dare attempt in either way, is he.

(Prologue to *Julius Caesar*, 1672)

THE occasion which Shakespeare, Euripides, and Fletcher have all taken is the same, grounded upon friendship; and the quarrel of two virtuous men, raised by natural degrees to the extremity of passion, is conducted in all three to the declination of the same passion, and concludes with a warm renewing of their friendship.* But the particular groundwork which Shakespeare has

* The references are to Euripides' *Iphigenia in Aulis* and Fletcher's *The Maid's Tragedy*. P.U.

taken is incomparably the best; because he has not only chosen two of the greatest heroes of their age, but has likewise interested the liberty of Rome, and their own honours, who were the redeemers of it, in this debate. And if he has made Brutus, who was naturally a patient man, to fly into excess at first, let it be remembered in his defence, that, just before, he has received the news of Portia's death; whom the poet, on purpose neglecting a little chronology, supposes to have died before Brutus, only to give him an occasion of being more easily exasperated. Add to this, that the injury he had received from Cassius had long been brooding in his mind; and that a melancholy man, upon consideration of an affront, especially from a friend, would be more eager in his passion than he who had given it, though naturally more choleric.

(from the preface to Troilus and Cressida, 1679)

COLLEY CIBBER

A farther Excellence in *Betterton* was, that he could vary his Spirit to the different Characters he acted. Those wild impatient Starts, that fierce and flashing Fire, which he threw into *Hotspur*, never came from the unruffled Temper of his *Brutus* (for I have more than once seen a *Brutus* as warm as *Hotspur*): when the *Betterton Brutus* was provok'd in his Dispute with *Cassius*, his Spirit flew only to his Eye; his steady Look alone supply'd that Terror which he disdain'd an Intemperance in his Voice should rise to. Thus, with a settled Dignity of Contempt, like an unheeding Rock he repelled upon himself the Foam of *Cassius*. Perhaps the very Words of *Shakespear* will better let you into my Meaning:

> *Must I give way and room to your rash Choler?*
> *Shall I be frighted when a Madman stares?*

And a little after,

> *There is no Terror, Cassius, in your Looks!* &c.

Not but in some part of this Scene, where he reproaches *Cassius*, his Temper is not under this Suppression, but opens into that Warmth which becomes a Man of Virtue; yet this is that *Hasty Spark* of Anger which *Brutus* himself endeavours to excuse.

But with whatever strength of Nature we see the Poet shew at once the Philosopher and the Heroe, yet the Image of the Actor's Excellence will be still imperfect to you unless Language could put Colours in our Words to paint the Voice with.

Et, si vis similem pingere, pinge sonum, [Ausonius, II 8 (Epigram xi)] is enjoying an impossibility. The most that a *Vandyke* can arrive at, is to make his Portraits of great Persons seem to *think*; a *Shakespear* goes farther yet, and tells you *what* his Pictures thought; a *Betterton* steps beyond 'em both, and calls them from the Grave to breathe and be themselves again. . . .

(from *An Apology for the Life of Mr Colley Cibber, Comedian*, 1740)

S. T. COLERIDGE

[II i 10–13.

> *Bru.* It must be by his death: and, for my part,
> I know no personal cause to spurn at him,
> But for the general. He would be crown'd:
> How that might change his nature, there's the question:]

This is singular – at least I do not at present see into Shakespeare's motive, the *rationale* – or in what point he meant Brutus's character to appear. For surely (this I mean is what I say to myself, in my present quantum of insight, only modified by my experience in how many instances I have ripened into a perception of beauties where I had before descried faults), surely nothing can seem more discordant with our historical preconceptions of Brutus, or more *lowering* to the intellect of this Stoico-Platonic tyrannicide, than the tenets here attributed to him, to *him*, the stern Roman republican; viz., that he would have no objection to a king, or to Caesar, a monarch in Rome, would Caesar be as good a monarch as he now seems disposed to

be. How too could Brutus say he finds no personal cause; i.e.
none in Caesar's past conduct as a man? Had he not passed the
Rubicon? Entered Rome as a conqueror? Placed his Gauls in
the Senate? Shakespeare (it may be said) has not brought these
things forward. True! and this is just the ground of my per-
plexity. What character does Shakespeare mean *his* Brutus to be?

(from marginalia on *Julius Caesar*, 1808(?))

WILLIAM HAZLITT

THE honest manliness of Brutus is . . . sufficient to find out the
unfitness of Cicero to be included in their enterprise, from his
affected egotism and literary vanity.

> O, name him not; let us not break with him;
> For he will never follow anything
> That other men begin.

His scepticism as to prodigies and his moralising on the
weather – 'This disturbed sky is not to walk in' – are in the same
spirit of refined imbecility.

Shakspeare has in this play and elsewhere shown the same
penetration into political character and the springs of public
events as into those of everyday life. For instance, the whole
design to liberate their country fails from the generous temper
of Brutus, and his overweening confidence in the goodness of
their cause and the assistance of others. Thus it has always been.
Those who mean well themselves think well of others, and fall a
prey to their security. The humanity and sincerity which dispose
men to resist injustice and tyranny render them unfit to cope with
the cunning and power of those who are opposed to them. The
friends of liberty trust to the professions of others, because they
are themselves sincere, and endeavour to secure the public good
with the least possible hurt to its enemies, who have no regard
to anything but their own unprincipled ends, and stick at nothing
to accomplish them. Cassius was better cut out for a conspirator.
His heart prompted his head. His habitual jealousy made him
fear the worst that might happen, and his irritability of temper

added to his inveteracy of purpose, and sharpened his patriotism. The mixed nature of his motives made him fitter to contend with bad men. The vices are never so well employed as in combating one another. Tyranny and servility are to be dealt with after their own fashion, or they will triumph over those who spare them.

(from *Characters of Shakespeare's Plays*, 1817)

EDWARD DOWDEN

CÆSAR passes by, and as he passes a soothsayer calls in shrill tones from the press of people, 'Beware the Ides of March'. Cæsar summons him forward, gazes in his face, and dismisses him with authoritative gesture, 'He is a dreamer; let us leave him: pass.' It is evidently intended that Cæsar shall have a foible for supposing that he can read off character from the faces of men:

Yond Cassius has a lean and hungry look.

Cæsar need not condescend to the ordinary ways of obtaining acquaintance with facts. He asks no question of the soothsayer. He takes the royal road to knowledge – intuition. This self-indulgence of his own foibles is, as it were, symbolized by his physical infirmity, which he admits in lordly fashion – 'Come on my right hand, for this ear is deaf.' Cæsar is entitled to own such a foible as deafness; it may pass well with Cæsar. If men would have him hear them, let them come to his right ear. Meanwhile, things may be whispered which it were well for him if he strained an ear – right or left – to catch. In Shakspere's rendering of the character of Cæsar, which has considerably bewildered his critics, one thought of the poet would seem to be this – that unless a man continually keeps himself in relation with facts, and with his present person and character, he may become to himself legendary and mythical. The real man Cæsar disappears for himself under the greatness of the Cæsar myth. He forgets himself as he actually is, and knows only the vast legendary power named Cæsar. He is a *numen* to himself, speaking of Cæsar in the third person, as if of some power above and behind his consciousness. And at this very moment – so ironical is the time-spirit – Cassius is cruelly insisting to Brutus upon all those infirmities which prove this god no more than a pitiful mortal.

BRUTUS is in his orchard alone. He has stolen away from Portia; he is seeking to master himself in solitude, and bring under the subjection of a clear idea and a definite resolve the tumultuary powers of his nature, which have been roused and thrown into disorder by the suggestions of Cassius. In the soliloquy of Brutus, after he has been left alone, will be found an excellent example of the peculiar brooding or dwelling style which Shakspere appropriated at this period to the soliloquies of men. The soliloquies of his women are conceived in a different manner. Of this speech Coleridge has said, 'I do not at present see into Shakspere's motive, his *rationale*, or in what point of view he meant Brutus' character to appear.' Shakspere's motive is not far to seek. He wishes to show upon what grounds the political idealist acts. Brutus resolves that Cæsar shall die by his hand as the conclusion of a series of hypotheses; there is, as it were, a sorites of abstract principles about ambition, and power, and reason, and affection; finally, a profound suspicion of Cæsar is engendered, and his death is decreed. It is idealists who create a political terror; they are free from all desire for blood-shedding; but to them the lives of men and women are accidents; the lives of ideas are the true realities; and, armed with an abstract principle and a suspicion, they perform deeds which are at once beautiful and hideous:

> 'Tis a common proof
> That lowliness is young Ambition's ladder,
> Whereto the climber-upward turns his face;
> But when he once attains the utmost round,
> He then unto the ladder turns his back,
> Looks in the clouds, scorning the base degrees
> By which he did ascend; so Cæsar may;
> Then, lest he may, prevent!

(from *Shakspere: A Critical Study of His Mind and Art*, 1875)

PAUL STAPFER

NOT only in body but also in mind was Cæsar becoming en-feebled in those last days of his life; he was superstitious and frightened, he had lost all foresight and firmness of purpose, and took refuge in a grandiloquent and empty declamation; his mental collapse was everywhere evident. And yet, when the conspirators put a violent end to this poor exhausted spirit, which was dying of itself, the Republic gained absolutely nothing: the Emperor is no more, but the Empire is begun – Cæsar is dead, long live Cæsar!

By this, Shakespeare, with a depth of insight and observation, before which thought stands astounded and abashed, meant to show that the days of liberty in Rome were irrevocably ended, and that for the future the cause of her bondage would no longer be the commanding genius of a ruler, but the inward alteration in the public mind and disposition. What must have been the bitterness of spirit experienced by Brutus when, in answer to his proclamation of liberty from the Forum, he heard the stupid people cry in their enthusiasm, 'Let him be Cæsar!' Had the empire depended only upon the genius of one man, Brutus, in killing Cæsar, might have saved the Republic, but in point of fact the Empire was rooted in the general state of things. It was in not perceiving this that the error of Brutus lay, and from this also resulted the utter failure of his enterprise. It is not the spirit of any one man, but the spirit of a new era about to begin – the spirit of *Cæsarism* – that fills Shakespeare's play and gives it its unity and moral significance, and therefore it is that this tragedy, in which Cæsar appears in only three scenes, and neither says nor does anything of importance, is called 'Julius Cæsar' and not 'Marcus Brutus'.

(from *Shakespeare and Classical Antiquity*, 1880)

R. G. MOULTON

THE assassination is accomplished, the cause of the conspirators is won: pity notwithstanding we are swept along with the current of their enthusiasm; and the justification that has been steadily rising from the commencement reaches its climax as, their adversaries dispersing in terror, the conspirators dip their hands in their victim's blood, and make their triumphant appeal to the whole world and all time.

> *Cassius.* Stoop, then, and wash. How many ages hence
>   Shall this our lofty scene be acted over
>   In states unborn and accents yet unknown!
> *Brutus.* How many times shall Cæsar bleed in sport,
>   That now on Pompey's basis lies along,
>   No worthier than the dust!
> *Cassius.*   So oft as that shall be,
>   So often shall the knot of us be call'd
>   The men that gave their country LIBERTY!

Enter a servant: this simple stage-direction is the 'catastrophe', the turning-round of the whole action; the arch has reached its apex and the Reaction has begun. So instantaneous is the change, that though it is only the servant of Antony who speaks, yet the first words of his message ring with the peculiar tone of subtly-poised sentences which are inseparably associated with Antony's eloquence; it is like the first announcement of that which is to be a final theme in music, and from this point this tone dominates the scene to the very end.

>   Thus he bade me say:
>   Brutus is noble, wise, valiant, and honest,
>   Cæsar was mighty, bold, royal, and loving,
>   Say I love Brutus, and I honour him;
>   Say I fear'd Cæsar, honour'd him, and lov'd him.
>   If Brutus will vouchsafe that Antony
>   May safely come to him, and be resolv'd
>   How Cæsar hath deserved to lie in death,
>   Mark Antony shall not love Cæsar dead
>   So well as Brutus living.

In the whole Shakespearean Drama there is nowhere such a swift swinging round of a dramatic action as is here marked by this sudden up-springing of the suppressed individuality in Antony's character, hitherto so colourless that he has been spared by the conspirators as a mere limb of Cæsar. The tone of exultant triumph in the conspirators has in an instant given place to Cassius's 'misgivings' as Brutus grants Antony an audience; and when Antony enters, Brutus's first words to him fall into the form of apology. The quick subtlety of Antony's intellect has grasped the whole situation, and with irresistible force he slowly feels his way towards using the conspirators' aid for crushing themselves and avenging their victim. The bewilderment of the conspirators in the presence of this unlooked-for force is seen in Cassius's unavailing attempt to bring Antony to the point, as to what compact he will make with them. Antony, on the contrary, reads his men with such nicety that he can indulge himself in sailing close to the wind, and grasps fervently the hands of the assassins while he pours out a flood of bitter grief over the corpse. It is not hypocrisy, nor a trick to gain time, this conciliation of his enemies. Steeped in the political spirit of the age, Antony knows, as no other man, the mob which governs Rome, and is conscious of the mighty engine he possesses in his oratory to sway that mob in what direction he pleases; when his bold plan has succeeded, and his adversaries have consented to meet him in contest of oratory, then ironical conciliation becomes the natural relief to his pent-up passion.

> Friends am I with you all and love you all,
> *Upon this hope, that you shall give me reasons*
> Why and wherein Cæsar was dangerous.

It is as he feels the sense of innate oratorical power and of the opportunity his enemies have given to that power, that he exaggerates his temporary amity with the men he is about to crush: it is the executioner arranging his victim comfortably on the rack before he proceeds to apply the levers. Already the passion of the drama has fallen under the guidance of Antony. The view of Cæsar as an innocent victim is now allowed full play upon our sympathies when Antony, left alone with the corpse, can drop the artificial mask and give vent to his love and vengeance. The success of the conspiracy had begun to decline as we marked Brutus's ill-timed generosity to Antony in granting him the funeral oration; it crumbles away through the cold unnatural euphuism of Brutus's speech in its defence; it is hurried to its ruin when Antony at last exercises his spell upon the Roman people and upon the reader. The speech of Antony, with its mastery of every phase of feeling, is a perfect sonata upon the instrument of the human emotions. Its opening theme is sympathy with bereavement, against which are working as if in conflict anticipations of future themes, doubt and compunction. A distinct change of movement comes with the first introduction of what is to be the final subject, the mention of the will. But when this new movement has worked up from curiosity to impatience, there is a diversion: the mention of the victory over the Nervii turns the emotions in the direction of historic pride, which harmonises well with the opposite emotions roused as the orator fingers hole after hole in Cæsar's mantle made by the daggers of his false friends, and so leads up to a sudden shock when he uncovers the body itself and displays the popular idol and its bloody defacement. Then the finale begins: the forgotten theme of the will is again started, and from a burst of gratitude the passion quickens and intensifies to rage, to fury, to mutiny. The mob is won to the Reaction; and the curtain that falls upon the third Act rises for a moment to display the populace tearing a man to pieces simply because he bears the same name as one of the conspirators.

The final stage of the action works out the development of an inevitable fate. The emotional strain now ceases, and, as in the first stage, the passion is of the calmer order, the calmness in this case of pity balanced by a sense of justice. From the opening of the fourth Act the decline in the justification of the conspirators is intimated by the logic of events. The first scene exhibits to us the triumvirate that now governs Rome, and shows that in this triumvirate Antony is supreme: with the man who is the embodiment of the Reaction thus appearing at the head of the world, the fall of the conspirators is seen to be inevitable. The decline of our sympathy with them continues in the following scenes. The Quarrel Scene shows how low the tone of Cassius has fallen since he has dealt with assassination as a political weapon; and even Brutus's moderation has hardened into unpleasing harshness. There is at this point plenty of relief to such unpleasing effects: there is the exhibition of the tender side of Brutus's character as shown in his relations with his page, and the display of friendship maintained between Brutus and Cassius amid falling fortunes. But such incidents as these have a different effect upon us from that which they would have had at an earlier period; the justification of the conspirators has so far declined that now attractive touches in them serve only to increase the pathos of a fate which, however, our sympathy no longer seeks to resist. We get a supernatural foreshadowing of the end in the appearance to Brutus of Cæsar's Ghost, and the omen Cassius sees of the eagles that had consorted his army to Philippi giving place to ravens, crows, and kites on the morning of battle: this lends the authority of the invisible world to our sense that the conspirators' cause is doomed. And judicial blindness overtakes them as Brutus's authority in council overweighs in point after point the shrewder advice of Cassius. Through the scenes of the fifth Act we see the republican leaders fighting on without hope. The last remnant of justification for their cause ceases as the conspirators themselves seem to acknowledge their error and fate. Cassius as he feels his death-blow recognises the very weapon with which he had committed the crime:

> Cæsar, thou art revenged,
> Even with the sword that kill'd thee.

And at last even the firm spirit of Brutus yields:

> O Julius Cæsar, thou art mighty yet!
> Thy spirit walks abroad, and turns our swords
> In our own proper entrails.
> (from *Shakespeare as a Dramatic Artist*, 1885)

GEORGE BERNARD SHAW

IT is when we turn to *Julius Cæsar*, the most splendidly written
political melodrama we possess, that we realize the apparently
immortal author of *Hamlet* as a man, not for all time, but for an
age only, and that, too, in all solidly wise and heroic aspects, the
most despicable of all the ages in our history. It is impossible for
even the most judicially minded critic to look without a revulsion
of indignant contempt at this travestying of a great man as a silly
braggart, whilst the pitiful gang of mischief-makers who destroyed him are lauded as statesmen and patriots. There is not a
single sentence uttered by Shakespear's Julius Cæsar that is, I
will not say worthy of him, but even worthy of an average
Tammany boss. Brutus is nothing but a familiar type of English
suburban preacher: politically he would hardly impress the
Thames Conservancy Board. Cassius is a vehemently assertive
nonentity. It is only when we come to Antony, unctuous volup-
tuary and self-seeking sentimental demagogue, that we find
Shakespear in his depth; and in his depth, of course, he is super-
lative. Regarded as a crafty stage job, the play is a triumph:
rhetoric, claptrap, effective gushes of emotion, all the devices of
the popular playwright, are employed with a profusion of power
that almost breaks their backs. No doubt there are slips and
slovenliness of the kind that careful revisers eliminate; but they
count for so little in the mass of accomplishment that it is safe
to say that the dramatist's art can be carried no further on that
plane. If Goethe, who understood Cæsar and the significance of
his death – 'the most senseless of deeds' he called it – had treated
the subject, his conception of it would have been as superior to
Shakespear's as St John's Gospel is to the Police News; but his
treatment could not have been more magnificently successful.
As far as sonority, imagery, wit, humor, energy of imagination,
power over language, and a whimsically keen eye for idiosyn-
crasies can make a dramatist, Shakespear was the king of dramatists. Unfortunately, a man may have them all, and yet conceive
high affairs of state exactly as Simon Tappertit did. In one of the
scenes in *Julius Cæsar* a conceited poet bursts into the tent of

Brutus and Cassius, and exhorts them not to quarrel with one another. If Shakespear had been able to present his play to the ghost of the great Julius, he could probably have had much the same reception. He certainly would have deserved it.

(from a review of Beerbohm Tree's production originally published in the *Saturday Review*, 29 January 1898)

PART TWO
Special Aspects

A. C. BRADLEY: (i) The Quarrel Scene

ONE purpose . . . of the quarrel scene between Brutus and Cassius (IV iii), as also of the appearance of Caesar's ghost just afterwards, is to indicate the inward changes. Otherwise the introduction of this famous and wonderful scene can hardly be defended on strictly dramatic grounds. No one would consent to part with it, and it is invaluable in sustaining interest during the progress of the reaction, but it is an episode, the removal of which would not affect the actual sequence of events (unless we may hold that, but for the emotion caused by the quarrel and reconciliation, Cassius would not have allowed Brutus to overcome his objection to the fatal policy of offering battle at Philippi).

The quarrel-scene illustrates yet another favourite expedient. In this section of a tragedy Shakespeare often appeals to an emotion different from any of those excited in the first half of the play, and so provides novelty and generally also relief. As a rule this new emotion is pathetic; and the pathos is not terrible or lacerating, but, even if painful, is accompanied by the sense of beauty and by an outflow of admiration or affection, which come with an inexpressible sweetness after the tension of the crisis and the first counter-stroke. So it is with the reconciliation of Brutus and Cassius, and the arrival of the news of Portia's death.

(ii) Brutus and Hamlet

IF we consider the tragedies first on the side of their substance we find at once an obvious difference between the first two and the remainder. Both Brutus and Hamlet are highly intellectual by nature and reflective by habit. Both may even be called, in a popular sense, philosophic; Brutus may be called so in a stricter sense. Each, being also a 'good' man, shows accordingly, when placed in critical circumstances, a sensitive and almost painful anxiety to do right. And though they fail – of course in quite different ways – to deal successively with these circumstances, the failure in each case is connected rather with their intellectual nature and reflective habit than with any yielding to passion. Hence the name 'tragedy of thought', which Schlegel gave to *Hamlet*, may be given also, as in effect it has been by Professor Dowden, to *Julius Caesar*. The later heroes, on the other hand, Othello, Lear, Timon, Macbeth, Antony, Coriolanus, have, one and all, passionate natures, and, speaking roughly, we may attribute the tragic failure in each of these cases to passion. Partly for this reason, the later plays are wilder and stormier than the first two. We see a greater mass of human nature in commotion, and we see Shakespeare's own powers exhibited on a larger scale. Finally, examination would show that, in all these respects, the first tragedy, *Julius Caesar*, is further removed from the later type than is the second, *Hamlet*.

These two earlier works are both distinguished from most of the succeeding tragedies in another though a kindred respect. Moral evil is not so intently scrutinised or so fully displayed in them. In *Julius Caesar*, we may almost say, everybody means well. In *Hamlet*, though we have a villain, he is a small one. The murder which gives rise to the action lies outside the play, and the centre of attention within the play lies in the hero's efforts to do his duty. It seems clear that Shakespeare's interest, since the early days when under Marlowe's influence he wrote *Richard III*, has not been directed to the more extreme or terrible forms of evil. But in the tragedies that follow *Hamlet* the presence of this interest is equally clear. In Iago, in the 'bad' people of *King Lear*, even in Macbeth and Lady Macbeth, human nature assumes shapes which inspire not mere sadness or repulsion but horror and dismay. If in *Timon* no monstrous cruelty is done, we still watch ingratitude and selfishness so blank that they provoke a loathing we never felt for Claudius; and in this play and *King Lear* we can fancy that we hear at times the *saeva indignatio*, if not the despair, of Swift. This prevalence of abnormal or appalling forms of evil, side by side with vehement passion, is another reason why the convulsion depicted in these tragedies seems to come from a deeper source, and to be vaster in extent, than the conflict in the two earlier plays. And here again *Julius Caesar* is further removed than *Hamlet* from *Othello*, *King Lear*, and *Macbeth*.

(iii) The Style

THE general style of the serious parts of the last plays from English history is one of full, noble, and comparatively equable eloquence. The 'honey-tongued' sweetness and beauty of Shakespeare's early writing, as seen in *Romeo and Juliet* or the *Midsummer-Night's Dream*, remain; the ease and lucidity remain; but there is an accession of force and weight. We find no great change from this style when we come to *Julius Caesar*,* which may be taken to mark its culmination. At this point in Shakespeare's literary development he reaches, if the phrase may be pardoned, a limited perfection. Neither thought on the one side, nor expression on the other, seems to have any tendency to outrun or contend with its fellow. We receive an impression of easy mastery and complete harmony, but not so strong an impression of inner power bursting into outer life. Shakespeare's style is perhaps nowhere else so free from defects, and yet almost every one of his subsequent plays contains writing which is greater. To speak familiarly, we feel in *Julius Caesar* that, although not even Shakespeare could better the style he has chosen, he has not let himself go.

(from *Shakespearean Tragedy*, 1904)

w. WARDE FOWLER: Old and New Ideas about Tragedy

THE idea that a good man could do incalculable harm from the best possible motives was, as far as I know, a new one in tragedy. True, that incalculable harm would not be found by Shakespeare in Plutarch; but he would come to the contemplation of the murder with other ideas than those of Plutarch – with the

* That play, however, is distinguished, I think, by a deliberate endeavour after a dignified and unadorned simplicity – a Roman simplicity perhaps.

inherited tradition of the overwhelming greatness of Caesar, and the appalling horror of the deed. Thus the contrast between the goodness of Brutus and the awful crime into which he was drawn would be far more vivid in his reading of the Life than in Plutarch's telling of it; and for the moment that contrast was a godsend – a delivery from all doubt as to the tragic possibilities of the story. And here at the same time was a new path opened out for the development of the tragic art. The crash of fate falling on a good man, brought on himself by his own blunders or self-deception or noble pride – by character issuing in action – this was an idea of human life and fortune suggesting most fascinating possibilities, such as neither Marlowe nor Shakespeare himself had ever yet thought of dealing with. I am strongly inclined to think that this [Plutarch's] Life of Brutus was in some degree a turning-point in Shakespeare's artistic life; it may be that some personal experience of his own was in his mind as he read it, and gave it special meaning for him; it may be that it attracted him to the character of Hamlet, which he used in his next tragedy, and which has so often been compared, rightly or wrongly, with that of Brutus.[1]

Yet none the less, in constructing the play, it was impossible for him to escape the necessity of making the murder of Caesar its central and dominating fact: Caesar bestrode the world like a Colossus, and the others are in comparison but ordinary men. And the play must bear his name not only because the common Englishman knew something of him and little or nothing of Brutus, but because his greatness was such that if his death were introduced into the play at all it must inevitably control the whole action. Caesar was not a king like Duncan – a king and little more; in *Macbeth* it is the murder of his king that dominates the action, but in our play it is the murder of *Caesar*. Duncan's death was not of vital importance to the world: Caesar's was the great fact of his time, and a man like Shakespeare reading these Lives could not possibly escape the conviction that it was so. The result of this conviction was that this tragedy stands apart from all the others in point of construction; the crisis, the turning point of the hero's fortunes, is a deed of such magnitude, and the murdered man is so great in his fall as in his life, that this crisis becomes itself a catastrophe, and the victim must give his name to the play. We have in fact in *Julius Caesar* the meeting-point of the old and the new ideas of tragedy. We have the sudden fall of a man of overwhelming greatness – this was the old idea, of which Marlowe's *Tamburlaine* may be cited as the type; and at the same time we have retribution falling upon a good man whose very goodness has made him wrong-headed in action – this is the new idea, which could be used in various ways in the tragedies that were to follow. The result on the play of this compromise between the old and the new is not wholly to its advantage. It falls too clearly into two parts, and neither part is perfect. A play with a double plan of construction, in which the crisis overbears the catastrophe in interest, must have given its author unusual trouble.

(from *Roman Essays and Interpretations*, 1911)

NOTE

1. Mr Gollancz has an interesting suggestion by way of connecting the two plays in his *Julius Caesar* (Temple edition (1896) preface, p. x). See also M. W. MacCallum, *Shakespeare's Roman Plays* (1910) p. 173.

c. h. herford: *Julius Caesar* and Ben Jonson's *Sejanus*

Shakespeare himself, to whom a really formless drama was from the first impossible, yet allows himself far greater structural liberties in the Histories than in any other branch of his plays. And when, at the beginning of the new century, he turned from England to Rome, it was to write dramas which were no longer 'Histories' even in name. In the Roman plays he evolved a true historical drama, structurally organic, yet sufficiently free and plastic to represent the complexity and movement of a great historic action. The structural mastery of the Roman plays is the more remarkable since he was here handling sources with far

closer fidelity than before. In *Julius Caesar* above all, essential
historicity was achieved without detriment to the most pellucid
simplicity of structure. And when Jonson sat down to write
Sejanus, *Julius Caesar* was still one of the resounding successes
of the day.

It is certain that *Julius Caesar* counted for much more than
Jonson would have acknowledged, or was aware of, in the making
of *Sejanus*. He planned his work, no doubt, in conscious and
even disdainful emulation. The splendid Roman triumph won
by the man of little Latin and less Greek, who 'wanted art', was
a challenge to his conscious superiority both in art and learning.
He had himself openly derided, if we may trust his report in the
Discoveries, a slip in the fluent language of Shakespeare's play.*
But Jonson's emulation was itself a tribute. His attempt to
outdo *Julius Caesar* rested in large part upon imitation. Shakespeare had led the way in historic drama founded upon the great
portraits in the ancient historians reproduced in detail. Jonson
did the same, only drawing upon more sources, and reading
them at first hand. Shakespeare represented a famous Roman
conspiracy, ending in the ruin of the conspirators. Jonson meant
to show what could be made of another Roman conspiracy by a
poet who had access to the greatest of Roman historians and could
render Tacitus in language as authentic and hardly less sinewy.
In *Julius Caesar* the creative or re-creative processes of Shakespeare are relatively unobtrusive. The matter is clarified and
ennobled, but not completely transfigured, like the matter of

*   Caesar did never wrong but with just cause.

The phrase is represented in our texts by the quite unexceptionable:

     Know, Caesar doth not wrong; nor without cause
     Will he be satisfied —

Jonson's version may caricature the original defect, but it is unlikely
that his criticism was wholly without ground. On the other hand,
Shakespeare may have written something like what Jonson says, and
have later amended it, perhaps in consequence of this very criticism.
No unfriendly animus could be inferred from that. But the correction
had in this case been made for many years, as Jonson must have known,
and it would remain noteworthy that he should ignore the fact.

Hamlet or *Othello*. Caesar himself is, in Shakespeare, almost a failure. It is hard to lay a finger on the point at which the divinity steals into his 'god-like' Romans. There is no romantic heightening of stature, no hint of legendary glamour, hardly any deliberate and palpable invention. Much of the alchemy consists in a mere sifting and straining away of disturbing elements, of confusing and insignificant incident, of vague or redundant traits, of the baser and poorer kinds of prose. It is not inexplicable that Jonson should have seen in *Julius Caesar* the loose brilliance of an amateur. He overlooked the miracles which even the unobtrusive touches of Shakespeare effect in that simplest of his masterpieces.

(from *Ben Jonson*, II (1925))

G. WILSON KNIGHT: The Death of Cassius

THERE is now a light-foot strength of spirit in Cassius: something fiery-strong, intangible, intractable to definition. He is yet strangely 'fresh of spirit' in disaster, in foreboding:

> Go, Pindarus, get higher on that hill;
> My sight was ever thick; regard Titinius,
> And tell me what thou notest about the field.
>
> (v iii 20)

Pindarus leaves him:

> This day I breathed first: time is come round,
> And where I did begin, there shall I end;
> My life is run his compass.   (v iii 23)

Cleopatra-like, he thus celebrates his birthday under the shadow of impending tragedy. And yet, this birth-remembrance yet lights this death with a sudden expectancy, a birth – a death and birth:

> Come down, behold no more.
> O, coward that I am, to live so long,
> To see my best friend ta'en before my face!
>
> (v iii 33)

A breathless expectancy indeed charges this scene. It is a positive, purposeful adventure, a stepping free, a death, like Cleopatra's, into love. Cassius the envious, the passionate, the lover, is now afloat on a love – Brutus before, now Titinius. Names are but symbols through which the spirit steps naked into the air and fire of love. Cassius gives Pindarus his last charge, the air aquiver with immortality. Like Antony, he bids his bondman remember the condition by which the saving of his 'life' has bound him to obedience:

> Come now, keep thine oath;
> Now be a freeman. . . .   (v iii 40)

'Life', 'freeman': what are these associations? In my reading of this scene I may be thought to tread a dangerous precipice. For only by irrationalities are my statements justified. But the associations here are powerful: the 'fire' perceived by Cassius, the love of Titinius – 'if thou lovedst me' – 'birth', 'shouts' of 'joy' (v iii 32), 'my best friend', 'saving of thy life', 'freeman': all this, together with the event which proves indeed that victory has been mistaken for failure, all stresses, not death, but life-in-death. The sight of mortality is 'ever thick'. The associations here contradict the logic: it is often the way of poetry. Cassius all but accomplishes the fiery splendour and conscious purpose of Cleopatra's death-in-love. His death is a thing of ecstasy and liberation. Pindarus will fly far 'where never Roman shall take note of him' (v iii 50). Safe and far, Pindarus or Cassius? Far from Rome. It is well that the purest essence of this play's poetry be spilled over his body:

> No, this was he, Messala,
> But Cassius is no more. O setting sun,
> As in thy red rays thou dost sink to-night,
> So in his red blood Cassius' day is set;
> The sun of Rome is set.   (v iii 59)

As the blood of the lover's heart streams out, the blood of republican Rome itself is spilt on the Parthian sands: and the crimson of the great sun drops level to honour with horizontal streams of fire the spirit of man victorious. This is the Shake-spearian sanction of love which has the universe at its bidding. Cassius is now crowned with a wreath of victory: our final, most vivid, association:

> *Titinius.* Why didst thou send me forth, brave Cassius?
>   Did I not meet thy friends? And did not they
>   Put on my brows this wreath of victory,
>   And bid me give it thee? Didst thou not hear their shouts?
>   Alas, thou has misconstrued every thing!
>   But, hold thee, take this garland on thy brow;
>   Thy Brutus bid me give it thee, and I
>   Will do his bidding. Brutus, come apace,
>   And see how I regarded Caius Cassius.
>   By your leave, gods: – this is a Roman's part:
>   Come, Cassius' sword, and find Titinius' heart.
>   (v iii 80)

'Heart' always in this play of fire and love. So Titinius crowns Cassius. 'Thy Brutus . . .'

>   Shall it not grieve thee dearer than thy death
>   To see thy Antony. . . .   (III i 197)

It is all one. This universe of kingly ambition, divided allegiances, envy, hostility, friendship – all is dominated and finally fused by love, the love and intimacy that beats here in imagery, incident, emotion, life, and death itself. So Titinius crowns Cassius, the lover, in death:

>   Brave Titinius!
>   Look, whether he have not crown'd dead Cassius!
>   (v iii 96)

Like Charmian over Cleopatra, he arranges the lover's crown, then hastens to follow his master. I have compared Cassius with the Duke in *Measure for Measure*; and now I relate his death to that of Cleopatra, to whom he is close in point of a certain romantic strength which solicits our respect apparently quite independently of any ethical judgement. What quality can we say binds these three? The Duke is the prince of ethical moralizers;

Cleopatra, the Queen of Courtezans. Yet all three possess a certain unique richness of soul and range of feeling: and in this they conquer.

(from *The Imperial Theme*, 1931)

J. E. PHILLIPS: Monarchic Principles

BRUTUS argues, Caesar has reached the extreme limits of the power delegated to him under the aristocratic form of government. At present the dictator at least formally observes the claims of the old order. Moved by ambition, however, he threatens, in seeking the crown, to reject in theory as well as in fact the system through which he rose to his position of authority:

> But 'tis a common proof
> That lowliness is young Ambition's ladder,
> Whereto the climber-upward turns his face;
> But when he once attains the upmost round,
> He then unto the ladder turns his back,
> Looks in the clouds, scorning the base degrees
> By which he did ascend. (II i 21–7)

For according to Brutus, the crown which Caesar desires is the symbol which distinguishes an absolute monarch from a governor limited by the final political authority of the corporate body of the nobility. By assuming the crown Caesar will transfer sovereign will in the state from the Senate to his own person, thereby fundamentally altering the theoretical structure of Roman political society. I believe that Brutus is thinking primarily of this effect of the crown on Caesar's political character and position (not on his private moral character, as does MacCallum) when he says:

> He would be crown'd:
> How that might change his nature, there's the question.
> It is the bright day that brings forth the adder,
> And that craves wary walking. Crown him? – that; –
> And then, I grant, we put a sting in him
> That at his will he may do danger with. (II i 12–17)

Sir Mark Hunter observes that 'To Brutus at one point it would almost seem that the forbidden thing was not so much the actual fact òf kingship as the name and symbol of royal rule.'[1] That, indeed, is the case. Brutus believes with the sixteenth-century advocate of limited monarchy, Buchanan, that rulers should be constrained 'to make use not of their own licentious wills in judgement, but of that right or privilege which the People had conferred upon them.'[2] Caesar, now a benefit to Rome, might become a menace when the crown establishes the sovereignty of his own 'licentious will' to run unlimited and unchecked to whatever lengths he desires. As Brutus reasons it out:

> So Caesar may;
> Then, lest he may, prevent. . . .
> . . . .
> Fashion it thus: that what he is, augmented,
> Would run to these and these extremities;
> And therefore think him as a serpent's egg
> Which, hatch'd, would, as his kind, grow mischievous,
> And kill him in the shell.   (II i 27–8, 30–4)

The use of such violence to preserve the sovereignty of the aristocracy in Rome is justified, Brutus maintains, because the welfare of the state demands it. The major premise with which his soliloquy opens reaffirms the high-principled honesty of his intentions: 'I know no personal cause to spurn at him But for the general.' (II i 11–12) Only by preventing the imminent accession of an absolute monarch can the common good be served.

Whatever the interpretation of this soliloquy – and any interpretation of so difficult and disputed a passage must be largely conjectural – the political scheme of the first half of the play seems fairly evident. On one side Shakespeare presents Roman political society flourishing under a *de facto* monarchy, with all of its degrees conforming to the pattern ordained by universal law. Against this he sets a group of men who are sincerely convinced that such political organization is a menace to the commonwealth and who believe that the earlier aristocratic government must be restored. With little prejudice so far manifest in either

direction Shakespeare brings these two concepts to test. Brutus'
words make clear Shakespeare's intention that the criterion to be
kept in mind in judging the efficacy and justice of any system of
government is the welfare of the society concerned. With these
principles established the resolution of the problem begins.

The conspirators act on their beliefs and Caesar is assassinated.
The consequences of their deed prove almost immediately the
fallacy of their political reasoning and indirectly reaffirm the
monarchic principles of society which Shakespeare seems consistently to have held. Its natural head gone, the Roman body
politic begins a mad run toward destruction. As MacCallum
phrases it, 'Brutus has brought about an upturn of society by
assassinating the one man who could organize that society.'[3]
Shakespeare does not leave to implication the political significance
of the action which follows the murder of Caesar. In his soliloquy
over the body of the dictator Antony forecasts the violence and
strife which will devastate the Roman commonwealth and
directly links this chaos with the death of the monarch:

> Woe to the hand that shed this costly blood!
> Over thy wounds now do I prophesy
>   .   .   .
> A curse shall light upon the limbs of men;
> Domestic fury and fierce civil strife
> Shall cumber all the parts of Italy;
> Blood and destruction shall be so in use
> And dreadful objects so familiar
> That mothers shall but smile when they behold
> Their infants quartered with the hands of war;
> All pity chok'd with custom of fell deeds;
> And Caesar's spirit, ranging for revenge,
> With Ate by his side come hot from hell,
> Shall in these confines with a monarch's voice
> Cry 'Havoc', and let slip the dogs of war;
> That this foul deed shall smell above the earth
> With carrion men, groaning for burial.
>
>   (III i 258-9, 262-75)

Later, in his funeral oration, Antony speaks again of Caesar's death in terms of its devastating effect on the commonwealth in general:

> O, what a fall was there, my countrymen!
> Then I, and you, and all of us fell down,
> Whilst bloody treason flourish'd over us.

(III ii 194–6)

Whatever his own motives, Antony's observations are sound from a political point of view. He recognizes the association between regicide and social chaos as almost any Elizabethan would recognize it.

(from *The State in Shakespeare's Greek and Roman Plays*, 1940)

NOTES

1. Sir Mark Hunter, in *Royal Society of Literature: Essays by Divers Hands*, x (1931) p. 120.
2. George Buchanan, *De iure regni apud Scotos* (translated, 1689) p. 13.
3. M. W. MacCallum, *Shakespeare's Roman Plays* (1910) p. 263.

S. MUSGROVE: Portia, Calpurnia, and the Buffer Scenes

CAESAR compares most unfavourably with Brutus when he meets him on his own ground, so to speak: when they are compared in the privacy of their studies. I refer to the two scenes (II i and II ii) where the two men are seen in conversation with their wives: and notice that each seems to have got the wife he deserves, Brutus the serious, noble and dignified Portia, and Caesar the superstitious, nervous and negative Calpurnia. Brutus has concealed from Portia the projected conspiracy from a typically unselfish motive – because he wishes to spare her anxiety; but she speaks to him as an equal – as 'Cato's daughter' – demanding as a right and as a tribute to her strength of character to know the reasons for his preoccupation. Brutus, accordingly, in a sudden flash of emotion, lets us know how dearly he holds

her, and the depth of true feeling which is concealed behind the
Stoic façade:

> You are my true and honourable wife;
> As dear to me as are the ruddy drops
> That visit my sad heart.   (II i 288–90)

Thus, it is natural for him to promise her that he will tell her
what she wishes to know:

> ... by and by thy bosom shall partake
> The secrets of my heart:
> All my engagements I will construe to thee,
> All the charactery of my sad brows.   (II i 305–8)

'All', notice – he will conceal from her nothing that is in his
heart. Contrast now Caesar and Calpurnia. She comes to him in
mortal terror, frightened like a child in the dark:

> O Caesar, these things are beyond all use,
> And I do fear them!   (II ii 25–6)

Or else, she scolds him like a shrew from the excess of her fear:

> You shall not stir out of your house to-day.
>   (II ii 9)

Finally, like Portia, she falls on her knees before him:

> Let me, upon my knee, prevail in this,
>   (II ii 54)

but Caesar does not, like Brutus, raise her with 'Kneel not,
gentle Portia', but replies testily:

> ... for thy humour, I will stay at home,
>   (II ii 56)

which, in modern English, means 'All right, I'll stay, if that's the
way you feel about it'. Observe, too, the general tone of Caesar's
replies to her requests. He neither treats her as an equal, as Brutus
had treated Portia, nor does he comfort her as her fearful nature
requires; instead, he speaks in his Olympian mode:

> What can be avoided
> Whose end is purposed by the mighty Gods?
> Yet Caesar shall go forth!   (II ii 26–8)

Or, like another statesman on another occasion, he addresses her
as though she were a public meeting:

> Cowards die many times before their deaths;
> The valiant never taste of death but once.
> Of all the wonders that I yet have heard,
> It seems to me most strange that men should fear,
> Seeing that death, a necessary end,
> Will come when it will come.   (II ii 32–7)

That is, Caesar feels the necessity of acting, of referring to himself
in the third person, of making splendid gestures even before his
wife. To me, that is the surest proof of the hollowness of his
character, and had not Calpurnia been such a silly woman, she
would have seen through him long ago: perhaps she did.

You will observe that the second of these two domestic scenes
does not follow immediately upon the first, but is separated from
it by a short scene between Brutus and Ligarius. This scene is
rather pointless in itself – it merely tells us how Ligarius' enthusiasm for the cause is so great that he has risen from a sick
bed to have a hand in 'any exploit worthy the name of honour' –
but its true function is to stand as a buffer between the two
domestic scenes. Were they to stand side by side with nothing to
separate them, the contrast would be too obviously artificial:
Shakespeare would be back at the primitive and unconvincing
formalism of early Elizabethan plays like *Gorboduc*, where the
good prince has a long conversation with the good counsellor,
and this is immediately followed by an equally long conversation
between the evil prince and his evil counsellor. Shakespeare
avoids this primitive technique by the use of this buffer scene.

While we are on this topic, we may pause and consider the
skill which Shakespeare exhibits in his use of other buffer scenes.
None of them, on a careless reading, seems to have much point;
we only realise their value when we try to read the play without
them. Take, for example, II iii and iv – the short Artemidorus

scene and the second Portia scene, in which Portia sends Lucius
to find out how the conspiracy is succeeding. These scenes serve,
mainly, to give the audience time to recover its breath after the
excitement of one of the tensest scenes in the play – the scene
in which Caesar is persuaded to visit the Senate-house – and to
prepare itself for the even greater excitement of the murder-scene.
Were the intervening scenes absent, the tension would be too
long drawn out, and so the appreciation of this part of the play
would suffer. They also have, of course, their own purposes to
serve: the Artemidorus scene to arouse our hopes, even against
our previous knowledge of events, by showing that Caesar still
has a chance if he will only take it; and the Portia scene to exhibit
the true womanliness of Brutus' wife, whom we have hitherto
seen only as a dignified and purposeful lady. Perhaps the best
example of the buffer scene is the introduction of Octavius'
servant at the end of III i, after the great speech of Antony's
beginning

> O, pardon me, thou bleeding piece of earth.

(III i 254)

This little scene is often omitted in modern representations –
very wrongly, for it performs no less than three very valuable
functions. First, it acts, like the two scenes mentioned a moment
ago, as a buffer, a relaxation between two moments of tension;
second, it advances the plot by hinting that Octavius is only
waiting for the right moment to seize power; and third – and
most important on the Elizabethan stage which, of course, had
no curtain – it gives Antony someone to help him carry the body
of Caesar from the stage.

(from an Australian English Association lecture, 1941)

E. M. FORSTER: *Julius Caesar*

WHILE I was considering what to say about *Julius Caesar*, I
happened to go to a school entertainment. It was a large primary
school, and the boys mostly came from working class homes;
little boys – the eldest couldn't have been fourteen. They acted

some scenes out of this very play. They did not act them well –
how should they? They had not had the time to rehearse, they
forgot their words and said them too fast, also there was not the
money to buy properties with: the Roman Senators wore towels
and curtains and anything they could scrounge and a solitary
garland of green cardboard was handed from Caesar to Brutus
and from Brutus to Antony as the occasion required. The audience
were more interested in identifying their offspring than in following the plot. Remarks could be heard such as, 'There he is, that
one's Tom', and there were squeals from babies who were lifted
up in their mothers' arms to see better, and seemed critical of
what they saw. I was critical myself – yet I had an odd feeling of
pleasure and of awe, and certain words of Cassius after the murder
came into my mind.

> How many ages hence
> Shall this our lofty scene be acted o'er,
> In states unborn and accents yet unknown!

If Shakespeare had been present with us in that school, he might
not have been flattered but he would not have been surprised,
for what he expected to occur has occurred: the play lives.

> O Julius Caesar! thou art mighty yet:
> Thy spirit walks abroad.

It was walking with us as well as circumstances permitted: it was
part of the civilisation of England and of all who read English.

The general immortality of Shakespeare is too vast a subject.
Let us keep to this particular play. Why has it caught on? It is
about some old Romans who murdered one of their number and
were finally defeated by his friends. The incident was chronicled
by a Greek historian, Plutarch, and Shakespeare read a translation of it and turned out a play somewhere about 1600. It seems
to have been a success from the first. And we to-day, though we
may not rank it with the Great Four – *Hamlet, Othello, Lear,
Macbeth* – always hail it as a typical example of his genius, and
are excited when the curtain rises.

It is exciting – that is one reason for its popularity. Although it is not carefully constructed like a Greek play or a classical French play, although it is not as cunning in its advance as *Othello* or *Macbeth*, yet it does succeed in startling us and holding us. It effects this by three well-timed explosions. The first of these explosions is of course the murder itself. The preparation for this is masterly – the growth of the conspiracy, omens, storms, apparitions, Portia's forebodings, Calpurnia's dream, the tempting of Caesar to the Senate House, the failure of Artemidorus to save him, the luring away of Antony: and then the deed. And the murder is followed by a second explosion: Antony's funeral speech. The excitement is revived and increased instead of dropping. After that indeed there is a lull and a failure to interest, until we come to the plains of Philippi and the third explosion: the quarrel in the tent between Brutus and Cassius. This is so unexpected, so natural psychologically and so touching that it produces a tremendous effect, and after it, his nerves all exhausted, Brutus beholds Caesar's ghost. I do not mean that these three explosions, these three famous scenes, are the only reason for the play's popularity. But they do provide the excitement, and if a drama does not excite the ordinary man it may satisfy its contemporaries, but it has no chance of being acted 'in states unborn and accents yet unknown'.

The second reason for popularity is the character drawing, and particularly the character of Brutus. Before I come to it, I am going to risk a generalisation about Shakespeare. He was an Elizabethan dramatist, and I do not think the Elizabethans were conscientious over their characters; they would often alter them in the middle in order to get on with the play. Beaumont and Fletcher contain glaring examples of this. Good men become bad and then good again: traitors turn into heroes and vice versa without any internal justification. And Shakespeare sometimes does it too. There is an example – not a glaring one – in this play, in the character of Casca. Casca first appears as extremely polite and indeed servile to Caesar. 'Peace ho! Caesar speaks,' he cries. Then he shows himself to Brutus and Cassius as a sour blunt contradictious fellow, who snaps them up when they speak and is grumpy when they invite him to supper. You may say this is subtlety on Shakespeare's part, and that he is indicating that Casca is a dark horse. I don't think so. I don't think Shakespeare was bothering about Casca – he is merely concerned to make the action interesting and he alters the character at need. Later on, during the thunderstorm, Casca becomes different again; he walks about with a drawn sword, is deeply moved by the apparitions, and utters exalted poetry. At the murder-scene he wounds Caesar in the neck, and then we hear of him no more. His usefulness is over. Contrast Shakespeare here with a modern writer, like Tolstoy. Tolstoy is conscientious over his characters, he has a personal responsibility to each of them, he has a vital conception of them, and though they are full of contradictions, those contradictions are true to life. Contrast Casca with Dolohov in *War and Peace*. Shakespeare often doesn't mind about his people. And when I am reading him one of my difficulties is to detect when he does mind and when he doesn't. This may be heresy on my part, but it seems to me that a great deal of Shakespearean criticism is invalid because it assumes that his characters are real people, and are never put in just to make the play go. The play's the thing, I suggest.

It is delightful when the characters are real, when Shakespeare does bother about them. Brutus is real, so is Cassius, so is Antony, so perhaps is Caesar himself. Brutus is an intellectual who can do things, who is not (like Hamlet) hampered by doubts. He can do things – but he always does them wrong: his advice is invariably fatal, from the moment of the murder down to the battle of Philippi. He cannot realise that men seek their own interests, for he has never sought his own, he has lived nobly among noble thoughts, wedded to a noble wife. He is kind to his servant. Everything he does is touched with fineness. Yet Brutus is not frigid. He just avoids being a prig. We are able to take him to our hearts. And with him is associated the worldly but far from contemptible Cassius. Those two speak the same language though they sometimes use different words. And against them is opposed Mark Antony– brilliant, sensuous, devoted to Caesar, but heartless otherwise, and treacherous. These three support the play. The character of Caesar is – difficult: Shakespeare does not present him sympathetically. He makes a few fine remarks like

> It seems to me most strange that men should fear:
> Seeing that death, a necessary end,
> Will come when it will come.

But goes on to talk bombast and to assert that he and Danger

> . . . are two lions litter'd in one day
> And I the elder and more terrible.

Do you detect a contemporary voice here? I do. It is Mussolini's. His infirmities are insisted on: his epilepsy, his deafness. He is pompous, conceited, showing-off, dictatorial. Indeed, some modern producers have stressed this and have presented *Julius Caesar* as a study in Fascism. But when Caesar is dead, his spirit is mighty, and haunts Brutus and wins. I don't know what to make of this. If Shakespeare were a modern writer I should be more clear about his conception. I should be certain that he has planned Caesar to be little in life and great in death. But, being an Elizabethan, is it possible that he may be altering Caesar as he alters Casca, for the sake of the play?

Excitement – and enough real people. Here are two of the reasons why *Julius Caesar* lives, and why, after more than three hundred years, it is acted by primary school boys. At the end of the performance to which I have referred, after Brutus, aged twelve, had suicided himself, and fallen with rather a thump, another of the children came forward, in his little brown suit, to speak the epilogue. The epilogue was not by Shakespeare. It ran as follows:

> I come to say our play is done
> We hope you have enjoyed the fun.

The child then retired. He had spoken briefly but justly. Shakespeare is fun. There are murders and ghosts, jealousy, remorse, despair, there is *Othello*, there is *Lear*, there is even *Timon of Athens* – but – how shall I put it? Shakespeare never grumbles. He denounces life but he never complains of it; he presents even its tragedies for our enjoyment.

(from *Two Cheers for Democracy*, 1951)

WILLARD FARNHAM: High-minded Heroes

Julius Caesar is a landmark not merely in the history of Shakespearean tragedy but in the history of English tragedy. Before Brutus there had been no tragic hero on the English stage whose character had combined noble grandeur with fatal imperfection. Heroes fatally imperfect there had been, as interest in tragic justice had grown and the medieval picture of a disorderly mortal scene ruled by Fortune had faded, but many of them had been villains or weaklings and all of them had been incapable of arousing profound admiration. Though Marlowe's Tamburlaine had achieved grandeur, it was of a kind not to be called noble, and he had achieved it by being free from any fatal imperfection except a mortal nature and thus by being a dubious tragic hero. In Brutus, then, Shakespeare discovered the noble hero with a tragic flaw. By that discovery he made it possible for English tragedy to reach a greatness hitherto attained only by Greek tragedy. All his tragedies written after *Julius Caesar* benefited by the discovery.

The heroes of *Julius Caesar, Hamlet, Othello,* and *King Lear* are blood brothers in their nobility. With all their faults they are nothing if not admirable characters. Shakespeare lavishes poetic power upon them to magnify them and give them an appeal to our hero-worshiping faculties, and we find that even Lear, though old age has had a sad effect upon his majesty, possesses that which commands esteem.

Probably the most significant thing one may say about these four heroes as admirable characters is that, however difficult it is to probe the meanings of their tragedies, it is not at all difficult to understand the hold their humanity has upon us. When they arouse our admiration, they do not leave us uncertain why they do so. Moreover, they arouse some measure of admiration in all of us who know them; no one of them creates among us a camp of condemners as well as a camp of praisers, for they are noble spirits in a simple sense of the word. If good and evil are mighty opposites in the finite universe, as Shakespeare often makes them in his tragedies, then Brutus, Hamlet, Othello, and Lear can be placed on the side of good, without debate and without involved justification. Each has plainly a bent toward good. Brutus and Hamlet have a consuming desire to further the cause of right, and Othello and Lear suffer the tortures of remorse when they realize the wrong they have done.

Because these heroes of Shakespeare's middle tragic world are at heart incorruptible, their tragic flaws do not reach into the centers of their characters. They are not deeply flawed, even though their flaws are fatal. The flaws of Brutus and Hamlet do not lead either hero to the doing of evil – that is, to the doing of evil according to the light in which their dramas are written. Shakespeare does not put Brutus in a class with Judas and make him worthy of a place in deepest Hell for treacherous betrayal of a master, as Dante does. In *Julius Caesar* the high-minded hero tries dutifully to do right, even by means of assassination, which for him is a form of judicial execution, and comes to ruin because of fatal mistakes in judgment growing out of faulty wisdom. Nor does Shakespeare make Hamlet guilty of sin in the seeking of a private revenge forbidden by God, as he might have made him. Hamlet, too, tries dutifully to do right, even by means of assassination, which in his case is enjoined by a primitive code of honor.

(from *Shakespeare's Tragic Frontier*, 1950)

JOHN HOUSEMAN: Filming *Julius Caesar*[1]

As our work progressed it was Joe Mankiewicz, the movie maker, who proved to be the conservative among us. He it was who held us most severely to a direct and smooth transition from playscript to screen-play; he who insisted, and then went on to demonstrate, that the diverse and special resources of the movie medium should be used not to supercharge or distort but to render Shakespeare's political thriller faithfully and imaginatively for the screen. When we had finished, we found, to our surprise, that we had adhered more closely not only to Shakespeare's text but also to Shakespeare's stage directions than would have been possible or desirable on a modern stage.

From the start we set ourselves one basic rule: that at no point must the words or the action of the drama be swamped by 'production' – either by spectacular mass or by irrelevant detail. For this reason, in spite of the studio's offer of Technicolor, we chose to film *Julius Caesar* in the familiar and concentrated dramatic tones of black and white.

Our costumes, while authentic in style, are simple and functional. Formal or informal, civilian or military, we tried to give the impression at all times that our actors were men wearing clothes, not characters wearing costumes.

Our sets are architectural: some small, some massive, but all, we trust, dramatically effectual. Our main stage, the Roman forum with the 'pulpit' and the long, steep flight of steps leading up to the pillared porch of the Capitol where Caesar is murdered, has the line and scope of great stage design. For years we have all been admiring Gordon Craig's magnificent theatrical conceptions while regretfully realising that their proportions could never be satisfactorily contained within the restricted frame of our modern proscenium arches. In the motion picture *Julius Caesar*, however, we have to a great extent been able to satisfy our hunger for heroic setting. And through the magic power of lens and microphone, registering every syllable and every facial expression, no matter how whispered the voice or how intimate the secret thought, the actors and their conflicts are never dwarfed by their surroundings. Rather, they gain from the set's great size and their own changing and controlled dramatic relation to it.

In sharp contrast to the official magnificence of the Capitol is the sweaty congestion of our Roman slums. Here, as in the later military scenes, it was action, not spectacle, we were after, dramatic reality rather than archaeological realism. (Not that we weren't pleased the afternoon Vittorio de Sica came onto our set and, walking up our dark and crooked street, asked if we had not copied it from an existing alley in present-day provincial Ferrara rather than from ancient Rome.)

While never deliberately exploiting the historic parallels, there were certain emotional patterns arising from political events of the immediate past that we were prepared to evoke – Hitler,

Mussolini and Ciano at the Brenner Pass; the assemblage at Munich; Stalin and Ribbentrop signing the Pact; and similar smiling conference-table friendships that soon ripened into violence and death. Also Hitler at Nuremberg and Compiègne, and later in the Berlin rubble; Mussolini on his balcony with that same docile mob massed below which later watched him hanging by his feet, dead. These sights are as much a part of our contemporary consciousness – in the *black and white* of newsreel and TV screens – as, to Elizabethan audiences, were the personal and political conflicts and tragedies of Essex, Bacon, Leicester and the Cecils.

There was another challenge of which we were aware, but of which, no matter how carefully we planned, little could be learned until we got into production: the proper visual and acoustical treatment of Shakespearean dialogue on the screen.

In one respect we were fortunate: the action of *Julius Caesar* is swift, concentrated, intense. Thus, we were spared some of the grievous problems that beset the film-maker who undertakes a *Hamlet*, a *Macbeth* or a *Lear*. The cinematic treatment of the soliloquies in *Julius Caesar* presented no hazard, for there are none. The words of Cassius as he watches Brutus' retreating figure and plans his next move to enmesh him, and of Brutus in his orchard at dawn awaiting the coming of the conspirators and reluctantly conceding the necessity for Caesar's murder, were not treated as soliloquies (with sound-track riding over a frozen close-up or the camera wandering across irrelevant scenery), but as highly charged dramatic speech.

The basic problem, of course, was how to transfer the dramatic action of a great playwright whose essential instrument of communication is the spoken word, to a medium in which the auditory is habitually subordinate to the visual. Beyond that, there was the problem of fixing in a permanent print, for projection before diverse audiences separated by time and place, words intended to be spoken directly by living actors to living audiences whose daily mood the actors could gauge and whose measure they could take at each performance. . . .

For all our planning and precaution it was inevitable, in

making such a picture, that new problems – visual and aural – should have been encountered right through to the last phases of editing and preparing the film for release.

We soon found that a Shakespearean scene, no matter how conventionally shot, is not subject to the normal laws of film cutting. With the intuitive skill of a sensitive editor watching new film running through his moviola, Jack Dunning soon discovered that a Shakespearean scene had certain general rules of its own, differing from those of other movies.

The reaction-shot, for instance, which has long been the basis of dramatic cutting in both silent and talking pictures, becomes a tricky thing to use in editing Shakespearean dialogue. Silent reactions, even when carefully planned by the director to fall in predetermined places during a long speech, were rarely used by the editor, who developed a strong reluctance – born not of veneration for the classics but of sound cutting instinct – to interrupt the line and cadence of a speech in the mouth of one character, by cutting away to the reaction of another. It struck him as arbitrary and false. And he was right. The film, as he worked on it, developed its own proper cutting-rhythm and form. The result was no less sharp or dramatic than other cutting – only different.

(from *Sight and Sound*, July–September 1953)

NOTE

1. The article in *Sight and Sound* (July–September 1953) from which these portions are taken incorporates two pieces by Mr Houseman published earlier in 1953 in *Theatre Arts Magazine*. P.U.

HERBERT BLAU: The Language of Casca

THE functioning of language in Elizabethan drama is, of course, too complex a subject to consider fully; but it would be worthwhile, in conclusion, to examine two marked characteristics in respect to what has been said so far:[1] the alternation of mood, and the variation from verse to prose. In the Elizabethan drama, whenever there is an alternation of mood, it is, as Eliot somewhere suggests, generally in the direction of humor, as in the scene in *Julius Caesar* were Casca recounts to Cassius and Brutus the refusal of Caesar to accept the crown thrice offered to him by Antony. The tone of this scene, with its ominous banter, is not entirely different from the one preceding it, in which Cassius sounds out Brutus's attitude toward Caesar. Yet the Casca scene is in prose and the latter in verse – the variation serving to label not only the change in tone, but the character of Casca and, even more important, the reduction in motive, the relaxed intensity of situation. In the first scene, Cassius had to speak carefully: consequently the formalization of his expression. With Casca – who speaks elsewhere in verse – the tone is that of the informal, half-mocking conversation of old friends, rhythmic nonetheless for its prose, because the tension is dormant, underlying the immediate situation and liable to manifest itself again in verse, which it does in the next exchange between Brutus and Cassius on Casca's exit.

The Casca scene is, then, a rhythmic and structural node in the Brutus–Cassius relationship. The language of the play is always in motion; the change from verse to prose has meaning beyond characterization. Poetry, in becoming character, becomes action – becomes in fact an appraisal of the very action it identifies.

(from *Modern Language Quarterly*, XVIII (1957))

NOTE

1. These are the two concluding paragraphs of Mr Blau's extended study of 'Language and Structure in Poetic Drama'. *Julius Caesar* is not elsewhere cited in Mr Blau's paper. P.U.

R. A. G. CARSON: The Ides of March[1]

CAESAR was now absolutely supreme; but at the close of the wars against the Pompeians his autocratic powers were, strictly speaking, constitutionally held. At the end of 45 B.C. he was for the fourth time dictator, and from misconceptions about the nature of this office much muddled thinking on Caesar's position derives. In modern political thought the term dictatorship means the exercise of unconstitutional supreme power; but in the Roman Republic the dictatorship was an office to which a man was constitutionally appointed at a crisis of the State's affairs. When the crisis was safely over, the dictator resigned his appointment, as Sulla had done. In Caesar's case, however, the appointment had been given him for life; and on some of his coins his portrait appears coupled with the title *dictator perpetuus*.

In addition, at the end of 45, Caesar was given the consulship, in normal times the chief annual magistracy of the Roman state, for a period of ten years. The *praefectura morum*, a reviewing authority which controlled entry into the Senate, was also now bestowed on him permanently. More to the point, it was Caesar alone who had command of armed forces.

As the year 44 opened, the great political question in men's minds, not least in that of Caesar himself, must have been how his supreme power was to be given a durable expression. Doubtless Caesar could have maintained his autocracy for his life-time; but the experience of the Civil Wars had shown that Roman political organization was inadequate to control and perpetuate a widespread empire. It must have been Caesar's purpose, as a statesman, to establish a system that would continue beyond his life-time. Contemporary sources, which Shakespeare followed in close detail, allege that Caesar's intended solution was the establishment of a monarchy.

This was a natural conclusion for contemporary society to reach, since throughout ancient history kingship was the only known form of continuing authority vested in the hands of one man. The Romans were sufficiently familiar with this conception through their recent wars of conquest in the East against the monarchs of the Hellenistic kingdoms, into which the empire of Alexander the Great had been divided. Indeed, Rome herself in her early days had had her own kings. But there was a political tradition in Rome, now several centuries old, of repugnance to the idea of kingship; and the allegation that Caesar meant to set up a monarchy was probably no more than a piece of propaganda, spread by the senatorial opposition and subsequently used to justify his assassination.

Because Caesar was murdered before he revealed his political plans, they have been a subject of speculation among many later historians. Some of the evidence produced by research has been interpreted as revealing monarchical ambitions on his part. The Hellenistic monarch was conceived to be not a mere mortal but a divine being who was worshipped as a god in his life-time. Ancient authorities relate that a cult of Caesar as Jupiter Julius was established while he was still alive, and that statues of Caesar were erected in temples, including one in a temple dedicated to the Clemency of Caesar. Since a cult of the deified Julius was zealously propagated by Octavian, for his own political reasons, after Caesar's murder, it is more than likely that hostile sources have conveniently ante-dated this practice. Indeed, the coins that picture the temple dedicated to the Clemency of Caesar can be shown to have been issued only after the Ides of March; for the reverse is shared with a coinage bearing the portrait of Mark Antony, wearing a beard, an indication, in a clean-shaven period, of mourning – and for whom but Caesar?

There is, of course, the incident at the feast of the Lupercalia on 15 February, when Mark Antony 'thrice presented him a kingly crown which he did thrice refuse'. There are two mysteries here. If Caesar had decided on a public ceremony of coronation, his purpose would hardly be deflected by a hostile reaction from the Roman plebs: his legions, after all, were drawn up just outside the gates of Rome. Yet this presentation and refusal are well attested. The presumption is that Caesar meant publicly to give the lie to the mounting rumours of his intention to become king. The second mystery is the crown itself. That Greek writers should describe it as a diadem is natural enough, for this was the head-dress of the Hellenistic kings; but Cicero, too, uses the same word. It was, perhaps, because of the close association of the diadem with Hellenistic monarchy that Caesar chose it as the symbol of the kingship that he would reject. The regalia worn by Caesar at the Lupercal – a purple robe and golden wreath – and the golden chair in which he sat, have all been taken as evidence of his kingly ambitions. This regalia is said to be that of the ancient Etruscan kings of Rome. In fact, Caesar's wreath on his coin portraits, in the artificial regularity of its leaves and the lack of ties at the back, is exactly that of gold wreaths of the Etruscan type. The wreath and the purple cloak were, however, also the insignia of the successful general celebrating a triumph; and they would be recognized as such by Caesar's contemporaries. Evidently the Romans did not connect this type of wreath, at least, with their ancient kings; for a coin, issued in the reign of Augustus a short time later, portrays one of these kings, Numa Pompilius, wearing a Hellenistic, and not an Etruscan, diadem.

The fact that a series of coins, bearing the portrait of Caesar, was issued in his life-time has been regarded as part of his plans to be recognized as king; for it is asserted that until this time the only living persons who had appeared on coins were the Hellenistic monarchs. This is not strictly true: portraits of two Romans of an earlier period have been identified on coins struck while they were still alive. Coins with the portrait of Scipio were issued during the war against Hannibal, and a series of gold staters was struck with the portrait of Flaminius, after his defeat of the Macedonians at the battle of Cynoscephalae in 197. These, indeed, were issued in the provinces, not in Rome. The practice at Rome had been to reserve the obverse of coins for the portraits of the gods, or of illustrious forbears of the moneying magistrates; but the general tendency was towards a commemoration that caught up with events. Sulla's head appeared on coins not very long after his death, and Pompey's within a few years of his decease. That Caesar's head appeared on coins while he was still alive was only to carry the trend a stage further. The surprising thing is that this had not happened earlier; and it does not necessarily indicate kingly aspirations on Caesar's part.

Much of the idealism that has been attributed by later political thought to the conspirators against the dictator can be discounted; Shakespeare truly says that they acted as they did 'in envy of great Caesar'. His autocratic position, and the likelihood that some such political arrangement would persist, spelt the end of power for the senatorial party. More important, it foreshadowed a close to the financial gains that proconsular office in the provinces had hitherto offered them. For practical reasons Caesar had to be removed.

Not all the names of the conspirators are known to us. Those who have been identified include not only members of the defeated Pompeian party, such as Cassius and Brutus, but also close associates of Caesar, such as Decimus Brutus, whom he had named in his will as his heir should Octavian not accept the inheritance. The secret of the conspiracy was well kept; and, although hints of it had leaked out, the rumours were not taken seriously, and Caesar even disbanded his special guard. The conspirators could not easily decide on the place and time for the assassination. But they saw that their opportunity would soon have passed, since in the early spring of 44 Caesar was on the point of leaving Rome for the Parthian war. The meeting of the Senate, called for the Ides of March in the theatre of Pompey, was finally chosen as the occasion. At this meeting, it was said, a further proposal to confer the kingship on Caesar would be debated.

The stories of warnings to 'beware the Ides of March', of dreams and other supernatural manifestations that caused Caesar, at the last minute, to ask Antony to postpone the meeting, indicate that some information about the proposed attempt had reached him. Decimus Brutus, however, was able to persuade him not to cancel the arrangements. At the entrance to the theatre, Antony was held in conversation by one of the conspirators, Trebonius. Caesar entered alone and took his place on his gilded chair. Tillius Cimber approached proffering a plea that Caesar should annul the sentence of banishment on his brother; the other conspirators thronged around, ostensibly joining Cimber to support his petition. When Caesar rejected it, Cimber ripped the toga from the dictator's shoulders, Casca stabbed him in the neck and, under a wild flurry of blows from the other conspirators, Caesar, wrapping himself in his toga, fell at the foot of the statue of his great enemy, Pompey.

Caesar was dead. The conspirators seem to have imagined that, once he had been slain, they would be hailed as liberators by the Senate and people. The senators, however, bolted in panic from the theatre; Antony, fearing for his life, made his escape; and the news of Caesar's murder cleared the crowds from the streets. The conspirators, unable to pursue their advantage, shut themselves up in the Capitol for safety.

The initiative was lost; and, after a day of uncertainty, the conspirators made an approach to Antony, the surviving consul, asking him to convene the Senate. From that moment their cause was doomed. The opening of negotiations with Antony, Caesar's colleague in the consulship, was a tacit recognition of the legality of Caesar's position. The Senate met in the Temple of Tellus, under Antony's presidency, and in the absence of the conspirators themselves. Even the short time that had elapsed since Caesar's murder had been sufficient for the senators to reflect on the consequences of repudiating Caesar's acts. For them not the least would be the disqualification and removal of many of their own order from the Senate. Just as persuasive was the knowledge that among Caesar's unfulfilled promises was one for the reward and settlement of his veterans, crowds of whom surrounded the meeting place. Caesar's acts were ratified, a general amnesty declared, and a public funeral decreed for the fallen head of state.

Since it was the custom, when a consul died in office, for his colleague to make a speech in his honour, it fell to Antony to deliver the funeral oration on 20 March. Antony's magnificent speech over the body of Caesar in Shakespeare's play may not accord closely with the sober truth of history; but it is the speech that he might well have wished to make. What Shakespeare has so well caught is Antony's attempt to allay the fears of the Senate and, at the same time, rouse the feelings of the mob, especially those of Caesar's veterans, and identify himself as the heir to Caesar's designs.

It had been planned that the body of Caesar should be removed from the Forum, when the funeral oration had been delivered, to the Campus Martius where, in the neighbourhood of the burial ground of the Julian family, a pyre had been prepared. But the crowd, wrought up by the ceremonies, by the reading of Caesar's will under which all benefited, and by Antony's speech, rushed to build their own pyre for Caesar in the Forum. There are picturesque accounts of wood torn from the Forum and surrounding buildings and heaped into a pile; of the veterans adding their wreaths of honour and weapons of ceremony, the participants in the processions their ceremonial robes, women their ornaments and children their toys. On this pyre the crowd burned Caesar's body. At the same time they fired the Senate house where he had been murdered. Caesar was dead; but none of the conspirators' other intentions had been accomplished. In his place for the moment stood Antony, with the support of Caesar's veterans; and already young Octavian was on his way from Greece to claim his inheritance. The Ides of March unleashed another decade, and more, of civil conflict, which finally destroyed the power of the senatorial class. Thus were created the circumstances in which Octavian, become Augustus, could establish the Roman Empire.

(from *History Today*, March 1957)

NOTE

1. Photographs of coins, etc., reproduced in the original article have been omitted. P.U.

M. M. MAHOOD: Words and Names in *Julius Caesar*

THE stage Shakespeare's thought about language had reached towards the turn of the century can best be seen in *Julius Caesar*. The dramatic conflict of that play is above all a conflict of linguistic attitudes. At one extreme there is Caesar himself, a superstitious man, who believes in the magic of his own name which is 'not liable to fear', and who tries to conjure with it by always speaking of himself in the third person. At the other extreme is the sceptic Cassius:

> *Brutus* and *Cæsar*: What should be in that *Cæsar*?
> Why should that name be sounded more then yours
> Write them together: Yours, is as faire a Name:
> Sound them, it doth become the mouth as well:
> Weigh them, it is as heauy: Coniure with 'em,
> *Brutus* will start a Spirit as soone as *Cæsar*.
>
> (I ii 141–6)

For both Cassius and Brutus, words are arbitrary symbols without properties of their own. Brutus so mistrusts the effective power of words, that he will have no oaths between the conspirators. Events at first justify the scepticism of Cassius, since Caesar's name proves no talisman to him. But there is an ominous irony in Brutus's words:

> We all stand vp against the spirit of Cæsar,
> And in the Spirit of men there is no blood.
> O that we then could come by Cæsars Spirit,
> And not dismember Cæsar!   (II i 167–70)

Words, the breathing spirit of men, are in fact the cause of much bloodshed in the remainder of the play, since the evocative power of Caesar's name is not dismembered but lives on as 'Caesarism'. The statement that '*Brutus* will start a Spirit as soone as *Cæsar*', coming from Cassius, is probably intentional irony, for he does not believe either name to have any magical power. But it is also negative dramatic irony. Brutus can *not* start a spirit because he lacks both Caesar's faith in the magic of words and Antony's knowledge of the connotative power of words. Brutus's address to the citizens approaches the Baconian ideal of establishing a just relationship between the mind and things: it is a pithy appeal to look at the facts. Its utter failure is indicated by the man in the crowd who cries out 'Let him be Cæsar'. Antony, on the contrary, has the skill not only to play upon the connotations of the word *Cæsar* but also, in the course of his oration, to strip the epithet *honourable* of all its normal connotations as it is applied to Brutus. Moreover, Caesar's word lives on in Caesar's will, and thus inflames the citizens to avenge his murder. The odd episode of Cinna the poet being lynched in error for Cinna the conspirator seems irrelevant, but in fact sums up a main theme of the play. There is everything in a name – for the ignorant and irrational. The fact that none of the characters in *Julius Caesar*, with the exception of Brutus, is morally 'placed' suggests that, while Shakespeare has cleared his thinking on language to the point where he knows words have no inherent magic but have immense connotative powers, the moral implications of his discovery, already suggested in *Richard II*, have yet to be explored. That exploration follows in the major tragedies, where the discovery that words are arbitrary signs and not right names is made by the heroes and the knowledge that the life of words is in their connotations is put to use by the villains.

(from Shakespeare's Wordplay, 1957)

ANNE RIGHTER: Acting and Play-acting

IN *Julius Caesar*, the idea of the actor's greatness works itself out in conjunction with the familiar theme of the Player King. In Casca's scornful description of the scene in which Mark Antony offers Caesar a crown before the assembled – and dubiously enthusiastic – populace of Rome, the common people 'clap him and hiss him, according as he pleas'd and displeas'd them, as they use to do the players in the theatre' (1 ii 256–60). As is usual with Shakespeare, the theatrical imagery in this speech expresses the insecurity of the ruler's position, a fatal division between individual and crown. The actors appear in *Julius Caesar* in another and more honorific guise, however, one which seems to reflect an attitude towards the Elizabethan theatre itself. Brutus actually bids the conspirators model themselves upon the players.

> Let not our looks put on our purposes,
> But bear it as our Roman actors do,
> With untir'd spirits and formal constancy.
>
> (II i 225–7)

Reality is enjoined to draw its strength from illusion, reversing the usual order. The actors are no longer the frail, shadowy figures of *Love's Labour's Lost* or *A Midsummer Night's Dream*; they are the creators and also the guardians of history. Immediately after the murder of Caesar the conspirators, bending down to bathe their hands in his blood, reflect even in the moment of violence upon the immortality which they have gained.

> *Cassius.* Stoop then, and wash. How many ages hence
>   Shall this our lofty scene be acted over
>   In states unborn and accents yet unknown!
> *Brutus.* How many times shall Caesar bleed in sport,
>   That now on Pompey's basis lies along
>   No worthier than the dust!　　　　　(III i 112–17)

In a sense, this passage belongs to that most traditional class of play images, the description of some situation or moment of time as potential material for drama. Yet it represents neither a sly, Plautine joke with the audience nor an excuse for any artificiality in the action. It serves, pre-eminently, to glorify the stage. The actors, Shakespeare's own companions and friends, have become the chroniclers of man's great deeds. It is in the theatre that the noble actions of the world are preserved for the instruction of future generations. Nothing quite like this attitude can be found in the plays of Shakespeare's contemporaries. Their work abounds with topical references, with the sort of comment on the London theatre which now requires an explanatory footnote. Only in non-dramatic literature, in the various apologies for the contemporary stage, does Shakespeare's enthusiasm find its echo. Thomas Nashe, in *Pierce Penilesse His Supplication to the Divell*, imagined fervently how it would

have joyed brave *Talbot* (the terror of the French) to thinke that after he had lyne two hundred yeares in his Tombe, hee should triumphe again on the Stage, and have his bones newe enbalmed with the teares of ten thousand spectators at least (at severall times), who, in the Tragedian that represents his person, imagine they behold him fresh bleeding. I will defend it against any Collian, or clubfisted Usurer of them all, there is no immortalitie can be given a man on earth like unto Playes.[1]

It is against the background of such a passage that one must see

not only the 'Roman actors' of *Julius Caesar* but also the trage-
dians of the city who arrive so suddenly at Elsinore, 'the abstract
and brief chronicles of the time' (*Hamlet*, II ii 518).

(from *Shakespeare and the Idea of the Play*, 1962)

NOTE

1. *Works of Thomas Nashe*, ed. R. B. McKerrow (1904–10) I 212.

ROLAND MUSHAT FRYE: 'The fault, dear Brutus . . .'

ACCORDING to Luther, 'a man without the spirit of God does
not do evil against his will, under pressure, as though he were
taken by the scruff of the neck and dragged into it, like a thief or
foot pad being dragged off against his will to punishment; but
he does it spontaneously and voluntarily'.[1] Calvin too deplores
the 'excuses' which men make to relieve themselves of responsibility, for he says that 'men cannot allege that the evil cometh
from anywhere else than themselves', while Hooker deplores 'that
secret shame wherewith our nature in itself doth abhor the de-
formity of sin, and for that cause [men] study by all means how
to find the first original of it elsewhere'.[2] These remarks sum-
marize the personal accountability insisted upon by the Christian
tradition and accepted by Iago when he tells Roderigo that "Tis
in ourselves that we are thus or thus . . . the power and corrigible
authority of this lies in our wills' (*Othello*, I iii 322 ff.). The latter
phrase sums up a commonplace idea which Calvin also expresses
when he declares that 'all sin results from our own will and
inclination',[3] while Edmund's ridicule of the notion that 'we
were villains on necessity, fools by heavenly compulsion' or
'by a divine thrusting on' similarly recalls a number of theological
expressions. Calvin teaches that 'if we sin, it does not happen
from compulsion, as though we were constrained to it by an
alien power' and that 'people with a bad conscience gain nothing
by pushing forward the providence of God as a screen for their

misdeeds',[4] while we have already noted Luther's caustic denial
that we do evil 'unwillingly and by compulsion' as though . . .
taken by the scruff of the neck and dragged into it'. Like Edmund's, too, is Calvin's attack on the astrological notion that
'all the evils wherewith the stars threaten us do proceed from the
order of nature, [so that] we must needs conceive this phantasy
that our sins are not the cause',[5] a treatment which in turn reminds us of Cassius' famous words in *Julius Caesar*:

> The fault, dear Brutus, is not in our stars,
> But in ourselves, that we are underlings.
>
> (I ii 140–1)
> (from *Shakespeare and Christian Doctrine*, 1963)

NOTES

1. Martin Luther, *The Bondage of the Will*, ed. J. I. Packer and
O.R. Johnston (1957) p. 107.
2. John Calvin, *Sermons on Deuteronomy*, trans. Arthur Golding
(1583) p. 1086a, and Richard Hooker, 'Fragments of an Answer', in
Works, ed. John Keble (New York, 1849) II 44.
3. Calvin, quoted in Wilhelm Niesel, *The Theology of Calvin*
(Philadelphia, 1956) p. 86.
4. Ibid. and Calvin, *Commentaries*, trans. J. Haroutunian (Philadelphia, 1958) p. 274.
5. Calvin, *Against Astrology Judicial*, trans. G. G[ylby] (1561)
sigs C7–C7ᵛ.

PART THREE

Longer Studies

Geoffrey Bullough

ATTITUDES TO CAESAR
BEFORE SHAKESPEARE (1964)

By the end of the classical epoch the main features of the chief characters in the fall of the Republic were well established. Usually two aspects of each of them were contrasted. Julius Caesar appeared as a man of paradox. On the one hand there was general agreement on his martial skill, energy, eloquence, power over his legions and the plebeians; on his kindness to his friends and soldiers, his moderation in diet, his frequent clemency. On the other hand he was widely regarded as capable of great ruthlessness, a despiser of religion, lustful, guileful, above all ambitious. Opinions were divided on whether he sought the Civil War and Pompey's death, but most ancient writers agreed that inordinate ambition was his lifelong driving-force; he could not bear to be second, and he wished to rule the state, possibly as hereditary monarch, certainly as a 'tyrant' in the Greek sense of the word. Though some writers thought his murder might be justified, the majority regarded it as a wicked act. The ambivalence found in Cicero and developed by Plutarch affected the whole Caesar-tradition, and we can see later historians striving towards a balanced view which would take account of both sides of his personality and career.

Few ancient historians considered the assassination as anything but a gross mistake fraught with evil consequences. The conspirators on the whole were condemned. Brutus shared the double reputation of Caesar. He was noble in his Republican and Stoic principles, yet he killed his benefactor, and though he did it for the best political motives the results proved him wrong. Either political circumstances or the gods themselves avenged Caesar within a short time. Antony also had two sides. He was a man of lax principles and loose life, yet he was Caesar's faithful friend and avenger. Afterwards he declined rapidly through his enmity towards Octavian and his luxurious life in Egypt, and he deserved his miserable fate at the hands of Caesar's heir, who himself combined the virtues of the avenger and peacebringer with a coldly calculating strain.

Thus already in the ancient world we can see a realization that the chief figures in the events between Pharsalia and Actium were men of mixed motives, with good and bad points in their public and private lives.

As Gundolf has shown, the Middle Ages found magic in the name of Caesar and attached it to many legends. In one he became the father of the fairy king Oberon by the fairy Morgana; in a poem on Huon of Bordeaux he was the son of the fairy Brünhilde and grandson of Judas Maccabaeus. Perceforest made his murder an act of private revenge by Brutus; elsewhere it was done by friends of Virgil because Caesar's daughter had laughed at the poet. Especially in France and Italy Caesar became a paladin like Hector, Aeneas, Alexander, King Arthur. He became one of the Nine Worthies* (though sometimes Pompey replaces him, as in *Love's Labour's Lost*, v 2). Having conquered many lands he was said to have founded many cities, Worms, Mainz, Ghent and Worcester. He built a Louvre in Paris, and the Tower of London (as Shakespeare's Prince Edward recalled in *Richard III*, III i 68–77):

> *Prince.* I do not like the Tower, of any place:
>   Did Julius Cæsar build that place, my lord?
> *Buckingham.* He did, my gracious lord, begin that place,
>   Which, since, succeeding ages have re-edified.
> *Prince.* Is it upon record, or else reported
>   Successively from age to age, he built it?
> *Buckingham.* Upon record, my gracious lord.
> *Prince.* But say, my lord, it were not register'd,
>   Methinks the truth should live from age to age,
>   As 'twas retail'd to all posterity,
>   Even to the general all-ending day.

* They were Hector, Alexander, Julius Caesar from the classical world; Joshua, David and Judas Maccabaeus from Hebrew story; Arthur, Charlemagne and Godfrey of Boulogne from the romances.

Alexander the Great was more easily regarded as a hero of romance, yet Caesar took to himself the qualities of the enchanter, the epic and chivalric hero. Emperors and popes traced their descent from him and boasted of their likeness to him; thus Boniface VIII wrote, 'I am Caesar, I am Emperor.' But although there were many who admired the column in Rome alleged to mark the tomb of his ashes, others remembered the fate of mortality:

> Cæsar, tantus eras quantus et orbis,
> Sed nunc in modico clauderis antro.

For many churchmen Caesar was an enemy of virtue. Anselm indeed called him an anti-Christ, like Nero and Julian the Apostate. St Thomas Aquinas in his *De Regimine Principum* (*c.* 1270) treated him as an abuser of power and as a moral example, now of mildness, now of cruelty, with no attempt at a historical view. Unlike these two Dante presented a favourable view of Caesar. In the *Inferno*, Canto IV, 'Cesare armato con gli occhi grifagni' ('Caesar, armed, with falcon's eyes') is seen in the green fields of the castle in Limbo, with Electra, Hector and Aeneas. In *Paradiso*, Canto VI 74–8, the spirit in Mercury, sketching the history of the Roman Empire, tells of Caesar's glory in war 'of such a flight as neither tongue nor pen could follow', and of Augustus' prowess.

Dante's aim being to advocate a unified rule against division and dissension, he naturally thought little of Brutus and Cassius and placed them in the lowest reach of the *Inferno* (Canto XXXIV 61–9) with Judas Iscariot, as traitors to their benefactors, each in one of the three mouths of Satan, 'Lo imperador del doloroso regno.' Cato however appears in *Purgatorio* as a hero of liberty. This extreme view of Brutus, with no palliation for his noble soul, was not common. Petrarch was in two minds about Brutus. In his *Trionfi* he praises Cicero the versatile orator, leader, writer, even more than Julius Caesar, whom he saw as a slave of Cupid and a friend of Fame. Cato and Brutus were to be admired as champions of liberty. Petrarch also wrote a work on famous men, of which the biography of Caesar formed half. Here in contrast with his awestruck admiration for Caesar, he takes a different view of Brutus – as ungrateful, treacherous and foolish. In the Renaissance this biography was often ascribed to one Julius Celsus and as such widely read, translated and copied. Petrarch did much to give the Caesar legend scholarly details and new admirers. Compared with him Boccaccio showed little historical sense, telling of Caesar's death in the *Amorosa Visione* and also in the *De Casibus Illustrium Virorum* which Chaucer used for the *Monk's Tale*.

> By wisedom, manhede, and by greet labour
> From humble bed to roial magestie
> Up roos he, Julius the conquerour,
> That wan al thoccident, by land and see
> By strength of hand, or elles by tretee,

and vanquished Pompey. Brutus and Cassius are evil men

> That ever hadde of his hye estaat envye.

Caesar's manliness and 'honesty' were shown when before he died he cast his mantle over his hips

> For no man sholde seen his privetee.

Chaucer's (or Boccaccio's) authorities were Lucan, Suetonius and Valerius Maximus for a history which showed that to Caesar and Pompey

> Fortune was first freend and sithe foo.

So Caesar's is a tragedy of changing Fortune, not of desert.

Against this view the Ciceronian tradition in the Renaissance restored the good name of Brutus as the lover of freedom. Poggio Bracciolini thought Caesar inferior to Cicero because he was a bad citizen and an evildoer.

The image of Caesar entered the minds of aspiring rulers in the sixteenth century. Henry VIII was praised by Erasmus for having Caesar's strength of will, Ptolemy Philadelphus' love of learning, Augustus' reason, Trajan's clemency, Theodosius' piety. In an age of great monarchs Caesar became a pattern, and Pedro

Mexia's *Lives of the Emperors from Caesar to Charles V* praised him lavishly. So did the *Life of Caesar* by Schiapollaria (1578). On the other hand Colet warned the King to imitate Christ rather than Caesar or Alexander. Martin Luther saw Caesar as a tyrant who destroyed the Roman commonwealth, and Montaigne, while admiring Caesar's writings and his humane qualities, also thought him an enemy of liberty. Jean Bodin viewed Caesar from a Machiavellian standpoint as exemplifying the art of rule, and saw his weaknesses as political rather than moral failings. A famous German historian Johan Carion, in his *Chronica* (1532; and often translated), having like some medieval writers ascribed Pompey's downfall to retribution for sacrilege in the Temple at Jerusalem, where he was said to have entered the Holy of Holies, describes the conspiracy against Caesar:

> Cassius, having been rebuffed in purchasing to be prætor in Rome, which he aspired to be, and moreover hating Cæsar, was the first to put forward that Cæsar must be killed, and by subtlety drew Brutus into that plot. Thereupon the authority of Brutus caused the others to join.

The death of Caesar, 'this great personage, must not only be placed among examples of the inconstancy of human things, but also of the ingratitude and disloyalty of men. For several of the murderers had been saved from death by Caesar, and (what is more) honoured with great riches and estates. Also his death did not put the Republic into better order, although Cicero and other Senators tried to make peace.' Carion proved by dates that Caesar could not possibly have behaved as a tyrant during the short interval between his arriving in Rome and his death. So he defended Caesar, but he thought little of his avengers – their triumvirate was filled with cruelty.

The other side was taken by G. Botero in the *Observations upon the Lives of Alexander, Caesar and Scipio* (trans. 1602). Caesar, wrote Botero,

> had placed the principalitie and signorie of Rome (or at least an extraordinarie and singular potencie) for the end of his thoughts and the reward of his labours.

He had been involved in many conspiracies against the Republic; he governed 'not as Consull, but as a Dictator'. His aim in collecting disgraced and bankrupt followers was because such men 'did wish with al their hearts, That the waters might bee troubled, and the state perturbed'. A cynical opportunist, he reconciled himself to his enemies for sheer expediency, using Crassus and Pompey to suppress the Senate's authority and to advance his own interests until he could do without them. Botero praises Caesar's energy in the war, and his principal military virtues, but writes more about the reasons for condemning him – 'his ambitious projects' and 'those meanes which hee used to attain thereunto', 'his annihilating of the authority of the Senat: and in oppressing of the Optimates, and the better sort of Cittizens; finally, in not making any difference twixt right and wrong'. In addition he succumbed to ambition, let himself be 'honoured above reason by flatterers and sycophants', and sought 'the Title and Crowne of a King'.

These two works sum up the opposite verdicts on Caesar. For the most part a balanced judgement was attempted by both schools of Renaissance historians, and it is not surprising therefore to find in the literary treatment of Julius Caesar before Shakespeare a weighing of pros and cons, a representation of good and bad characteristics.

Renaissance educationists and writers of 'courtesy-books' frequently illustrated their ethical teaching from ancient history. In *The Governour*, a book which Shakespeare seems to have known well, Sir Thomas Elyot claimed that Lucan was 'very expedient to be lerned' for his account of the Civil Wars (I x). A noble heart should be 'trayned to delite in histories', and to 'begynne with Titus Livius'. Livy was valuable for the study of war. 'Julius Cesar and Salust for their compendious writynge, to the understandynge whereof is required an exact and perfect jugement', should be reserved till a later stage of study (I xi). 'Also there be dyvers orations, as well in all the bokes of the said autors as in the historie of Cornelius Tacitus, which be very delectable, and for counsayles very expedient to be had in memorie.'

Discussing the several qualities of a good prince Elyot uses Caesar's swimming at Alexandria to illustrate physical prowess (I xvii), praises his industry (I xxiii), his learning (I xxv), his placability (II vi), his diligence 'as well in commune causes as private, concernynge the defence and assistance of innocents' (III x). Under Affability he ascribes the discontent with Caesar and the plot against him to Caesar's own fault in withdrawing from Affability – a view which Shakespeare may possibly have recalled in his portrayal of Caesar as pontifical, critical of Cassius etc., and lacking in the geniality found in Pescetti's *Il Cesare*. Elsewhere Pompey and Caesar are made illustrations of Ambition, a 'vice following Magnanimitie'. Brutus and Cassius are treated as examples of disloyalty.

As Professor T. J. B. Spencer has shown[1] in a perceptive essay, 'The really important and interesting and relevant political lessons were those connected with *princes*' and 'in spite of literary admiration for Cicero, the Romans in the imagination of the sixteenth century were Suetonian and Tacitan rather than Plutarchan'. Various factors contributed to this. Under the Tudor régime civil war was regarded as the worst of public evils and an ever-recurring possibility, so the history of Rome under Caesar and the Triumvirate was a terrible illustration of the results of internecine strife, personal ambition and intrigue, a perfect Mirror for Magistrates. Moreover an age which regarded a benevolent monarchy as the most desirable form of government and distinguished this from selfish tyranny and democracy – as witness many other treatises beside Fulke Greville's on that subject – found it easy to agree that both the gods and human needs brought about the replacement of the Roman Republic by the Roman Empire. Caesar's arrogation of more than kingly privileges to himself might be reprehended, but the bringing of the world under Augustus' wise and peaceful rule could be seen as a lesson for Tudor and Jacobean England.[2] So the translator of Appian saw the fate of Julius Caesar's murderers as an *exemplum* of 'How God plagueth them that conspire againste theyr Prince' and declared his wish 'to affray all men from disloyaltie toward their Soveraigne', while his title page advertised his book as providing 'finally, an evident demonstration, that peoples rule must give place, and Princes power prevayle'.

In an age of princes the works of Suetonius and Tacitus were topical, and full of salutary lessons. The conflicts at imperial courts were not only more easily understood than the earlier history of Rome, but more sensational, appealing to the Elizabethans' love of luxury, cruelty, revenge and exemplary justice. Hence works like Richard Reynolds' *Chronicle of all the noble Emperours of the Romaines, from Julius Cæsar orderly*, ... (1571). Yet the number of histories of Rome written in the sixteenth century was few compared with the number of editions of the Roman historians themselves, and no later Emperor outshone the glory of Pompey and Caesar.

The English attitude to Julius Caesar preserved its medieval ambivalence, and his popularity owed perhaps as much to the fact that the British withstood his invasions as to his versatile genius and terrible fate. In his *Preface* to his *Mirror for Magistrates* (1559) Baldwin declared that 'it were ... a goodlye and a notable matter to search and dyscorse one whole storye from the fyrst beginning of the inhabitynge of the yle', but the first edition, starting where Lydgate left off, had nothing about the early history of Britain. In the additions made by John Higgins in 1574 however this gap was partially filled by sixteen tragedies from early British history which included the tragedy of *Cordila*, Lear's daughter, and *Perrex* (told in *Gorboduc*) and concluded with the tale of Nennius, 'a worthy Britayne, [who] the very paterne of a valiaunt, noble, and faithful subjecte encountring with Julius Caesar at his firste comming into this Islande, was by him death wounded, yet nathelesse he gate Caesar's swoorde: put him to flighte: slewe therewith Labienus a Tribune of the Romaynes, endured fight till hys countreymen wan the battayle, died fiftene dayes after'.

The story of Irenglas in the 1575 edition likewise told of the time

> When *Cæsar* so with shamefull flight recoylde,
> And left our *Britayne* land unconquerde first
> (Which only thought, our realme & us, t'ave spoild).

For the definitive edition of the Baldwin–Higgins *Mirror* in 1587, the tragedy of *Caius Julius Cesar* was added along with those of Nero, Caligula and other Romans. In this poem Caesar's ghost explained his inclusion in a work of British history by his invasions and conquest of Britain, and went on to describe not only these but also his triumphs over the Pompeians and his death at the hands of 'the traitor Brutus' and other envious traducers of his fame. His fall was also due to Fortune and to Jove's justice, because of the thousands whose deaths he had caused. . . . There is no evidence that Shakespeare used [this dreary piece], but he may have glanced through *The Mirror* while writing *Julius Caesar*, since Cassius' 'The fault dear Brutus lies not in our stars . . .' may be a recollection of that other rebel Glendower who in his Complaint declares, 'For they be faultes that foyle men, not their fates' (cf. IV 203).

There is no evidence that Roman themes found any popularity on the public stage before Shakespeare, although the Revels Accounts mention several pieces performed at court by child-actors between 1574 and 1581. Roman plays came next from members of the court circle revolving round Sidney's sister, Mary Countess of Pembroke, and their attempts to naturalize French Senecanism in closet drama. In writing *Julius Caesar* Shakespeare may well have been the initiator of a fashion in the popular theatre.

SOURCE: *Narrative and Dramatic Sources of Shakespeare*, V (1964).

NOTES

1. 'Shakespeare and the Elizabethan Romans', in *Shakespeare Survey*, 10 (1957).

2. Cf. J. E. Phillips, *The State in Shakespeare's Greek and Roman Plays* (New York, 1940) ch. ix.

Norman Rabkin

STRUCTURE, CONVENTION, AND MEANING IN *JULIUS CAESAR* (1964)

STANDING over the corpse of Julius Caesar at the climax of Shakespeare's tragedy, Mark Antony exclaims, 'O pardon me, thou bleeding piece of earth, / That I am meek and gentle with these butchers.'[1] Most critics have recognized in Antony's words an ironic refutation of Brutus' wishful imagining of the assassination:

> Let's be sacrificers, but not butchers, Caius.
> We all stand up against the spirit of Caesar,
> And in the spirit of men there is no blood.
> O that we then could come by Caesar's spirit,
> And not dismember Caesar! But alas,
> Caesar must bleed for it. And gentle friends,
> Let's kill him boldly, but not wrathfully;
> Let's carve him as a dish fit for the gods,
> Not hew him as a carcass fit for hounds.
>
> (II i 166–74)[2]

It should be noted that Antony refutes not only Brutus, but also Caesar. For the dictator, tempted by Calphurnia's dream not to go to the Capitol on the Ides of March, has been persuaded to ignore the dream by Decius' equally ritualistic and idealized interpretation of a spectacularly bloody incident:

> Your statue spouting blood in many pipes,
> In which so many smiling Romans bathed,
> Signifies that from you great Rome shall suck
> Reviving blood, and that great men shall press
> For tinctures, stains, relics, and cognizance.
> This by Calphurnia's dream is signified.   (II ii 85–90)

Two things interest us here, the emphasis put upon the blood shed at the turning point of the play and the surprising parallelism between Brutus' and Caesar's visions of it. The blood, as I hope to show later, is a key to the meaning of the play. But in order fully to understand it we must first see the significance of the similarity between what Brutus and Caesar make of it. Like other such commanding touches in Shakespeare, the similarity is a crucially important element of an intricate and highly meaningful design. Before coming back to the turning point of the play, I should like to explore that design.

Watching *Julius Caesar*, ii ii, the audience should be troubled by a sense of *déjà vu*; that sense, traced back to its causes, becomes increasingly troublesome. The scene presents the titular hero of the play for the first time as protagonist of a scene; the action focuses on him more than it has done heretofore. Similarly, the preceding scene has for the first time allowed the action to focus on the real hero of the tragedy. Though it is more than fitting that the play concentrate on its two great opponents on the eve of its climactic day, dramatic heightening alone will not explain the mysterious and graceful thoroughness with which the second scene repeats the action of the first.

ii ii begins, at the home of its protagonist, late in the night before the fatal Ides of March, as Caesar, his sleep disturbed, calls his servant:

> *Caesar.* Nor heaven nor earth have been at peace to-night.
>   Thrice hath Calphurnia in her sleep cried out,
>   Help ho, they murder Caesar! Who's within?
>   *Enter* SERVANT
> *Servant.* My lord.
> *Caesar.* Go bid the priests do present sacrifice,
>   And bring me their opinions of success.
> *Servant.* I will my lord.   [*Exit*

Immediately we recall the opening of ii i:

> *Brutus.* What Lucius ho!
>   I cannot, by the progress of the stars,
>   Give guess how near to day. Lucius, I say!

I would it were my fault to sleep so soundly.
What Lucius, when? Awake, I say; what Lucius!
            Enter LUCIUS
Lucius. Called you my lord?
Brutus. Get me a taper in my study, Lucius.
    When it is lighted, come and call me here.
Lucius. I will my lord.   [*Exit*

As night gives way to morning in II ii, Caesar, like Brutus in the preceding scene, greets as honored friends a group of conspirators. At the end of each scene, each antagonist has overcome his scruples and is asserting, in the presence of members of the conspiracy, his readiness to go to the Capitol. And in each scene the wife of its central figure, concerned about the consequences of her husband's behavior, assumes the position of suppliant: Calphurnia addresses Caesar 'upon my knee' (II ii 54), Portia Brutus 'upon my knees' (II i 270).

Striking enough; more so when we discover that Shakespeare has taken some pains to make his scenes appear thus constructed after a single pattern. Granville-Barker finds it necessary to apologize for the appearance of a conspirator at the end of II i. 'We may question', he remarks, 'why, after a vibrant climax, Shakespeare so lowers the tension for the scene's end.'[3] Only one advantage is gained by Brutus' departure in the company of Ligarius: the parallel with the end of the next scene. Moreover, Shakespeare has altered the material he found in his sources in such a way as to emphasize the similarity between the scenes. To cite a small instance, Plutarch describes Caesar as sending to the soothsayers after Calphurnia has spoken to him, but Shakespeare represents him doing so, in response to her sleeptalking, before she enters the scene. Again no dramatic advantage is gained; the only importance of the change is that it allows Caesar's scene to open with a brief dialogue between protagonist and servant. More notable than these details, however, is the fact that the scene in Brutus' house does not exist in Plutarch's *Life* of Brutus: it is rather a composite of several scenes in which Brutus confers with the conspirators, decides who can be trusted, plans the assassination, *goes to visit C. Ligarius*, and fences with Portia's suspicion that something is in the wind. Even the dialogue with Portia, which Shakespeare bases closely on Plutarch, does not occur in the *Life* on the night before the Ides. The idea of parallel scenes in the two homes then is very much Shakespeare's own.

Such paralleling might of course be intended, like the scenes in the French and English camps on the eve of Agincourt in *Henry V*, to draw our attention to a contrast. We should expect to find dramatic differences between the characters of Brutus and Caesar, oppositions between notions and modes of behavior that might help point up the significance of the assassination. But when we begin to consider the Brutus of II i and the Caesar of II ii, we encounter some difficulty.

Watch Brutus, for example, as he refuses to join in an oath with the other conspirators:

> No, not an oath. If not the face of men,
> The sufferance of our souls, the time's abuse –
> If these be motives weak, break off betimes,
> And every man hence to his idle bed.
> So let high-sighted tyranny range on,
> Till each man drop by lottery. But if these,
> As I am sure they do, bear fire enough
> To kindle cowards, and to steel with valour
> The melting spirits of women; then countrymen,
> What need we any spur, but our own cause,
> To prick us to redress? What other bond
> Than secret Romans, that have spoke the word,
> And will not palter. And what other oath
> Than honesty to honesty engaged,
> That this shall be, or we will fall for it?   (II i 114–28)

Here is Brutus the ardent republican, the ideal Roman, the man of action whose passionately maintained conception of honor makes him the first of a line of Shakespearean tragic heroes whose intensity of vision is almost their defining quality. Such a Brutus were easy enough to contrast to a self- and time-serving Caesar. Brutus is right: what good is an oath which merely ornaments an action conceived in honor and love of country? Moreover he is right practically: any member of the band so inclined could

break the oath to his own advantage and warn Caesar, and none
does so in the absence of an oath. Oaths then are meaningless.

As Brutus' tirade goes on, however, a new note enters:

> Swear priests and cowards and men cautelous,
> Old feeble carrions, and such suffering souls
> That welcome wrongs; unto bad causes swear
> Such creatures as men doubt; but do not stain
> The even virtue of *our* enterprise,
> Nor th' insuppressive mettle of *our* spirits,
> To think that or *our* cause or *our* performance
> Did need an oath. . . .   (II i 129–36; italics mine)

The suggestion of vanity here increases immediately as Brutus
mistakenly refuses to consider the possible aid that Cicero's
oratory might give his cause. As Cassius, Casca, and Cinna
advance arguments Brutus says nothing. Then Metellus, not
knowing his man, uses terms predictably repellent to Brutus to
propose that Cicero may profitably be thought of by the populace as the leader of the conspiracy:

> O let us have him, for his silver hairs
> Will purchase us a good opinion,
> And buy men's voices to commend our deeds.
> It shall be said, his judgement ruled our hands;
> Our youths and wildness shall no whit appear,
> But all be buried in his gravity.   (II i 144–9)

Whether touched as under the circumstances he cannot afford
to be by the crassness of Metellus' language, or wounded by the
thought that Cicero will get credit for the leadership of the
conspiracy, Brutus is wrong here, and his answer, that Cicero
will not deign to join another man's cabal, is trivial, though his
politic friends quickly agree with him.

Immediately follows what Plutarch, in North's translation,
called Brutus' 'first fault':* to the horror of every literate member
of the audience Brutus blithely rejects the proposal to murder

* Significantly Shakespeare has moved this moment from its original
place in the narrative just after the assassination to the present scene on
the eve.

Mark Antony. The speech in which he justifies his decision reveals a Brutus who parodies the sensible idealist of the preceding oration on honor, a man capable of blinding himself to practical realities through the casuistic use of analogy (Antony is merely the limb of a mystical body whose head is Caesar, and Antony will be unable to act once the head is off), and of a mystical mumbo-jumbo whose foolishness is pointed up by Brutus' tolerant condescension immediately afterwards to Cassius' superior worldly knowledge. The most famous lines in Brutus' speech describe his vision of the murder, and constitute the speech which is to be refuted by Mark Antony. The irony of Brutus' unworldly self-deception would be considerable in any context, but here, in an argument for the fatal preservation of Antony's life, it is unmistakable. The audience will recall these words shortly when Antony stands before the 'dish fit for the gods' and calls the conspirators 'butchers'.

We have just seen Brutus, then, at his best and his worst, a virtuous man whose vices – not very serious vices, perhaps: vanity, inability to notice the vicious motives of those about him, a capacity to be deceived by analogies of his own making – undercut but do not vitiate the nobility of the character he demonstrates. Because his character is so mixed, it will be difficult to contrast him to the Caesar of any one scene; the expectations of contrast aroused by the parallelism between ii i and ii will have to be disappointed. What then can be the point of the symmetry?

Let us turn now to a central moment in ii ii. Caesar's servant has left to bring him the priests' opinions of success, and Calphurnia is imploring her husband to remain in his house. To her descriptions of the night's portents, lines calculated to terrify the audience as well as Caesar, the dictator wisely remarks that fate cannot be avoided, and that these predictions 'Are to the world in general, as to Caesar' (ii ii 29). Calphurnia replies that such portents obviously 'blaze forth the death of princes', and Caesar responds with his most famous lines:

> Cowards die many times before their deaths,
> The valiant never taste of death but once.
> Of all the wonders that I yet have heard,

> It seems to me most strange that men should fear,
> Seeing that death, a necessary end,
> Will come when it will come.   (II ii 32–7)

Like Brutus' speech against oaths in the preceding scene, Caesar's stoical pronouncement is charged with Roman nobility. And like that speech of Brutus', it degenerates immediately from magnificence to bluster, culminating in inflated self-adulation ironic in the context. For as the servant returns with an absolute sign that Caesar should not go forth, Caesar announces:

> The gods do this in shame of cowardice.
> Caesar should be a beast without a heart
> If he should stay at home today for fear.
> No, Caesar shall not. Danger knows full well
> That Caesar is more dangerous than he.
> We were two lions littered in one day,
> And I the elder and more terrible.
> And Caesar shall go forth.   (II ii 40–7)

For the rest of the scene Caesar's behavior alternates between hyperbolic self-esteem such as this and suggestions of the sense of dignity appropriate to the greatest of Romans. At Caesar's best we see him, like Brutus earlier, ironically employing fine rhetoric to support a mistaken decision.*

The resemblance between Brutus and Caesar is sketched in other ways through these two scenes. In II i we watch Brutus succumbing to the skillful flattery of Cassius and company, who gaily subscribe despite their trepidations to Brutus' refusal to kill Antony. Ironically this episode is followed by Decius' account of the way he flatters Caesar: by praising him for hating flatterers. Already we may be noting the fact that both Brutus and

---

* The change in tone is unmistakable. It puzzled Hazlitt, who remarked in a note that 'we do not much admire the representation here given of Julius Caesar, nor do we think it answers the portrait given of him in his Commentaries' (New Variorum edition of *Julius Caesar*, ed. H. H. Furness, Jr (2nd ed., Philadelphia, 1913) p. 118). On the discrepancies in Caesar's behavior in this scene, see John Palmer, *Political Characters of Shakespeare* (1945) pp. 38–9.

Caesar are – at least sometimes – susceptible to false praise. II ii points up the similarity when Decius' flattery finally persuades Caesar to attend the day's exercises. Like the climax of Brutus' foolishness in the preceding scene, in fact, Caesar's vanity is here demonstrated in his fatally capricious acceptance of the interpretation of the blood that is about to be shed.

The juxtaposition of two such characterizations in two consecutive, crucial, and astonishingly similar scenes prods us to realize that Caesar and Brutus share a striking number of qualities. Both are great men who put country before self: Brutus' concern for the general good is dramatically mirrored in the crucial capacity for self-abnegation which Caesar shows when he refuses to hear Artemidorus' suit on the grounds – not those of his prototype in Plutarch – that 'What touches us ourself shall be last served' (III i 8). Yet in both selflessness is intertwined with a self-destructive vanity and a tendency to play to the galleries: witness the language of Caesar's rebuff to Artemidorus, or of Brutus' haughty remark to Cassius:

> There is no terror, Cassius, in your threats;
> For I am armed so strong in honesty,
> That they pass by me, as the idle wind,
> Which I respect not.   (IV iii 66–9)

Significantly Brutus is perceptive enough at this point to see a falling off in Cassius, yet not perceptive enough to recognize worse failings in himself; thus he can reproach Cassius first for contaminating the bleeding of mighty Julius with money illegitimately raised, and second for not sending some of it to him ('For *I* can raise no money by vile means' (IV iii 70)),* A like balance of perception and self-righteous blindness is apparent in Caesar from the outset: thus he sees better than Antony that the lean Cassius is not to be trusted, only to cancel out his observation with the fatuous 'I rather tell thee what is to be feared, / Than what I fear; for always I am Caesar' (I ii 211–12). Both sapient

* On the ambiguity of Brutus' moral standards here, see Palmer, *Political Characters*, p. 50.

men, Caesar and Brutus alike sacrifice wisdom to egotism. Both
generous men, Brutus with Cassius and Caesar with Metellus
Cimber are alike predictably unable to relax a self-destructive
moral rigidity.

In neither case is Shakespeare cynically deriding a great man
for his weaknesses, large or small. Only a Cassius, never re-
covered from the shock of realizing that all men are mortal,
could despise Caesar for being a poor swimmer. Shakespeare
wants us rather to recognize them as flawed giants. Even in
II i and II ii, where we learn more to their detriment than Mark
Antony and Cassius ever know, Brutus and Caesar are presented
to our admiration. Brutus is altruistic, courageous, compassion-
ate, and gentle with Ligarius, steadfastly noble in his recognition
that oaths are superfluous and that honor should rule the conspiracy. Caesar too is courageous, contemptuous of cowards, a
splendid Roman. If Brutus is unwilling to accept as a member
of the conspiracy that Cicero who will 'purchase us a good
opinion', Caesar will not 'send a lie' to the Senate to put a
favorable light on his absence (II ii 115). More than their suscepti-
bility to flattery and self-deception, their irrationality in deciding
and rigidity in decision, and their posturing, we remember their
largeness of soul, the courage with which they meet their ends,
and – once again the strange link between them – their stoicism.
Perhaps most startling of all the similarities, Caesar's famous
expostulation on 'death, a necessary end' looks forward directly
to Brutus'

> Fates, we will know your pleasures.
> That we shall die we know, 'tis but the time,
> And drawing days out, that men stand upon
> (III i 98–100)

and

> O that a man might know
> The end of this day's business ere it come!
> But it sufficeth that the day will end,
> And then the end is known.   (V i 123–6)

What can be Shakespeare's meaning in so carefully identifying Brutus with Caesar, slayer with slain? Ernest Schanzer has demonstrated how the ambiguity in Caesar's character fulfills the purpose of 'showing up the futility and foolishness of the assassination', and he argues persuasively that 'the whole second part of the play is an ironic comment on Brutus'

> We all stand up against the spirit of Caesar,
> And in the spirit of men there is no blood. . . .'

This is the function as well of an elaborate parallel which above all totally discredits Brutus' picture of the significance of the assassination. For if at best Caesar is to be replaced by his mirror image, what will the great eruption have accomplished? By making us see the similarity between Brutus and Caesar, Shakespeare has made the assassination rather a criminal mistake, as such recent critics as Palmer and Schanzer regard it, than an act of public virtue. The course taken by the events of the last Acts implies that *Julius Caesar* is designed as a criticism of Brutus' action and as the embodiment of a despairing political quietism not evident in Shakespeare's earlier plays. But the similarly ambiguous presentations of the great antagonists are not the only key to the play's meaning: for, by a brilliant manipulation of convention which no member of his first audience could have missed, Shakespeare brings us even more powerfully in the last Acts to understand the meaning of Brutus' crime.

Let us return to the play's pivotal moment, where we began: Mark Antony's answer to Brutus' naïve idealization of the shedding of Caesar's blood. As everyone knows, *Julius Caesar* seems to start over as a new play at this point. Much recent criticism holds that the point of the second half of the tragedy is the triumph of 'Caesarism'; Professor Schanzer has effectively refuted MacCallum, Dover Wilson, and the rest on this matter;[4] but his discussion of the ghost does not fully account for the events which comprise the last Acts of the tragedy. What really happens at the moment of Antony's speech over Caesar's body is that the play changes its terms to those of a convention that at once gives new meaning to the reality with which Brutus thinks he has been dealing and informs the audience of the course events are to take. One is dubious about Brutus' grasp of the nature of things when he admonishes his fellow conspirators that the carving of Caesar can spill its victim's blood without constituting murder. He is deceived by his own logic, and, as we have already seen, this wishful self-deception is directly answered by Mark Antony's definition of the murderers as 'butchers'. At precisely this point in the plot, as Brutus bids his companions bathe their hands in Caesar's blood, the play changes its course:

> A curse shall light upon the limbs of men;
> Domestic fury, and fierce civil strife,
> Shall cumber all the parts of Italy.
> Blood and destruction shall be so in use,
> And dreadful objects so familiar,
> That mothers shall but smile when they behold
> Their infants quartered with the hands of war;
> All pity choked with custom of fell deeds;
> And Caesar's spirit ranging for revenge,
> With Ate by his side, come hot from hell,
> Shall in these confines, with a monarch's voice,
> Cry havoc, and let slip the dogs of war,
> That this foul deed shall smell above the earth
> With carrion men, groaning for burial.
>
> (III i 262–75)

Mark Antony here calls up the world of revenge tragedy. No member of an audience remembering the *Ur-Hamlet* and *Titus Andronicus*, still in love with *The Spanish Tragedy* and within a year of seeing the first performance of *Hamlet*, could have missed Shakespeare's point; but nothing is more ephemeral than theatrical convention, and today only a familiarity with plays long dead and with such scholarship as Professor Bowers' *Elizabethan Revenge Tragedy* can make us understand what the first audience realized instantaneously. Antony reminds us, as we look at Caesar's blood, what blood on the stage can mean; and it is the moral law of that imaginary world which controls the rest of the play's events: the evil that men do lives after them, a bloody act committed to pay ambition's debt promptly incurs a further debt that must be paid, the ghost of a murdered man stalks his murderers, the sword of the revenger will not go up again 'till Caesar's three and thirty wounds / Be well avenged: or till another Caesar / Have added slaughter to the sword of traitors' (v i 53–5). In the bloody world of revenge tragedy an audience knows precisely how to evaluate the part of each actor: Brutus, the first criminal, who must trade his life for his crime; Mark Antony, the hero-revenger, who is no sooner a hero than by the inner dynamics of his role he is the villain of the piece.

The logic of the revenge conventions justifies the title of a play in which the titular hero is out of the way before the third Act has barely got under way: Caesar is the moving force of the tragedy. The action of the play makes clear sense in terms of revenge tragedy. From the moment of the murder Brutus is marked as victim, and historical process will operate on the principle that blood will have blood. Morality is irrelevant: the efficient avenger must dissemble, disclaiming the very rhetoric he employs, urging indiscriminate mischief to take what course it will because the only way back to rest is through the spilling of blood. And because morality is irrelevant, the high principles on which the noblest of the conspirators moved become a mockery. Mark Antony is deeply and movingly touched by the death of his friend, but his responsive action is utterly without the lofty end of Brutus' bloody act. The principle of his action is opportunism. Where we know the populace to be 'blocks, ... stones, ... worse than senseless things' (I i 41), he can appeal, as Brutus never deigned to do, to their vanity: 'You are not wood, you are not stones, but men' (III ii 147). Where Brutus hesitates to kill Caesar despite what he takes to be an immediate danger to Rome, and refuses (however foolishly) to kill Antony himself, Mark Antony damns with a spot his sister's son, only to please a fellow triumvir for whom he has utter contempt. The point is clear: by committing an act which makes possible the dialectic of the revenge play, Brutus has automatically removed from history the feasibility of that high-minded governance to which he dedicates his life. Because of his crime against established order, success will now go to the calculating. In such a world as he has made possible, one's chances for survival are in direct proportion to one's skill at seizing the main chance; moral passion is of no value. And so as *Julius Caesar* closes it is not even the hot-blooded Antony, but the icily opportunistic Octavius who inherits Brutus' followers and makes the final disposition.

As he was to do, though with a difference, in *Hamlet*, and unlike his predecessors in the genre, Shakespeare used revenge tragedy to create the moral universe, the philosophical base, of his play. In the world of *Julius Caesar*, the conventions establish a dramatically convincing representation of a universe, governed by inexorable law, in which events are brought about not according to man's idealistic intentions but deterministically by their own logic. The ghost stalking Brutus at Philippi calls up a cosmic order in which Brutus' wishful planning is totally irrelevant. 'Indeed,' the sage Cicero has warned us at the outset, 'it is a strange disposed time. / But men may construe things after their fashion, / Clean from the purpose of the things themselves' (1 iii 33–5). Caesar's superstition, his trust of his own personal majesty, his willing self-deception, and Brutus' naïve idealism, speciously leading him to the fatal sparing of Antony as well as to the unwarranted killing of Caesar, are signs of such construing, answered finally by the irrefutable truth of historical fact played out in time. The lover, the lunatic, and the poet, Shakespeare has told us, see to the truth of things by the tricks of strong imagination, supplying through inner vision the sense and purpose that the seeing eye cannot provide. In the world of antique history, he clearly implies, such vision is worse than futile. Troilus may argue that things are as they are valued, but Hector's contention that value lies not in the will but in the fact is confirmed by a world in which Cressida is what time proves her to be, not what Troilus posits her to be.

Such a world, in which history, not man, is the determining force, is enunciated by Brutus when he erroneously uses his perception to justify battle at Philippi:

> There is a tide in the affairs of men,
> Which taken at the flood leads on to fortune;

> Omitted, all the voyage of their life
> Is bound in shallows and in miseries.
> On such a full sea are we now afloat,
> And we must take the current when it serves,
> Or lose our ventures.   (IV iii 218–24)

The irony that Brutus is wrong about the particular application of his insight serves only to support his generalization. His wisdom here is undercut only by his failure to realize that the flood cannot be gauged by the reasoning mind. In a world governed by necessity, plans, whether noble or otherwise, have little effect on the course of events. Brutus and Cassius believe that history is amenable to reason. Cassius' intuitions may tend to be more accurate and his plans more successful in the short range, but in the long range both men succumb to a historical process over which they have no control, while success, as we have seen, goes to the opportunist who does not plan but irresponsibly allows mischief to take its own course, and from him to Octavius, who initiates no action but simply waits to gather the fallen fruit.

Making his point in yet another way, Shakespeare shows us that even the man who attempts to live by reason is determined by irrational elements within himself that he cannot recognize. Thus the great soliloquy in which Brutus contemplates the killing of Caesar begins with a decision already made – 'It must be by his death' – and proceeds through a set of rationalizations that reveal the utter absence of foundation for Brutus' fears. The proud and independent Brutus – like the proud and independent Caesar, subject, as we have seen, to skillful flattery – bases his action as much on the shrewd innuendo of Cassius as on the formulations of his own reason, and, noble though he is, shows by the eve of Philippi a degeneration – manifest in his querulousness, his new eagerness to finance his campaign with ill-got money as long as he has not raised the money himself, and his exaggerated priggishness with the newly sympathetic Cassius – which demonstrates clearly that even character is determined more by process than by abiding and shaping inner principles.

Brutus' ultimate wisdom, the only statement he ever makes to

which the play offers no contradictory answer, is his recognition
that the end is known only when the day has ended. Significantly
this realization brings him precisely to Caesar's position: death,
the necessary end, will come when it will come. In the fact, not
men's construing, is the meaning. Man is only actor, not playwright, and as actor he may not even, in the terms of *Julius Caesar*,
know the conventions of the play in which he acts. In Cassius'
ebullient words as the conspirators bend over the body of Caesar,
Shakespeare makes mortifyingly explicit the fundamental irony
of his tragedy:

> Stoop then, and wash. How many ages hence
> Shall this our lofty scene be acted over,
> In states unborn and accents yet unknown.
>
> (III i 111–13)

But by this point Shakespeare has made us party to his irony: he
has let us see and consider before the assassination the identity
between Caesar and Brutus which is at the center of the play.
Confronted with a body of historical material which meant a
great many things to a great many people, yet characteristically
motivated by the artist's desire to transform the raw materials
of historiography into the coherent form of significant art,
Shakespeare has experimented with both structure and convention in *Julius Caesar*. By creating virtually *ex nihilo* a surprising
parallelism between two crucial scenes, and by turning at its
climax what promised to be a tragical history into a revenge play,
he has twice directed our responses towards the meaning that is
the vital principle of the play.

SOURCE: *Journal of English and Germanic Philology*, LXIII (1964).

NOTES

1. III i 254–5. All citations are to the text of *William Shakespeare:
The Complete Works*, ed. C. J. Sisson (New York, n.d.).
2. e.g. Ernest Schanzer, 'The Tragedy of Shakespeare's Brutus', in

Journal of English Literary History, XXII (1955) vii; Brents Stirling, *Unity in Shakespearean Tragedy: The Interplay of Theme and Character* (New York, 1956) p. 41 *et passim*.

3. Harley Granville-Barker, *Prefaces to Shakespeare* (Princeton, 1947) II 386.

4. Ernest Schanzer, 'The Problem of *Julius Caesar*', in *Shakespeare Quarterly*, VI (1955) 307–8.

A number of longer footnotes have been omitted. P.U.

J. I. M. *Stewart*

CHARACTER AND MOTIVE IN
JULIUS CAESAR (1949)

SCHÜCKING'S[1] first discovery about Shakespeare's characters is this: that the dramatist frequently makes them speak of themselves with an unnatural objectivity, in order that the audience may easily understand their rôles. To this insufficiently dramatic technique Schücking gives the name of direct self-explanation.

In a modern theatre, he says, monologue commonly purports to reflect a realistic psychological process. The character, isolated on the stage, thinks aloud and so admits us to his mind. Elizabethan dramatic technique in this particular, however, is influenced by a close connection between stage and audience. The actor stands in the midst of the spectators and frequently addresses them directly. Schücking regards this as clumsy, crude and likely to be artistically fatal: 'The whole dramatic composition and the illusion connected with it may in this manner be absolutely destroyed.' And moreover in these circumstances the monologue is something quite other than with us and more primitive; what is offered is simple information on the play, not necessarily to be conceived as part of any authentic mental disposition. It is as if the actor held up his finger to suspend the action, turned to the audience with a 'Make no mistake! I am the villain of the piece', and then stepped back into his part. If we misunderstand this we shall feel obliged to explain in some subtle fashion what is merely an arbitrary device for keeping a simple audience on the rails.

And this non-realistic method of giving information, which extends too into the dialogue, is a signpost which will set us on the highway to a better understanding of the dramatist. 'The primitiveness and a certain childishness' manifested here 'is apparent, less distinctly, perhaps, but recognisable on closer

scrutiny, in the whole mechanism of the Shakespearian drama.'
Direct self-explanation and its implications, therefore, have for
Schücking's argument something of the crucial significance that
obscenity and verbal trifling have for Bridges's; they afford a
preliminary hint that in Shakespeare's drama as a whole 'all the
details of the technique are more harmless, simple, unsophisti-
cated, than we are inclined to imagine'. And this important
principle is sufficiently evidenced in *Julius Caesar.*

When Brutus himself declares that it would be an honour to
be slain by Brutus we are likely, Schücking says, to view his
speech as in bad taste and as a sign of arrogance; nevertheless
here, and where Brutus describes himself as 'arm'd so strong in
honesty', it is far from Shakespeare's intention to suggest a
strain of boastfulness; we are merely being reminded of how the
dramatist requires us to regard this character. And so with much
that is put in the mouth of Caesar: when he announces that he is
fearless this is no more than the handiest way of telling the
audience that Caesar *is* fearless; even when Caesar reiterates that
he is fearless the same consideration continues to apply. Indeed,
Caesar is a particularly good example of the way in which
failure to understand this simplicity leads to the misinterpreting
of a character. For on the main outlines of what is intended – a
figure wholly heroic and ideal – we cannot possibly go wrong,
unless we ignore the principle of direct self-explanation, thereby
falling into 'a gross misunderstanding of Shakespeare's art-form
which characterises all Shakespearian criticism of the last hundred
years'. If – once more – we interpret in a spirit of psychological
realism all that Caesar has to say of himself we shall receive an
unsympathetic impression of his character, not designed by
Shakespeare. And we are asked to note some of the passages
upon which such an unsympathetic impression will be based.

> . . . I feare him not:
> Yet if my name were lyable to feare,
> I do not know the man I should avoyd
> So soone as that spare *Cassius* . . .
> I rather tell thee what is to be fear'd,
> Then what I feare: for alwayes I am *Caesar*.

Of all the Wonders that I yet have heard,
It seems to me most strange that men should feare,
Seeing that death, a necessary end
Will come, when it will come.

        . . . Danger knowes full well
That *Caesar* is more dangerous than he.
We are two Lyons litter'd in one day,
And I the elder and more terrible.

I could be well mov'd, if I were as you,
If I could pray to moove, Prayers would moove me:
But I am constant as the Northerne Starre,
Of whose true fixt, and resting quality,
There is no fellow in the Firmament.
The Skies are painted with unnumbred sparkes,
They are all Fire, and every one doth shine:
But, there's but one in all doth hold his place.
So, in the World; 'Tis furnish'd well with Men,
And Men are Flesh and Blood, and apprehensive;
Yet in the number, I do know but One
That unassayleable holds on his Ranke,
Unshak'd of Motion: and that I am he,
Let me a little shew it, even in this:
That I was constant *Cymber* should be banish'd,
And constant do remaine to keep him so. . . .
Hence: Wilt thou lift up Olympus?

In a modern play, Schücking points out, we should suspect
that a man who talked so much about his fearlessness had secret
doubts as to his own courage, and on the strength of other of
these speeches we should call Caesar a boaster and a mono-
maniac; but Shakespeare's is not a modern technique, and we
must regard the self-characterisation of Caesar as being more
naïve dramatically than has hitherto been supposed by the critics.
The information which Caesar gives of himself is meant by
Shakespeare to correspond exactly with the facts, and there is
no intention of charging Caesar with the odium of vanity or
vainglory because he says these things. We might as well so
charge those figures of primitive conventional art which have

scrolls hanging from their mouths describing the moral qualities they represent. And certainly we shall misinterpret Shakespeare if we do not acknowledge that, confusingly and inartistically, he mingles this alien element with the predominant realism of his representation.

So much for Schücking's contention here. Let us examine it.

We may well begin by asking whether the confusion and lack of artistry predicated by the critic is something we recognise. Has it ever formed part of our imaginative experience of the play? If not – if it is merely something excogitated by a commentator in his study – an explanation of the discrepancy may lie in this: that Shakespeare's art holds a swift complexity not readily to be overtaken by a merely pedestrian criticism, and that his dramatic construction, far from being more primitive than we commonly allow, actually has more subtlety than is readily discernible. 'The simplicity of *Julius Caesar*', Mr Wilson Knight says, 'is a surface simplicity only. To close analysis it reveals subtleties and complexities which render interpretation difficult.' And the speeches objected to by Schücking are valid, I think, upon each of two planes upon which Shakespeare builds: the simple, outward and heroic plane upon which men 'show themselves to the world like figures on a stage'; the complex and inward plane along which we are drawn to a knowledge of 'the hidden man'. There are, in a sense, two plays.

Consider first the simpler play. Plutarch's is a story-book of which the foundation is character strongly and simply conceived, and the people so created leap straight from the page. From the first eight hundred words of the life of Caesar Shakespeare would learn three things, each conveyed through the medium of narrative: Caesar was fearless; he was possessed of a histrionic streak and fond of making speeches; he was ruthless. And what later emerges is equally simple. Caesar had a covetous desire to be called king, and was resisted by Brutus – a man (the first page of the life of Brutus tells us) who had

framed his manners of life by the rules of vertue and studie of Philosophie, and having imployed his wit, which was gentle and constant, in attempting of great things: me thinkes he was rightly made and framed unto vertue.

To Brutus men referred what was noble in the attempt against Caesar; Brutus was of gentle and fair condition; he bore a noble mind to his country. But his friend and fellow-conspirator, Cassius, was not so well given and conditioned, being often carried away from justice by gain, and suspected of making war more for absolute power than liberty. Brutus believed that Caesar would establish a tyranny hateful and fatal to Rome; he therefore subordinated his personal feelings, joined the conspirators, fought valiantly and died nobly. Cassius fought valiantly too, for though not so good a man he was full of Roman virtue. Nor were their adversaries ignoble: Antony took a big personal risk at the prompting of loyalty and Octavius spoke with magnanimity of fallen foes.

In all this, and in Plutarch's sense of the effective and defining incident, the popular dramatist's work is half done. The outwardness, not in the least 'crude' or 'primitive', which makes *Julius Caesar* so admirable for reading in schools, translates the simple and heroic quality of the prose narrative. To object here to Brutus's stern and proud rebuke of Octavius:

> *Octavius.* I was not borne to dye on *Brutus* Sword.
> *Brutus.* O if thou wer't the Noblest of thy Straine,
>   Yong-man, thou could'st not dye more honourable –

or to the hard ring, as of bronze upon marble, of Caesar's speeches already cited, is to bring forward criteria altogether inappropriate to the imaginative effect at which the dramatist at this level aims; one might as well take exception to

> I am *Ulysses Laertiades*,
> The fear of all the world for policies,
> For which, my facts as high as heaven resound.

For every age instinctively recognises as a right expression of μεγαλοψυχία speech of this sort in personages heroically con-

ceived. 'I love the name of Honor, more than I feare death.' Here
would be an inappropriate and boastful remark for a professor
to offer in a seminar-room, but we need scarcely boggle over it as
it is torn from Brutus hard upon the 'Flourish, and Shout' which
may mean that Caesar has been crowned. For, primarily, this is a
direct and manly play; and one filled with straight talk.

But the play exists in depth. And when we achieve insight
into that depth we have not been jostled from a primitive play
into fragments of another and incongruous kind of play, as the
'realist' argument would maintain; rather we have been led, as a
reflective mind before the spectacle of nature may be led, to
view the ambiguities and complexities which perennially lie
behind that simple and idealised pageant of himself which is
native to man. Nor do we find, in this fuller play, that the speeches
of Brutus and Caesar lack propriety.

Shakespeare's Brutus has nobility and great beauty – but
Dante would have found that no figure in all the dramas commits
a darker crime. How came Brutus to join the conspirators? There
is an element of unresolved mystery here, strongly underlined
in that groping soliloquy in the orchard upon which so much
commentators' ink has been spilt. It is clear that he is concerned
for his own disinterestedness. He fumbles after some interpretation of the situation whereby it shall appear to be the whole
body of the people who are endangered by tyranny. Yet his
final adherence to the plot is insufficiently considered and a
matter of obscure emotions at play behind the stoic mask. Is it
because he does not acknowledge the lure of the pedestal that
he is, for all his nobility, intellectually dishonest? At least there
is a great blindness in the deed to which he gives his name and
arm. Politically it is futile: committed in the name of sacred
equality, it leads directly to a situation in which the populace
shout for Brutus as king, Brutus must dominate Cassius, and
Antony expounds the subordinate rôle of Lepidus to an Octavius
who will eventually leave Antony himself no rôle whatever.
Ethically it is indefensible, for 'the principles of true politics
are but those of morality enlarged', and the only refuge that all
these Romans have amid their tooth-and-claw public struggles

is in their private loyalties and domestic affections; their only ultimate salvation would have been in working outward from these. Committed thus, Brutus is constrained to defend positions the falseness of which must always be on the fringes of his consciousness. The people whom he harangues as having by Caesar's death escaped the shame of bondage are the same politically untroubled mechanicals who in the first scene were so inexpugnably cheerful beneath the censures of Flavius and Marullus. Cassius, whom he berates for extortion, he has also to reproach for failing to send needed money. Caesar, upon whose death he had agreed because of the corruption that power *might* bring, he comes to persuade himself had been 'strucke . . . but for supporting Robbers'. Self-deception gathers around him and in the end he is reduced to that spiritually desperate condition distinguished by Mr T. S. Eliot as cheering oneself up:

> My heart doth joy, that yet in all my life,
> I found no man, but he was true to me.

A Roman thought! But Caesar's last words had been 'Et tu, Brute' – and uttering them he had muffled up his face and struggled no more. . . . And so when Brutus tends something to insist on his honour he is no more stepping out of himself to give us a bare notice of Shakespeare's intention at this level than is Antony when he harps ironically on the same endowment. For one who is seemingly a philosopher and a statesman Brutus has acted with too little of reason and self-scrutiny, and too much of precipitancy. But, like Romeo, he 'thought all for the best', and his sole buckler is this same honour – his conviction that he is 'arm'd so strong in honesty' that the tempests unloosed about him and within him are but idle wind. The conception steals rather often from his thoughts into his speech. But it is a travesty of our experience to declare that unless Shakespeare and direct self-explanation be called in to absolve Brutus from the responsibility of these utterances we are confronted with a character marked by vanity and boastfulness. What is behind this strain in his speeches is the instinct of a man over the threshold of whose awareness a terrible doubt perpetually threatens to lap.[3]

For Schücking, as we have seen, Shakespeare's Caesar is simply the great figure of popular tradition, 'the Noblest man that ever lived in the Tide of Times'. But he is this figure not so much dramatically created as baldly announced by the method of direct self-explanation. Now, on this simple interpretation, why does Shakespeare here manipulate his material as he does? For, first, he modifies Plutarch to give Caesar a more striking nobility, magnanimity; for example, Plutarch's Caesar is prevented from reading Artemidorus's scroll by the press of people around him, whereas Shakespeare's Caesar is disinclined to do so when told that it deals with merely personal matters. Secondly, Shakespeare modifies Plutarch to give Caesar more of infirmity, both bodily and spiritual. Thus Plutarch's notable swimmer becomes the overconfident weakling who has to be rescued by Cassius whom he had challenged. And again, in Plutarch we are told that Calpurnia had not formerly been superstitious but was become so, but in Shakespeare this is transferred to Caesar:

> he is Superstitious growne of late,
> Quite from the maine Opinion he held once.

In these modifications it appears to me that Shakespeare is creating his *two* Caesars, the popular and the deeper Caesar; and is leading the judicious to discern that the overwhelming, immediate and public Caesar is the creation of an inflexible will, is a rigid mask which has proved so potent that its creator himself can scarcely regard it but with awe. Indeed in Plutarch there is a hint for this, since we are told that Caesar's whole life was 'an emulation with himself' – so North renders it – 'as with another man'. And the force of the struggle may be judged by the exhaustion it has brought. Caesar's utterances marvellously carry the impression of one physically fretted to decay, and opposing to the first falterings of the mind an increasingly rigid and absolute assertion of the Caesar idea. As petulance, superstitious dread, vacillating judgment, a lifetime of sternly repressed fears gather for their final assault, he marks them, as Brutus could never do, with all the wary prescience of a great general, and opposes to their threat the inexpugnable *vallum* of a marmorean rhetoric:

> But I am constant as the Northerne Starre.

It is much nearer to boastfulness and vainglory than to direct self-explanation – and yet it is not boastfulness and vainglory either. We are aware, indeed, that an ailing and inwardly faltering man is here vindicating a fiction with sounding words; but we are aware too, as Caesar is, of the power of the fiction. Caesar has created Caesarism and he speaks as the embodiment of this. It is something which cannot but escape the daggers of the conspirators, for it is an idea and mocks their thrusts:

> 'Tis heere.
> > 'Tis heere.
> > > 'Tis gone.
> We do it wrong, being so Majesticall
> To offer it the shew of Violence,
> For it is as the Ayre, invulnerable,
> And our vaine blowes, malicious Mockery.

A grand irony of the play, indeed, lies here. 'To think of Caesar as now no more than an empty shell, reverberating hollowly, the life and virtue gone out of him,' writes Mr Granville-Barker, 'must weaken the play a little; for will it be so desperate an enterprise to conspire against such a Caesar?'[3] But in just this consists the tragedy of Brutus. He has killed – and with inglorious ease – an old man, his friend, grown slightly ridiculous in the task of keeping physical and intellectual infirmity at bay. But the spirit at which he thinks to strike has only a deceptive habitation in the man who still speaks so resolutely – with so histrionic a note, indeed – in its accents. The spirit has gone out abroad over the earth, and on the field of Philippi is mighty yet.

The Elizabethans were concerned about politics, if only because politics might at any time intimately affect their lives. And politics at Elizabeth's court meant substantially the interplay of a small number of personalities – of personalities often sufficiently enigmatic, the historian now feels. Everyone had a motive for attempting some insight into these – for how many fortunes might turn, say, upon a true understanding of the Earl of Essex! – and this would make for some niceness of observation in the emotional hinterland of public professions. Moreover the Elizabethans, when their education permitted it, delighted in historical parallels, and many of them would be prepared to bring to a Roman history an eye not less penetrating than that which they carried to Whitehall. If we do, therefore, take historical ground there seems no *a priori* case against Shakespeare's having desired to gratify an important section of his audience with a somewhat more delicate analysis of the springs of political action than Plutarch immediately suggests. In short, the 'Elizabethan' Shakespeare (Schücking's, I mean) cannot well be brought up in support of a primitivist interpretation of drama treating of the interior mechanisms of statescraft. For here the audience had a strong practical stake in sophistication – far stronger than Coleridge or Andrew Bradley ever had. Why, then, does criticism take the course it sometimes does, contriving to ignore much of the finer light and shade that Shakespeare casts over his picture?

Perhaps there is regularly in the human mind some impulse to reject the artist's or scientist's psychological penetration where this conflicts with the simplifying and idealising formulations of a culture. And Shakespeare here has a discomfiting realism; he disconcerted many romantic critics and set them to reassuring reverie. Thus the Brutus whose personal relationships are so beautiful and whose politics are so insufficient, so fatally of the unexamined life, the Brutus of whom Shakespeare's sombre portrait, sparsely touched by compassion, is so subtle and so fine, was discarded for Swinburne's 'very noblest figure of a typical and ideal republican in all the literature of the world'.[4] It is an interpretation that meets difficulty as soon as there is a careful scrutiny of the text. But to solve the problem by declaring that theatrical conditions permitted Shakespeare to work only in simple blacks and whites, and that what remains perplexing on this view is simply the consequence of a technique imperfectly dramatic and personative, is to reject in the name of historical 'realism' that true realism, that deep and sensitive anatomy of the hidden man, which lies so often behind the outwardness and simplicity of Shakespeare's drama popularly viewed.

SOURCE: *Character and Motive in Shakespeare* (1949).

NOTES

1. The references to Schücking are to Levin Schücking's *Character Problems in Shakespeare's Plays* (1922). P.U.
2. I am indebted here to Sir Mark Hunter's 'Politics and Character in Shakespeare's *Julius Caesar*' (in *Royal Society of Literature: Essays by Divers Hands*, X (1931)), surely one of the best essays on the play.
3. H. Granville-Barker, *Prefaces to Shakespeare, First Series* (1927) p. 83.
4. Swinburne's description of Brutus is in *A Study of Shakespeare* (1879) p. 159.

L. C. Knights

PERSONALITY AND POLITICS
IN *JULIUS CAESAR* (1965)

SHAKESPEARE wrote *Julius Caesar* in 1599, and the play was first performed in the new theatre, the Globe, which Shakespeare's company, the Lord Chamberlain's Men, had recently had built on the Bankside. Shakespeare, of course, got the material for his play from Plutarch's *Lives* of Caesar and Brutus. But, just as in gathering material for the English historical plays from Holinshed, he selected only what he needed as an artist dealing with the universal stuff of human nature, so here his purpose is not simply to reconstruct the historical situation in Rome in the year 44 B.C. The historical material is of interest only for what Shakespeare makes of it. That he made of it a pretty exciting drama is witnessed by the fact that the play is still being performed today, still capable of holding audiences not all of whom are compelled by the exigencies of university examinations. It is exciting; it is richly human; it holds the attention. It also happens to be an important work of art – which means that through the forms of a dramatic action it focuses a particular vision of life: the sequence of events, the dialogue, the interplay of different characters, are held together by an informing 'idea', so that all these elements contribute not solely to an evening's entertainment but to an imaginative statement about something of permanent importance in human life. What, at that level of understanding, is *Julius Caesar* 'about'? That is the question to which I want to attempt an answer.

Before tackling that question directly, there are two matters I want to touch on – one concerning the play's structure, the other its substance: they are, in fact, closely related. The action of *Julius Caesar* turns on a political murder, the assassination of Caesar, which takes place in Act III, scene i – right in the middle of the play. Before the murder, attention is focused on the origin and development of the conspiracy – Caesar on one side, Cassius, Brutus, and half a dozen more, on the other. After the murder, attention is focused on the struggle between the conspirators (Brutus and Cassius) and the successors of Caesar (Octavius Caesar and Antony), on the failure and disintegration of the republican cause. It is possible to see a blemish here: the climax, it can be said, comes too early, and when Caesar has disappeared from the action, Shakespeare only contrives to hold our interest by such *tours de force* as Antony's oration and the quarrel between Brutus and Cassius. In fact, however, the play forms a coherent and tightly woven whole. The murder of Caesar is, if you like, the axis on which the world of the play turns. Up to that event, we are shown one half of that world, a hemisphere; as soon as the daggers are plunged into Caesar's body the world of the drama turns, and fresh scenes and landscapes come into view: but it is still one world. Dropping the metaphor, we may say that the interests aroused in the first part find their natural fulfilment in the second: that there is nothing in the presented action of the last two and a half acts (and action includes psychological as well as physical action) that is not a revelation of what was implicit, but partly concealed, in the conspiracy itself. There is no question here of a broken-backed play in which flagging interest must be maintained by adventitious means. The play is as much of a unity as *Macbeth*; and, like *Macbeth*, though less powerfully, it reveals the connexion between observable events in the public world and their causes in the deeper places of personal life – matters not so easily observed except by the eye of the poet.

My second preliminary observation concerns the nature of the interest enlisted by this play. In dealing with *Julius Caesar*, as indeed with other of Shakespeare's plays, there is a particular temptation to be guarded against – that is, the temptation to abstract from the play certain general issues and to debate them either in the abstract or in a context which Shakespeare has not provided for them. Criticism of *Julius Caesar* is sometimes confused by considerations that apply either to the historical situation at Rome at the time of Caesar's assassination, or else to specifically twentieth-century political situations, and the play is debated as though Shakespeare were putting before us the question of whether dictatorship or republicanism were the more desirable form of government. He is doing nothing of the kind; and perhaps the first thing to notice is how much of possible political interest the play leaves out. There is no hint of, say, Dante's conception of the majesty, the providential necessity, of the empire which Caesar founded. On the other hand, there is nothing that can be interpreted as a feeling for the virtues of aristocratic republicanism – in the way, for example, some of the first makers of the French Revolution felt when they invoked Roman example. We are not called on to concern ourselves with whether 'Caesarism' is, or was, desirable or otherwise. Instead, there is a sharp focus on a single, simple, but important question – on what happens when personal judgment tries to move exclusively on a political plane, where issues are simplified and distorted. I may say, in passing, that if we want a wider context for the play, we shall find it not in a realm of political speculation foreign to it, but in those other plays of Shakespeare – they include such different plays as *Troilus and Cressida* and *Othello* – where the dramatist is posing the question of how men come to deliver themselves to illusion, of how they construct for themselves a world in which, because it is not the world of reality but a projection of their own, they inevitably come to disaster. This means, of course, that the play offers no solution – it offers no material for a solution – of the question, Empire or Republic? dictatorship or 'liberty'? Shakespeare is studying a situation, bringing the force of his imagination to bear on it, not offering solutions, or not, at all events, political ones.

Yet – and this brings me to the substance of what I want to say – *Julius Caesar* does have important political implications. It takes up Shakespeare's developing preoccupation with the relation between political action and morality. 'Politics', I know, is an exciting word, and 'morality' is a dry word. But what I mean is this: – Politics are the realm where, whatever the particular interests involved, the issues are to some extent simplified and generalized, and therefore seen in abstract and schematic terms. Morality – and I mean essential living morality, not just copy-book maxims – has to do with the human, the specific and particular. Martin Buber, in his great book, *I and Thou*, has made us familiar with an important distinction – between the world of 'thou' (the world of relationship) and the world of 'it' (the world where things, and even people, are treated simply as objects, and manipulated accordingly). For the politician there is a constant temptation to lose sight of the 'thou' world, and Martin Buber's distinction may help us here.

Julius Caesar is a play about great public events, but again and again we are given glimpses of the characters in their private, personal, and domestic capacities. Caesar is concerned for his wife's barrenness, he faints when he is offered the crown, he 'had a sickness when he was in Spain', he listens to Calpurnia's dreams and fears. Brutus causes his wife concern about his health; we are told of his disturbed sleep; we see him forgetting his public cares and ensuring, with real tenderness, that his boy Lucius gets some needed sleep. And much more to a similar effect. Now Shakespeare at this time was nearing the height of his powers – *Hamlet* is only a year or two away – and it is unlikely that he put in these domestic scenes and glimpses because he didn't know what else to do. It is obvious that we are intended to be aware of some sort of a *contrast* between public life and private, and commentators have, in fact, noticed this. They point, for example, to the contrast between Caesar the public figure and Caesar the man:

> . . . for always I am Caesar.
> Come on my right hand, for this ear is deaf.

When Brutus, in his 'gown' (the symbol of domestic privacy) speaks gently to his boy, we are told that this 'relieves the strain' of the tragic action. And every account of the characters includes some reference to those aspects of Caesar, Brutus, and Cassius that are revealed in their more intimate moments and hidden or disguised in public. What seems not to have been recognized is the cumulative effect of these and many other reminders of a more personal life – the important part this pervasive but unobtrusive personalism plays, or should play, in our evaluation of the public action.

That we are intended to be aware of the characters as men, of the faces behind the masks, is clear enough. We may notice in passing that on occasion the contrast is emphasized in visual terms. At the beginning of II ii, according to the stage-direction that makes every schoolboy laugh, Caesar enters 'in his night-gown' (a dressing-gown, or house-coat); then, as the conspirators prevail over his wife's entreaties, 'Give me my robe, for I will go.' Not only are all the main figures at some time divested of their public robes – those 'robes and furr'd gowns' that, according to King Lear, 'hide all' – and allowed to appear as husbands, masters of households and friends, but they all, in turn, empha-size each other's personal characteristics. 'He was quick mettle when he went to school,' says Brutus of Casca. A principal reason why Cassius thinks Caesar isn't fit for his exalted position is that he, Cassius, is the stronger swimmer, and that Caesar, like the rest of us, was hot and cold and thirsty when he had a fever. And although Antony, addressing the crowd, deliberately makes emotional capital out of Caesar's mantle, 'I remember', he says,

> The first time Caesar ever put it on;
> 'Twas on a summer's evening, in his tent,
> That day he overcame the Nervii,

the touch of particularity, of revealed privacy, is intended for us, the audience, as well as for the Roman crowd. We notice, too, how often the word 'love' appears in this play. I haven't made a count, but it must be about two dozen times, which is perhaps rather surprising in a political play. Again and again the characters speak of their love – their 'dear love' or their 'kind love' – for each other, just as they seem to find a special satisfaction in referring to themselves as 'brothers'. Now the effect of all this is not only one of pathos or simply irony. The focus of our attention, I have said, is the public world: from the arena of *that* world, personal life – where truth between man and man resides – is glimpsed as across a gulf. The distance between these two worlds is the measure of the distortion and falsity that takes place in the attempt to make 'politics' self-enclosed.

The attempt – the attempt to make public action and public appearance something separate and remote from personal action – is common to both sides. Caesar constantly assumes the public mask. It seems to be a habit with him to refer to himself in the third person as 'Caesar'; and there is his speech, so charged with dramatic irony, when, immediately before the assassination, he rejects the petition of Metellus Cimber:

> I could be well mov'd if I were as you;
> If I could pray to move, prayers would move me;
> But I am constant as the northern star,
> Of whose true-fix'd and resting quality
> There is no fellow in the firmament . . .
> So in the world; 'tis furnish'd well with men,
> And men are flesh and blood, and apprehensive;
> Yet in the number I do know but one
> That unassailable holds on his rank,
> Unshak'd of motion: and that I am he,
> Let me a little show it. . . .

What this means, in the case of Caesar, is that in the utterance and attitude of the public man we sense a dangerous tautness. In the case of Brutus, a parallel divorce between the man and the statesman results in something more subtle and more interesting. That a particular bond of affection unites Caesar and Brutus, the play leaves us in no doubt. Almost the first words that Brutus speaks of Caesar are, 'I love him well', and when, after the murder, he insists again and again that Caesar was his 'best lover', there is no need to doubt his 'sincerity' in the ordinary sense of the word. So, too, Cassius tells us, 'Caesar doth bear me hard; but he loves Brutus'; and Mark Antony:

> For Brutus, as you know, was Caesar's angel:
> Judge, O you Gods! how dearly Caesar lov'd him.
> This was the most unkindest cut of all. . . .

It is this Brutus, the close friend of Caesar, who wrenches his mind to divorce policy from friendship; and the way in which he does it demands some attention.

It is, of course, true that on matters of public policy you may have to take a firm stand against men whom on other grounds you like and respect: you can see this in the government of a university, for example, as well as in the government of a state. Is Brutus doing more than follow this principle to a necessary conclusion? Well, yes, I think he is. For the moment I want to put on one side the scene in which Cassius (in Brutus's own words later) 'whets' him against Caesar, and ask your attention for the long soliloquy at the opening of Act II in which Brutus reviews his own motives and intended course of action. This is what he says:

> It must be by his death: and for my part,
> I know no personal cause to spurn at him,
> But for the general. He would be crown'd:
> How that might change his nature, there's the question.
> It is the bright day that brings forth the adder;
> And that craves wary walking. Crown him! that!
> And then, I grant, we put a sting in him,
> That at his will he may do danger with.
> The abuse of greatness is when it disjoins
> Remorse from power; and, to speak truth of Caesar,
> I have not known when his affections sway'd
> More than his reason. But 'tis a common proof,
> That lowliness is young ambition's ladder,
> Whereto the climber-upward turns his face;
> And when he once attains the upmost round,
> He then unto the ladder turns his back,
> Looks in the clouds, scorning the base degrees
> By which he did ascend. So Caesar may:
> Then, lest he may, prevent. And, since the quarrel
> Will bear no colour for the thing he is,
> Fashion it thus; that what he is, augmented,
> Would run to these and these extremities;
> And therefore think him as a serpent's egg
> Which, hatch'd, would, as his kind, grow mischievous,
> And kill him in the shell.

Now it is a principle of Shakespearean, indeed of Elizabethan, stage-craft, that when a character, in soliloquy or otherwise, develops a line of argument – as when Faustus, in Marlowe's play, produces a number of specious reasons for dismissing the traditional sciences – we are expected to follow the argument with some attention. Not, of course, that we follow such a speech merely as logicians. We are dealing with drama, which means that when a character expounds, say, his reasons for a course of action, what he says is intended to reveal some aspect of what he stands for and is committed to as a human being. And we are dealing with *poetic* drama, which means that even in an expository speech we are aware of much more than can be formulated in conceptual terms. But we do not, on this account, switch off our intelligence or such powers of logical thought as we may possess. As Virgil Whitaker says in his book, *Shakespeare's Use of Learning*, 'Like Marlowe, Shakespeare expected his audience to be able to detect a fallacy in reasoning.' With this in mind, let us turn back to Brutus's soliloquy. It is a curious argument, in which qualities known in direct contact between man and man ('I know no personal cause to spurn at him') are dismissed as irrelevant to public considerations; and it is precisely this that gives the air of tortuous unreality to Brutus's self-persuadings – full as these are of subjunctives and conditional verbs, which run full tilt against the reality that Brutus himself acknowledges:

> The abuse of greatness is when it disjoins
> Remorse from power; and, to speak truth of Caesar,
> I have not known when his affections sway'd
> More than his reason. . . .*

but:

> since the quarrel
> Will bear no colour for the thing he is,
> Fashion it thus. . . .

On this Coleridge shrewdly commented that what Brutus is really saying is that he 'would have no objection to a king, or to

---

* It may not be unnecessary to comment that 'remorse', here, means pity, and 'affections' passions.

Caesar as a monarch in Rome, would Caesar but be as good a monarch as he now seems disposed to be'. In Brutus's mind, however, *what is* is now completely lost in a cloud of mere possibilities:

> And, since the quarrel
> Will bear no colour for the thing he is,
> Fashion it thus; that what he is, augmented,
> Would run to these and these extremities;
> And therefore think him as a serpent's egg
> Which, hatch'd, would, as his kind, grow mischievous,
> And kill him in the shell.

Caesar is already, as Brutus describes him later, 'the foremost man of all the world'; he is not still 'in the shell', neither is he 'young ambition'. But it is by sophistries such as these that Brutus launches himself on what Clarendon was to call 'that fathomless abyss of Reason of State'.

Shakespeare, of course, was a very great psychologist, and what the play also shows – and I want to dwell on this for a moment before returning to the scene of Brutus's crucial choice and its consequences – is that personal feelings, which Brutus tries to exclude from his deliberations on 'the general good', are, in fact, active in public life. But they are active in the wrong way. Unacknowledged, they influence simply by distorting the issues. The famous quarrel scene between Brutus and Cassius certainly has this ironic significance. It is, of course, Cassius, in whom the 'taboo on tenderness' is strongest – who is scornful of 'our mothers' spirits' (I iii 83) and despises Caesar for behaving 'as a sick girl' (I ii 127) – who here displays the most pronounced 'feminine' traits – 'that rash humour which my mother gave me' (IV iii 119). That the whole thing contrives to be touching should not obscure the fact that the causes of the quarrel – they had mainly to do with money – did demand a more impersonal consideration. Now the relevance of this is that it is above all in Cassius that the springs of political action are revealed as only too personal. What nags at him is simply envy of Caesar: 'for my single self', he says to Brutus,

> I had as lief not be as live to be
> In awe of such a thing as I myself. . . .
>   . . . And this man
> Is now become a god, and Cassius is
> A wretched creature and must bend his body
> If Caesar carelessly but nod on him.

Caesar, he says to Casca, is:

> A man no mightier than thyself or me
> In personal action, yet prodigious grown.

And it is this man who acts as tempter to the 'idealizing' Brutus, skilfully enlisting what Brutus feels is due to his own 'honour'. I do not wish here to pursue the temptation scene in any detail; but that it *is* temptation the play leaves us in no doubt. At the end of the long, skilfully conducted second scene of the first Act, Cassius is left alone and reveals his thoughts about the man whom we can only call, at this stage, his dupe:

> Well, Brutus, thou art noble; yet, I see,
> Thy honourable mettle may be wrought
> From that it is dispos'd; therefore 'tis meet
> That noble minds keep ever with their likes;
> For who so firm that cannot be seduc'd?

Editors disagree about the meaning of these lines. Some would have it that Cassius means that the noble disposition of Brutus may be, as it were, wrenched from truth by his friendship with Caesar, the dictator: the man of republican virtue should 'keep ever' with those like-minded to himself. It may be so; but I find it hard *not* to read the lines as a firm 'placing' comment on Cassius's own relations with Brutus: 'For who so firm that cannot be seduc'd' – by specious reasoning? The most we can say for Cassius is that his appeals to Roman 'honour', to the 'nobility' of his associates, are not simply laid on for the benefit of Brutus, but are part of his own self-deception. The banished feelings have come in by the back door, thinly disguised by much talk of 'honour'.

It is of course true that the play does not present Caesar as
an ideal ruler, and I myself think that Shakespeare would have
agreed with Blake's gnomic verse:

> The strongest poison ever known
> Came from Caesar's laurel crown.

But when Brutus, the man of honour and high moral principles,
accepts Cassius's arguments and enters the world of the conspirators, he enters a topsyturvy world – a world where 'impersonal'
Reasons of State take the place of direct personal knowledge; and
at the same time true reason, which is a function of the whole
man, has given way to obscure personal emotion. Shakespeare
leaves us in no doubt of the confusion of values and priorities in
that world. We have noticed how often love and friendship are
invoked in this play, indicating what men really want and need.
What we also have to notice is how often the forms of friendship
are exploited for political ends. When Caesar is reluctant to go
to the Senate House, Decius inveigles him with protestations of
'dear dear love', and the conspirators drink wine with their victim
before leading him to the Capitol; Brutus kisses Caesar immediately before the killing; Antony talks much of love and shakes
hands all round as a way of deceiving the conspirators. It is this,
therefore, that explains our sense of something monstrous in the
action, symbolized by the storms and prodigies, and made fully
explicit by Brutus in his garden soliloquy – for it is time to return
to that – when, deserting the actual, he has given himself to a
phantasmagoria of abstractions.

At this point, Brutus's self-communings are interrupted by
his boy, Lucius, who brings him a letter – one of many such,
purporting to come from the citizens of Rome, asking for redress
at his hands, but, as we know, manufactured by Cassius. 'O
Rome!' says Brutus, not knowing that the letters do not represent 'Rome' at all,

> O Rome! I make thee promise;
> If the redress will follow, thou receiv'st
> Thy full petition at the hand of Brutus!

Then, as Lucius goes off once more to see who is knocking at the
gate in the darkness:

> Since Cassius first did whet me against Caesar,
> I have not slept.
> Between the acting of a dreadful thing
> And the first motion, all the interim is
> Like a phantasma, or a hideous dream:
> The genius and the mortal instruments
> Are then in council; and the state of man,
> Like to a little kingdom, suffers then
> The nature of an insurrection.

The indications here – the insomnia, the fact that Brutus is, as
he has said earlier, 'with himself at war' – are, if we remember
Macbeth, clear enough. And the signs of a mind at war with
itself, attempting to batten down its own best insights, which
yet refuse to disappear, continue into Brutus's musings as the
muffled conspirators are announced:

> O conspiracy!
> Sham'st thou to show thy dangerous brow by night,
> When evils are most free? O! then by day
> Where wilt thou find a cavern dark enough
> To mask thy monstrous visage? Seek none, conspiracy;
> Hide it in smiles and affability:
> For if thou path, thy native semblance on,
> Not Erebus itself were dim enough
> To hide thee from prevention.

Conspiracy is not only 'dangerous', it is 'monstrous', associated
with night and darkness, with evils and Erebus. As J. I. M.
Stewart has said, Brutus's words are those of a 'man over the
threshold of whose awareness a terrible doubt perpetually
threatens to lap'.

Brutus, of course, is not a deliberate villain as Macbeth is;
but like Macbeth he is presented as losing his way in a nightmare
world – 'like a phantasma', something both horrible and unreal,
'or a hideous dream'. In other words, Brutus's wrong choice
not only leads to wrong action, it delivers him to a world of

unreality, for the 'phantasma', far from ending with the acting of the 'dreadful thing', extends beyond it. As the play proceeds, we are made aware not only of a complete lack of correspondence between the professed intentions of the conspirators and the result of their act, but of a marked element of unreality in the world which they inhabit. Let us take two examples, for Shakespeare provides them, and he presumably intended that we should take notice of what he provides.

Shakespeare often puts before the audience two different aspects of the same thing, or suggests two different angles on it – sometimes, but not always, in juxtaposed scenes. He makes no obvious comment, but the different scenes or passages play off against each other, with an effect of implicit comment, for the audience itself is thus enlisted in the business of evaluation and judgment. I think of such things as Falstaff's description of his ragged regiment, following hard on the heels of Hotspur's heroics about warfare, in the First Part of *Henry IV*; or the way in which, in *Antony and Cleopatra*, the summit meeting on Pompey's galley is followed immediately by a glimpse of the army in the field, with some irony from a soldier about the High Command. In *Julius Caesar*, the murder of Caesar is not only presented on the stage, it is described both in prospect and in retrospect. You all remember the way in which Brutus envisages the action to the conspirators in the scene with which we have been dealing. Pleading that Antony may be spared, he says:

> Let us be sacrificers, but not butchers, Caius.
> We all stand up against the spirit of Caesar;
> And in the spirit of men there is no blood:
> O! that we then could come by Caesar's spirit,
> And not dismember Caesar. But, alas!
> Caesar must bleed for it. And, gentle friends,
> Let's kill him boldly, but not wrathfully;
> Let's carve him as a dish fit for the gods,
> Not hew him as a carcass fit for hounds. . . .

Is that the way political assassinations are carried out? Before the battle of Philippi, Brutus taunts Antony, 'you very wisely threat before you sting', to which Antony retorts:

>Villains! you did not so when your vile daggers
>Hack'd one another in the sides of Caesar;
>You show'd your teeth like apes, and fawn'd like hounds,
>And bow'd like bondmen, kissing Caesar's feet;
>Whilst damned Casca, like a cur, behind,
>Struck Caesar on the neck.

Antony, of course, speaks as a partisan of Caesar, but the energy of the verse ('your vile daggers Hack'd one another in the sides of Caesar') leaves us in no doubt that Antony's account is nearer to actuality than Brutus's fantasy of a ritualistic sacrifice.

My second example is of even greater importance, for it concerns the whole sequence of events in the second half of the play – consequences, I want to insist once more, that are shown as flowing directly from what Brutus and the rest commit themselves to in the first part. As soon as Julius Caesar falls, Cinna cries out:

>Liberty! Freedom! Tyranny is dead!
>Run hence, proclaim, cry it about the streets.

And Cassius:

>Some to the common pulpits, and cry out
>'Liberty, freedom, and enfranchisement!'

Then, as something of the mounting bewilderment outside the Capitol is conveyed to us ('Men, wives, and children stare, cry out and run As it were doomsday'), Brutus enforces the ritualistic action of smearing themselves with Caesar's blood:

>Stoop, Romans, stoop,
>And let us bathe our hands in Caesar's blood
>Up to the elbows, and besmear our swords:
>Then walk we forth, even to the market-place;
>And, waving our red weapons o'er our heads,
>Let's all cry, 'Peace, freedom, and liberty!'

The irony of that hardly needs comment, but the play does, in fact, comment on it with some pungency. I suspect that what I am going to say will be obvious, so I will be brief and do little

more than remind you of three successive scenes. When, after
the murder, Brutus goes to the Forum to render 'public reasons'
for Caesar's death, it is his failure in the sense of reality, of what
people really are, that gives us the sombre comedy of his oration:
so far as addressing real people is concerned he might as well
have kept quiet. 'Had you rather Caesar were living, and die all
slaves, than that Caesar were dead, to live all free men?' he asks,
and much more to the same effect. To which the reply is successively:

> – Live, Brutus! live! live!
> – Bring him with triumph home unto his house.
> – Give him a statue with his ancestors.
> – Let him be Caesar.

After this, the response of the crowd to Antony's more con-
summate demonstration of the arts of persuasion comes as no
surprise: it is:

Revenge! – About! – Seek! – Burn! – Fire! – Kill! – Slay! – Let
not a traitor live!

Mischief, in the words of Antony's cynical comment when he has
worked his will with the crowd, is indeed afoot; and the very
next scene – the last of the third Act – gives us a representative
example of what is only too likely to happen in times of violent
political disturbance. It shows us the death of an unoffending
poet at the hands of a brutal mob:

> – Your name, sir, truly.
> – Truly, my name is Cinna.
> – Tear him to pieces; he's a conspirator.
> – I am Cinna the poet, I am Cinna the poet.
> – Tear him for his bad verses, tear him for his bad verses.

The frenzied violence of this, with its repeated, 'Tear him, tear
him!' is followed at once by a scene of violence in a different
key. If the mob is beyond the reach of reason, the Triumvirs,
Antony, Octavius, and Lepidus, are only too coldly calculating
in their assessment of political exigencies:

Antony. These many then shall die; their names are prick'd.
Octavius. Your brother too must die; consent you, Lepidus?
Lepidus. I do consent —
Octavius.　　　　　　　　　Prick him down, Antony.
Lepidus. Upon condition Publius shall not live,
　　Who is your sister's son, Mark Antony.
Antony. He shall not live; look, with a spot I damn him.
　　But, Lepidus, go you to Caesar's house;
　　Fetch the will hither, and we shall determine
　　How to cut off some charge in legacies.

And, when Lepidus goes off on his errand, Antony and Octavius discuss the matter of getting rid of him, before they turn their attention to combating the armies now levied by Brutus and Cassius. These, then, are the more or less explicit comments on Brutus's excited proclamation:

> And, waving our red weapons o'er our heads,
> Let's all cry, 'Peace, freedom, and liberty!'

That peace and liberty could be bought with 'red weapons' was the illusion: the reality is mob violence, proscription, and civil war.

In following the story through to its end, Shakespeare was, of course, bound to follow his historical material; but, as an artist, he made this serve his own purposes. Many of you must have noticed how often Shakespeare, in his greater plays, makes the outward action into a mirror or symbol of events and qualities in the mind or soul: *Macbeth* is perhaps the most obvious instance of this. The last Act of *Julius Caesar* certainly follows this pattern. Even before the battle of Philippi Brutus and Cassius appear like men under a doom; and, although defeat comes to each in different ways, it comes to both as though they were expecting it, and prompts reflections, in themselves or in their followers, that clearly apply not merely to the immediate events but to the action as a whole. Cassius asks Pindarus to report to him what is happening in another part of the field ('My sight was ever thick,' he says), and, on a mistaken report that his messenger is taken by the enemy, kills himself. On which the comment of Messala is:

> O hateful error, melancholy's child!
> Why dost thou show to the apt thoughts of men
> The things that are not? O error! soon conceiv'd,
> Thou never com'st unto a happy birth,
> But kill'st the mother that engender'd thee.

Harold Goddard, in his interesting chapter on *Julius Caesar*, says of this, 'The whole plot against Caesar had been such an error.'[1] We may add further that the play also enforces the close connexion between error and a supposed perception of 'things that are not'. As Titinius says to the dead Cassius a moment later, 'Alas! thou hast misconstrued everything.' As for Brutus, defeated and brought to bay with his 'poor remains of friends', he senses that this is no accident of defeat but the working out of the destiny to which he committed himself long before:

> Night hangs upon mine eyes; my bones would rest,
> That have but labour'd to attain this hour.

And then, as he runs on his own sword:

> Caesar, now be still:
> I kill'd not thee with half so good a will.

These last ten words – if I may quote Goddard once more – 'are the Last Judgment of Brutus on a conspiracy the morality of which other men, strangely, have long debated'.[2] Earlier in the play, you may remember, Cicero had commented on certain portents and men's interpretation of them:

> But men may construe things after their fashion,
> Clean from the purpose of the things themselves.

That seems to me an anticipatory summing-up of Brutus's whole political career, as the play presents it.

Let me repeat once more, Brutus was not, in any of the ordinary senses of the word, a villain; he was simply an upright man who made a tragic mistake. The nature of that mistake the play, I think, sufficiently demonstrates. Brutus was a man who thought that an abstract 'common good' could be achieved with-

out due regard to the complexities of the actual; a man who tried
to divorce his political thinking and his political action from what
he knew, and what he was, as a full human person. Many of us
remember the idealizing sympathy felt by liberal young men in
the 1930s for the Communist cause. There had, it was felt, been
excesses, but as against the slow cruelty of a ruthless competitive
society, its degradation of human values, even violence might
seem like surgery. 'Today', said W. H. Auden, in his poem
'Spain' (1937):

> Today the inevitable increase in the chances of death;
> The conscious acceptance of guilt in the necessary murder.

That, of course, was written before the Russian treason trials of
1938 and the subsequent purges, and Auden subsequently re-
wrote the lines; but they serve to illustrate the matter in hand.
'General good', said Blake, 'is the cry of the scoundrel and the
hypocrite; he who would do good to another must do it in
minute particulars.' There is some exaggeration in the first half
of that aphorism, but it contains a profound truth, sufficiently
demonstrated in many eminent figures in history. Shakespeare
demonstrates it in the figure of a man who was neither a scoundrel
nor a hypocrite:

> This was the noblest Roman of them all:
> All the conspirators save only he
> Did that they did in envy of great Caesar;
> He only, in a general honest thought
> And common good to all, made one of them.
> His life was gentle, and the elements
> So mix'd in him that Nature might stand up
> And say to all the world, 'This was a man!'

Shakespeare offers little comfort to those who like to consider
historical conflicts in terms of a simple black and white, or who
imagine that there are simple solutions for political dilemmas.
In the contrast between the 'gentle' Brutus and the man who, for
abstract reasons ('a general honest thought'), murdered his friend
and let loose civil war, Shakespeare gives us food for thought

that, firmly anchored in a particular action, has a special relevance for us today, as I suspect it will have at all times.

SOURCE: *Further Explorations* (1965).

NOTES

1. Harold Goddard, *The Meaning of Shakespeare* (Chicago, 1951) I 329.
2. Ibid.

G. Wilson Knight

THE EROTICISM OF
JULIUS CAESAR (1931)

WE are forced by the play's symbolic effects to see the action largely through the eyes of Brutus. That we may do this, Caesar is also shown to us as he appears to Brutus: he is both man and demi-god curiously interwoven. But it will be clear that Brutus' failure to unify his knowledge of Caesar is a failure properly to love him, love being the unifying principle in all things, regularly opposed in Shakespeare to disorder, treachery, evils of all kinds: this is the continual music–tempest contrast throughout the plays. And Brutus' failure to love his friend, Caesar, is one with his worship of abstract 'honour'. Therein we have the key to his acts: he serves 'honour' always in preference to love. Both his 'love' for Caesar and his 'honour' are given exact expression. Cassius asks Brutus if he would not have Caesar made king:

> I would not, Cassius; yet I love him well.
> But wherefore do you hold me here so long?
> What is it that you would impart to me?
> If it be aught toward the general good,
> Set honour in one eye and death i' the other,
> And I will look on both indifferently:
> For let the gods so speed me as I love
> The name of honour more than I fear death.
>
> (I ii 82)

This love Brutus sacrifices to his 'honour'.

The rest of the play illustrates his attitude. Honour first, love second. His anxieties have made him forget 'the shows of love to other men' being 'himself at war' (I ii 46–7). Portia is distressed at his lack of kindliness. He has risen 'ungently' from their bed; last night he 'suddenly arose' at supper, and paced the

room 'musing and sighing'. Questioned, he stared at her 'with
ungentle looks', stamped 'impatiently', and dismissed her 'with
an angry wafture' of his hand (II i 237–51). So she pits the
strength of love against his schemes of honour:

> . . . and, upon my knees,
> I charm you, by my once-commended beauty,
> By all your vows of love and that great vow
> Which did incorporate and make us one,
> That you unfold to me, yourself, your half,
> Why you are heavy, and what men to-night
> Have had resort to you. . . .   (II i 270)

She wins her fight – for the moment – and draws from him the
deep emotion of:

> You are my true and honourable wife,
> As dear to me as are the ruddy drops
> That visit my sad heart.   (II i 288)

And she herself knows the meaning of honour and courage. She
has given herself a 'voluntary wound' to prove her constancy.
Brutus, hearing this, prays the gods to make him worthy of 'this
noble wife' (II i 302). The Brutus–Portia relation is exquisitely
drawn. It reminds us of Hotspur and Lady Percy. But Hotspur
was stronger, more single in purpose, and, in a sense, more wary
than Brutus: he gave away no secrets, whereas Brutus' surrender
to Portia came near ruining the conspiracy. It is to be noted that
'honour' is so strong in Brutus that Portia knows she must play
up to it, show herself courageous, possessing a sense of 'honour'
like his. Brutus' obsession, almost to absurdity, with this thought
is further evident from his long speech, prolixly expanding the
idea that an oath is unnecessary to bind Romans to a noble
enterprise:

> . . . what other bond
> Than secret Romans, that have spoke the word,
> And will not palter? and what other oath
> Than honesty to honesty engaged,
> That this shall be, or we will fall for it?   (II i 124)

Again, he nearly ruins his own cause: we may relate to this 'oath' speech the fact that some one has given away details of the conspiracy to Popilius Lena and Artemidorus. Brutus is ever out of touch with practical affairs, which is natural in a man so devoted to an ethical abstraction. He unwisely refuses to let Antony be slain; perhaps also unwisely objects to the inclusion of Cicero among the conspirators. He is, in fact, a disintegrating force in the conspiracy, just as he is a disintegrating force to Rome: without him, the conspiracy might well have been successful, and we should then give final sanction to Cassius' rather than Antony's view of Caesar. Here we see the profound poetic necessity of Caesar's apparent weakness: it justifies Cassius' whole-hearted hostility. Cassius and Antony are both order-forces, love-forces in the play: Cassius' hate of Caesar is one with his love of his excellently arranged conspiracy, and his love of the conspiracy is a practical, efficient thing, as efficient as Antony's love of Caesar. Brutus loves primarily nothing but 'honour', but many things with secondary affection: Cassius, Portia, Caesar, the conspiracy. Brutus is thus divided in mind, in outlook. He is 'with himself at war' (I ii 46); in him

> the state of man,
> Like to a little kingdom, suffers then
> The nature of an insurrection.   (II i 67)

All the disorder-symbols in the play, all our ideas of disorder and disruption in reading it, our two-fold and indecisive vision of two Caesars – demi-god and dolt – are to be related closely to Brutus, rather than to Cassius or Antony. They enjoy a oneness of vision, a singularity of purpose: Brutus does not.

Brutus throughout continues his honourable course. He is aptly praised by Ligarius:

> Soul of Rome!
> Brave son, derived from honourable loins!
>   (II i 321)

All the conspirators respect him for his 'honour'. He slays Caesar boldly, without wavering, in the cause of honour. Antony sends a message, asking to interview the conspirators:

> Brutus is noble, wise, valiant and honest,
> Caesar was mighty, bold, royal and loving:
> Say I love Brutus and I honour him;
> Say I fear'd Caesar, honour'd him and loved him.
>
> (III i 126)

Brutus promises him safety by his 'honour' (III i 141); then assures him he can give him ample 'reasons' for Caesar's death. He thinks ever in terms of cold abstract processes of reason, and, unlike Antony and Cassius, ever fails in contact with the rich warm life of reality. Thus he ever misjudges men: he lets Antony speak at Caesar's funeral. He is half-hearted: neither a good conspirator like Cassius nor a good lover like Antony. Next, Brutus gives his 'public reasons' (III ii 7) for Caesar's death in his speech to the citizens. Again, he emphasizes 'honour':

Romans, countrymen, and lovers! hear me for my cause, and be silent, that you may hear: believe me for mine honour, and have respect to mine honour, that you may believe: censure me in your wisdom, and awake your senses, that you may the better judge. If there be any in this assembly, any dear friend of Caesar's, to him I say, that Brutus' love to Caesar was no less than his. If then that friend demand why Brutus rose against Caesar, this is my answer: – Not that I loved Caesar less, but that I loved Rome more . . .

(III ii 13)

This speech exactly exposes the love–honour dualism in Brutus' experience. Both before and after Caesar's death, we find Brutus' 'honour' conflicting with his loves: and always this failure to unify his experiences results in disorder, failure. He trusts to his abstractions pitifully: here he expects the citizens to be convinced by cold reasoning. One breath of Antony's passion, one sight of Caesar's mutilated body, will dispel that effect. So Antony's speech drives Brutus and Cassius from Rome.

Brutus shows himself cold in his quarrel with Cassius. The rights and wrongs of the matter are hard to decide and not important. Both appear faulty: Brutus has 'condemned' a friend of

Cassius on a paltry charge, Cassius has refused money to Brutus, or so it seems. Brutus, however, can scarcely with any justice both blame Cassius for accepting bribes and for refusing himself money. His want is due to his own refusal to raise money 'by vile means' (IV iii 71). Thus to desire a loan from Cassius is clearly to justify Cassius' use of bribery. However, the issue is vague. But a general truth emerges. Brutus is still hampering success by continued regard for his 'honour'. Cassius, less scrupulous, shows, as always, more warmness of heart. Cassius is always in touch with realities – of love, of conspiracy, of war: Brutus is ever most at home with his ethical abstractions. He treasures to his heart the 'justice' of his cause:

> Remember March, the Ides of March remember:
> Did not great Julius bleed for justice' sake?
> What villain touch'd his body, that did stab,
> And not for justice? What, shall one of us,
> That struck the foremost man of all this world
> But for supporting robbers, shall we now
> Contaminate our fingers with base bribes,
> And sell the mighty space of our large honours
> For so much trash as may be grasped thus?
> I had rather be a dog, and bay the moon,
> Than such a Roman.   (IV iii 18)

The quarrel is exquisitely human and pathetic. As their cause fails, these two 'noble' Romans – the word 'noble' is frequent in the play – begin to wrangle over money. Brutus starts by his noble apostrophe to 'justice': but soon we feel his primary anxiety is a very practical one – lack of gold:

> *Brutus.*   ... I did send
>   To you for gold to pay my legions,
>   Which you denied me: was that done like Cassius?
>   Should I have answer'd Caius Cassius so?
>   When Marcus Brutus grows so covetous,
>   To lock such rascal counters from his friends,
>   Be ready, gods, with all your thunderbolts
>   Dash him to pieces!

Cassius.   I denied you not.
Brutus. You did.
Cassius. I did not: he was but a fool
    That brought my answer back. . . .   (IV iii 75)

We may observe, with reference to Brutus' self-idealization here, that, if he did not deny Cassius gold, he certainly ignored his letters on behalf of Lucius Pella. This quarrel marks the failure of Brutus and Cassius. Their impending joint failure is forecast in this inner dissension. Also it suggests the failure of ideals unrelated to practical expediency: Brutus' ship of 'honour' dashes on the hard rocks of finance. It is pathetic, human, and exactly true. At last their dissension is healed by Cassius' love. Brutus' coldness thaws. As with his wife earlier, a deeper loyalty replaces his frigid abstractions:

> Do what you will, dishonour shall be humour.
>
>   (IV iii 109)

Next Brutus again reverts to abstractions: this time his prided stoic philosophy:

Cassius. I did not think you could have been so angry.
Brutus. O Cassius, I am sick of many griefs.
Cassius. Of your philosophy you make no use,
    If you give place to accidental evils.
Brutus. No man bears sorrow better. Portia is dead.

          (IV iii 143)

Cassius is to 'speak no more of her' (IV iii 158). The news is corroborated by Messala. Brutus hears it a second time; there is no possibility of mistake. Again, he receives it dispassionately, to Cassius' wonder:

> I have as much of this in art as you,
> But yet my nature could not bear it so.
>
>   (IV iii 194)

'Art.' Brutus makes life a long process of 'art', almost 'fiction'. He aspires to impossibilities and unrealities, carries a great burden of 'honour' and 'nobility' through life: which honour is

continually troubled by the deeps of emotion which he shares
with Antony and Cassius. He is only outwardly cold. Throughout his story love is intermittent with the iron calls of honour.
Caesar, Portia, Cassius (whose conspiracy he ruins, whose
soldiership he hampers) – his love for all has been sacrificed to
honour in one way or another. But that love itself need not be
questioned. It is deep; its organ notes are pure:

> *Brutus.*   Noble, noble Cassius,
>   Good night, and good repose.
> *Cassius.*   O my dear brother!
>   This was an ill beginning of the night:
>   Never come such division 'tween our souls!
>   Let it not, Brutus.
> *Brutus.*   Everything is well.
> *Cassius.* Good night, my lord.
> *Brutus.*   Good night, good brother.
>   (IV iii 232)

'Brother' is emphasized. Notice how Cassius is always ready to
humble himself to Brutus – 'my lord'. Their practical failure is
here clearly heralded: but a victory has been realized in Brutus,
a victory for love. Left alone, he asks Lucius to play to him.
Lucius' care-free purity of youth always touches Brutus' heart to
words which suggest here – both in Act II and Act IV – a more
spontaneous love than any he shows to other people. He always
speaks gently to him: 'Bear with me, good boy, I am much
forgetful' (IV iii 255), and 'I trouble thee too much, but thou art
willing' (IV iii 259). Lucius is sleepy. He knows the dreamless
sleep that holds no torment, unlike the phantasma of Brutus'
divided soul. He has already 'slept':

> *Brutus.* It was well done; and thou shalt sleep again;
>   I will not hold thee long: if I do live,
>   I will be good to thee.   (IV iii 263)

There is 'music and a song'. So music, with Brutus' love for his
boy, are blended here: music and love, healing, unifying spells
casting momentary peace on Brutus' divided soul. The boy
sleeps:

> If thou dost nod, thou break'st thy instrument;
> I'll take it from thee; and, good boy, good night.
>
> (IV iii 271)

That is one extreme: extreme of peace, love and music, realities Brutus has banished, repressed. He pays for his momentary heaven. Swiftly its opposing hell returns. The 'evil' in his soul accuses him:

> *Brutus.*   ... Art thou any thing?
> Art thou some god, some angel, or some devil,
> That makest my blood cold and my hair to stare?
> Speak to me what thou art.
> *Ghost.* Thy evil spirit, Brutus.   (IV iii 278)

There is no prolonged peace for Brutus. His life, in the play, has been 'like a phantasma or a hideous dream' (II i 65), due, like nightmare, to a divided consciousness; 'evil' none the less potent for its deriving its existence from the clash of two positive goods: 'honour' and 'love'.

Brutus is ever obsessed with his 'honour'. Octavius mocks Brutus and Cassius as 'traitors', saying he was not born to die on Brutus' sword. To which Brutus replies:

> O, if thou wert the noblest of thy strain,
> Young man, thou couldst not die more honourable.
>
> (V i 59)

He often refers to himself in a strain which repels by its egoism:

> ... think not, thou noble Roman,
> That ever Brutus will go bound to Rome;
> He bears too great a mind.   (V i 111)

Curiously, this contradicts his words just spoken that suicide is 'cowardly'. His life is one long contradiction, one long abstraction. This boast is of the same order as his boast in the quarrel scene:

> There is no terror, Cassius, in your threats,
> For I am arm'd so strong in honesty
> That they pass by me as the idle wind,
> Which I respect not.   (IV iii 66)

He is so enwrapped in a sense of his own honour that others can make no headway against his will. The conspirators always give way to him. Cassius cannot resist his self-haloed personality ever. He submits to Brutus' judgement as to coming down from the hills to meet Octavius and Antony: the event is disaster. Even in the fight 'Brutus gave the word too early' (v iii 5). Brutus is a continual hindrance, usually exactly because of his exaggerated sense of honour. Yet he rouses our admiration by his consistency, his steadiness of purpose in serving a figment of his own mind. Even when he finds Cassius dead, he shows little emotion. Yet we feel deep surges unspoken:

> I shall find time, Cassius, I shall find time.
>
> (v iii 103)

Strangely, though through his life he has banished the softer joys of love, when at the end he knows his enterprise to be an utter failure, Caesar's spirit victorious, he joys in the thought of friendship:

> The ghost of Caesar hath appeared to me
> Two several times by night; at Sardis once,
> And, this last night, here in Philippi fields:
> I know my hour is come.   (v v 17)

Therefore –

> Countrymen,
> My heart doth joy that yet in all my life
> I found no man but he was true to me.
> I shall have glory by this losing day
> More than Octavius and Mark Antony
> By this vile conquest shall attain unto.
> So fare you well at once; for Brutus' tongue
> Hath almost ended his life's history:
> Night hangs upon mine eyes; my bones would rest,
> That have but labour'd to attain this hour.   (v v 33)

Into the darkness of death he takes the simple joy that his followers have been true to him. There is resignation here, a knowledge of failure, an acceptance of tragedy. The things he valued have played him false. He has 'dismembered' Caesar, but has not 'come by' his 'spirit', partly because he himself from the first made that unreal mental division of Caesar the man and Caesar the imperial force in Rome. So Caesar's disembodied 'spirit', his ghost, Brutus' own creation, pursues Brutus to his death. And the long torment of division in Brutus' soul is closed, the wounding dualism healed in death, an easy 'rest'; and in thoughts of his friends' faith. Love, at the last, quietly takes him, honour-wearied, by the hand, into the darkness. But even in his dying he is anxious for 'honour'. 'Thy life hath had some smatch of honour in it' he says to Strato (v v 46), when asking him to hold his sword.

Antony speaks a noble eulogy over his body. Octavius will have it 'order'd honourably' (v v 79). Honour always. But Antony is right in saying Brutus slew Caesar 'in a general honest thought' (v v 71), though he may be wrong in attributing only 'envy' to the rest. Brutus is sincere throughout. He unwaveringly pursues an ethical ideal which appears somewhat bloodless in this play of imperial glory, pulsing love, envy, ambition. Though bloodless, it yet sheds blood. Brutus lets his abstraction loose in the world of reality: he will not render Caesar what is Caesar's and offer his ideal to God. Thus he is the only force properly 'ethical' in the play: the rest act by emotion. Yet this ethical cast of thought itself creates division and disorder in his mind, in his view of Caesar under the two aspects, man and ruler:

> It must be by his death, and for my part
> I know no personal cause to spurn at him,
> But for the general. (II i 10)

He is himself confused in this speech – as we, too, are confused by the two Caesars, till Antony's strong love creates the Caesar we know. Like Caesar himself, he is anxious as to this tremendous power coming to the friend he loves. What change may it work? All the disorder-symbols of the play are to be related to Brutus' divided allegiances. The vision of naked spirit flaming over Rome is a projection of Brutus' own spirit-abstraction unharmonized with life. It cannot be too strongly emphasized that the conspiracy without Brutus might have been a life-force, a creating of order, not a destruction. So he ruins first Caesar, then the cause of his own party. Antony wins over the citizens by ringing the changes on Brutus' favourite slogan, 'honour':

> So are they all, all honourable men.
>
> (III ii 89)

Love's mockery of 'honour'. Over and over again he drives it in: 'Brutus is an honourable man' (III ii 87 and 99), 'Sure, he is an honourable man' (III ii 104) – and again at lines 129, 132, 216, 218. Again,

> I fear I wrong the honourable men
> Whose daggers have stabbed Caesar; I do fear it.
>
> (III ii 156)

Brutus' honour pains and slays Portia, drives Cassius in their quarrel almost to madness, while Brutus remains ice-cold, armed appallingly in 'honesty'. He shows little emotion at his dear ones' death. You can do nothing with him. He is so impossibly noble: and when we forget his nobility he becomes just 'impossible'. Thus when he would for once solace himself for a while with Lucius – his truest love – and Lucius' music, his 'evil spirit' denies his right to such relief. This incident corresponds exactly to the irruption of Banquo's ghost into Macbeth's feast. Macbeth especially desecrates hospitality, Brutus love. Neither may enjoy what they destroy. Brutus has put love from him. He rides roughshod over domestic happiness, like Macbeth. His acts disturb Portia, dislocate meals and sleep. So, too, Caesar and Calpurnia are roused from bed, and Caesar's hospitality desecrated. Cassius, on the contrary, invites people to dinner. The contrast is important. Such pursuit of an ethical ideal in and for itself, unrelated to the time and people around, is seen at the last to be perilous. It is a selfishness. His ethic is no ethic, rather a projection of himself. A phantasma of his own mind. Like Macbeth he projects his mental pain on his country. He alone bears the responsibility of Caesar's death, since he alone among the conspirators sees – and so creates – its wrongfulness; he alone bears the burden of the conspiracy's failure. He only has a guilty conscience – anguished by an 'evil spirit'. But Cassius, at the last, is 'fresh of spirit' (v i 91). And yet, Brutus has glory by his losing day. He suffers, not because he is less than those around him but because he is, in a sense, far greater. He is the noblest Roman of them all. He suffers, and makes others suffer, for his virtue: but such virtue is not enough. Virtue, to Brutus, is a quality to be rigidly distinguished from love. Love, in fact, ever conflicts with it. He denies the greatest force in life and the only hope in death. He thus fails in life and dies sadly, pathetically searching at the end for some one 'honourable' enough to slay him. He has starved his love on earth: he thinks at the last of his faithful friends, would take what crumbs he can to solace him in the darkness.

SOURCE: *The Imperial Theme* (1931).

Leo Kirschbaum

SHAKESPEARE'S STAGE BLOOD
(1949)

IN order to show how unprepared present-day sensibility is for blood scenes in Shakespeare, let me quote from a well-known modern critic:

Brutus addresses us through a wrapping of rhetoric, of public speech. And this wrapping is around the imageries of blood and sleep which are so prominent in the play – so prominent, and yet, if one remembers *Macbeth*, so remote from contact with us. The blood that smears the entire surface of *Macbeth* is physical; we see, feel, and smell it. Not so with Caesar's blood; it is 'noble' and 'costly' because Caesar was the foremost man of all the world, but it remains a metaphor, a political metaphor, distant from the experience of our senses. It may be significant that it can pour from Caesar's statue as well as from his body (II ii 76–9), and that when he falls at the base of Pompey's statue it too runs red. There is as much real blood in *Julius Caesar* as there is in stone.[1]

Examine, however, the scene of Caesar's murder. Calpurnia had dreamt, says Caesar,

> she saw my Statue
> Which like a Fountaine, with an hundred spouts
> Did run pure blood: and many lusty Romans
> Came smiling, & did bathe their hands in it:

This dream becomes an actuality. Immediately after the tyrannicide, the conspirators are highly excited. Suddenly Brutus bends to the bleeding corpse.

> Stoope Romans, stoope,
> And let vs bathe our hands in *Caesars* blood
> Vp to the Elbowes, and besmeare our Swords:
> Then walke we forth, euen to the Market place,

> And wauing our red Weapons o're our heads,
> Let's all cry Peace, Freedome, and Liberty.
> *Cassius.* Stoop then, and wash. How many Ages hence
> Shall this our lofty Scene be acted ouer,
> In State vnborne, and Accents yet vnknowne?
> *Brutus.* How many times shall *Caesar* bleed in sport,
> That now on *Pompeyes* Basis lye[s] along,
> No worthier then the dust?
> *Cassius.* So oft as that shall be,
> So often shall the knot of vs be call'd,
> The Men that gaue their Country liberty.
> *Decius.* What, shall we forth?
> *Cassius.* I, euery man away.
> *Brutus* shall leade, and we will grace his heeles
> With the most boldest, and best hearts of Rome.
> *Enter a Seruant.*

That the indicated actions were indeed done and exploited full-view of the audience is indicated by succeeding references. Antony speaks of

> your Swords; made rich
> With the most Noble blood of all this World.
> I do beseech yee, if you beare me hard,
> Now, whil'st your purpled hands do reeke and smoake,
> Fulfill your pleasure.

Brutus says to him:

> Though now we must appeare bloody and cruell,
> As by our hands, and this our present Acte
> You see we do: Yet see you but our hands,
> And this, the bleeding businesse they haue done:

Antony stretches out his hand to each of the death-dealers:

> Let each man render me his bloody hand.
> First *Marcus Brutus* will I shake with you;
> Next *Caius Cassius* do I take your hand;
> Now *Decius Brutus* yours; now yours *Metellus*;
> Yours *Cinna*; and my valiant *Caska*, yours;
> Though last, not least in loue, yours good *Trebonius.* . . .
> That I did loue thee *Caesar*, O 'tis true:

If then thy Spirit looke vpon vs now,
Shall it not greeue thee deerer then thy death,
To see thy *Antony* making his peace,
Shaking the bloody fingers of thy Foes?

The bathing of the hands in Caesar's bloody corpse and the smearing of the swords are, then, not metaphorical at all. They are naturalistic stage effects *coram populo* deliberately meant by Shakespeare for actual production and undoubtedly achieved at the Globe. It is interesting to inquire what past and present critics and producers have done with Shakespeare's intentions here.

In his text, Pope assigned the 'Stoope Romans, stoope,' speech to Casca and wrote: 'In all the editions this speech is ascribed to Brutus, than which nothing is more inconsistent with his mild and philosophical character.' Theobald thought Pope 'more nice than wise' in this change:

Brutus esteemed the death of Caesar a sacrifice to liberty; and as such gloried in his heading the enterprize. Besides, our author is strictly copying history. 'Brutus and his followers, being yet hot with the murder, marched in a body from the Senate-house to the Capitol with their drawn swords, with an air of confidence and assurance.' – Plutarch, *Caesar*, #45. And: 'Brutus and his party betook themselves to the Capitol, and in their way shewing their hands all bloody, and their naked swords, proclaiming liberty to the people.' – Ibid., *Brutus*, #13.

Upton (1746) wrote:

This was agreeable to an ancient and religious custom. So in Æschylus we read that the seven captains, who came against Thebes, sacrificed a bull, and dipped their hands in the gore, invoking at the same time the gods of war, and binding themselves with an oath to revenge the cause of Eteocles (*Seven Against Thebes*, verse 42). . . . By this solemn action Brutus gives the assassination of Caesar a religious air and turn.

Capell, too, thought the action 'solemn'.

For the action which is ushered in by these words we have seen a preparative [in that passage] where the same speaker opposes shedding any more blood but only Caesar's, which, in his idea, was an offering to the goddess he worshipped most – public liberty; and from this idea results the action proposed by him; such action having many examples in ancient sacrifices, the more solemn particularly, as this is thought, by the speaker.

In the nineteenth century Knight made some shrewd comments:

We have seen the stoic Brutus . . . gradually warm up to the great enterprise of asserting his principles by one terrible blow, for triumph or for extinction. The blow is given. The excitement which succeeds is wondrously painted by the poet, without a hint from the historian. The calm of the gentle Brutus is lifted up, for the moment, into an attitude of terrible sublimity. It is he who says: 'Stoop, Romans, stoop. . . . Let's all cry, Peace, Freedom, and Liberty!' From that moment the character flags; the calmness returns; something also of the irresolution comes back. Brutus is too high-minded for his position.[2]

In his essay on *Julius Caesar* Granville-Barker, surprisingly, seems to evade the problem of the blood-bath as stage effect:

We have the helter skelter of the moment after Caesar's fall; Brutus is the only figure of authority and calm. . . . Let them sign themselves ritual brothers – and in whose blood but Caesar's? . . . We need not doubt Brutus' deep sincerity for a moment. . . . And he anoints himself devotedly. Then Cassius, febrile, infatuate: Stoop, then, and wash. . . .[3]

How the audience is to get the notion of a solemn religious sacrifice from the shocking gory effect is not explained by the above critics.[4] The silence of most editors and critics, the pious explanations of others, seem indicative of some kind of turning away from the unseemly. None of them appears willing to face the scene in its own maculate terms.

The critics are in line with the producers. Eighteenth and nineteenth century productions did not contain the lines and action we have been discussing. In *Shakespeare and the Actors, The Stage Business in His Plays (1660-1905)*, A. C. Sprague informs us:

Brutus bids the conspirators stoop with him and bathe their hands in Caesar's blood. 'Stoop then and wash,' Cassius replies. But on the stage this was seldom done. What is more the lines themselves were quietly altered, the idea underlying the changes, which vary in different editions, being always that these dignified Romans were *not* to 'stoop and wash'.

In Bell's edition [1774], lines 111 ff. (including Rowe's direction, 'Dipping their swords in *Caesar's* blood') are quoted, as 'seldom delivered on the stage'.[5]

As Knight recognized, there is no warrant in the source for the blood-bathing action. Nevertheless, North's Plutarch may have suggested it. In the life of Brutus, we read that when the conspirators were stabbing Caesar, 'so many swords and daggers lighting upon one body, one of them hurt another, and among them Brutus caught a blow on his hand, because he would make one in murdering of him, and all the rest also were every man of them bloodied'. Afterwards, 'Brutus and his consorts, having their swords bloody in their hands, went straight to the Capitol, persuading the Romans as they went to take their liberty again.' Antony shows the common people 'Caesar's gown all bloody'. In the life of Caesar, the victim 'was hacked and mangled among them, as a wild beast taken of hunters'. He was driven 'against the base whereupon Pompey's image stood, which ran all of a gore-blood till he was slain'. 'Brutus and his confederates . . ., being yet hot with this murther they had committed, having their swords drawn in their hands, came all in a troop together out of the Senate, and went into the market-place . . . boldly holding up their heads like men of courage, and called to the people to defend their liberty. . . .' The plebeians later see Caesar's body 'all bemangled with gashes of swords'. In the life of Antony, 'he unfolded before the whole assembly the bloody garments of the dead, thrust through in many places with their swords, and called the malefactors cruel and cursed murtherers'.[6] It has been suggested that Shakespeare's source for the blood-wash may have been a passage in the life of Publicola in which the conspirators plan to seal their pact by sacrificing a man, drinking his blood, and shaking hands in his bowels.[7]

Shakespeare, therefore, invented the blood-bath, deliberately gave the proposal for it to Brutus, and followed it with the invention of the bloody handshaking action with Antony.

What, then, are Shakespeare's intentions? They are, of course, multiple. If proper attention is paid to the above lines and stage effects as integral parts of Shakespeare's design, much revelatory criticism will undoubtedly ensue. I think we can be fairly sure of the five following glosses: (1) Shakespeare introduces a scene which in its novelty and brutality excites the spectators and grasps their attention. (2) He underscores the fact that the conspirators are bloodthirsty men – even if the audience has already allowed that the motives of some of them were initially respectable. All murder is in the act savage and inhuman, Shakespeare is saying. Whether or not killing ever justifies the doctrine of a bad means serving a good end, the merciless rending of a man is an obscene performance. (3) As Pope saw, that Brutus should suggest the blood-bath comes as a shock. And that is exactly Shakespeare's intention. However they may disagree in particulars, all commentators on Shakespeare's play regard Brutus as a man who does not understand himself or others. That the dignified and gentle Brutus should propose the ghastly procedure of the conspirators bathing their hands in the blood of Caesar's body wrenches the mind. It emphasizes the disorder in the man. The major lesson of Shakespeare's history plays is so simple that its tremendous significance may be overlooked. It is this: *History is made by men*. How frightening this premise really becomes when we see the noble Brutus suddenly turn into a savage! (4) The conspirators openly degenerate precisely at that juncture where Antony begins to fashion the ensuing events. As Moulton,[8] seconded by Granville-Barker,[9] points out, the entrance of Antony's servant is the turning point of the play. (5) The blood of Caesar begins to spread. As critics have noted, the implications of his death overshadow the rest of the drama. He is mighty yet. The dreadful blood which we see covering the hands of the conspirators, then touching Antony's hand, then staining the exhibited mantle, then turning the witless plebeians into destroyers – this is the symbol and mark of the blood and destruction which is to flow through the rest of the play, overwhelming the conspirators' plans, accomplishing Antony's promise to Caesar's butchered corpse.

SOURCE: *Publications of the Modern Language Association of America*, LXIV (1949).

NOTES

1. Mark Van Doren, *Shakespeare* (New York, 1939) p. 185.

2. These quotations are from the New Variorum edition of *Julius Caesar*, ed. H. H. Furness, Jr (Philadelphia and London, 1913) pp. 145–6.

3. *Prefaces to Shakespeare* (Princeton, 1946–7) II 389–90. I like neither Granville-Barker's juggling of the order of the speeches nor his highly subjective interpretation. Why he believes Brutus comes off well in this scene and Casca and Cassius do not is not made clear. Cf. 'Our sympathy with Brutus has next to weather the murder, through the planning and doing of which he stalks so nobly and disinterestedly and with such admirable self-control' (p. 355) and 'Butchered by Casca, sacrificed by Brutus – these two doings of the same deed are marked and kept apart – Caesar lies dead' (p. 388). But for another play Granville-Barker *can* see the functional significance of a horror scene: 'Shakespeare then deals the dreadful blow to Gloucester. The very violence and horror of this finds its dramatic justification in the need to match in another sort – since he could not hope to match it in spiritual intensity – the catastrophe to Lear' (I 274).

4. When critics interpret the blood wash in III i as awe-inspiring ritual, they must be recalling (as Capell indicates) the passage in II i in which Brutus advises the conspirators not to kill Antony along with Caesar. But the critics are then contaminating III i with II i and confusing intention with act. The least one can say of the blood bath is what John Palmer says (my italics): 'Brutus [carries] to *dreadful extremes* the sacrificial mood in which he struck the fatal blow' (*Political Characters of Shakespeare* (1945) p. 14).

5. (Cambridge, Mass., 1945) pp. 321, 427. That an earlier stage tradition was faithful to Shakespeare may be indicated by Voltaire's words in 1731 concerning a London production in which he saw Brutus speak to the mob, 'tenant encore un poignard teint du sang de Cesar' (quoted ibid., p. 323). 'Tree . . . used the business [of blood

washing] (Irving's eagerly awaited comment on his production was
'H'm – yes – too much blood!') and, when Antony shakes hands with
the conspirators, "Casca with rude intent and purposeful cruelty
smirches with a crimson stain the arm of butchered Caesar's friend" '
(pp. 321–2). Percy Simpson tells us a bit more about the Tree production: 'Gathering round the body, the conspirators reddened their
hands in blood – a graphic touch usually omitted in acting copies, as
its significance depends upon a hunting custom long obsolete. . . .
As each man "rendered him [Antony] his bloody hand", the blunt
Casca wiped off the stains on Antony's wrist, and he repressed a rising
look of horror' (Furness, Variorum edition, p. 443).

6. *Shakespeare's Plutarch*, ed. C. F. Tucker Brooke (1909) I 133–7,
101–4, II 22.

7. See Furness, Variorum edition, p. 296; North's Plutarch (1579),
reprinted by Shakespeare Head Press, 1928 I 265.

8. *Shakespeare as a Dramatic Artist* (1906) pp. 197–8.

9. Op. cit., II 366, 390.

Brents Stirling

RITUAL IN *JULIUS CAESAR* (1956)

MODERN readers are prone to find the tragedy of Brutus in his rigid devotion to justice and fair play. Many members of the Globe audience, however, believed that his virtues were complicated by self-deception and doubtful principle. In sixteenth-century views of history the conspiracy against Caesar often represented a flouting of unitary sovereignty, that prime point of Tudor policy, and exemplified the anarchy thought to accompany 'democratic' or constitutional checks upon authority. Certain judgments of Elizabethan political writers who refer to Brutus are quite clear upon this point.[1] Although naturally aware of his disinterested honor and liberality, contemporary audiences could thus perceive in him a conflict between questionable goals and honorable action, a contradiction lying in his attempt to redeem morally confused ends by morally clarified means. The Elizabethan tragedy of Brutus, like that of Othello, is marked by an integrity of conduct which leads the protagonist into evil and measures him in his error.

The distinction between modern and Elizabethan views of *Julius Caesar* is not the point of our inquiry, but it is a necessary beginning, for the older view of Brutus determines both the symbolic quality and the structure of the play. I hope to show that a sixteenth-century idea of Brutus is as thoroughly related to Shakespeare's art as it is to his meaning.

When a dramatist wishes to present an idea, his traditional method, of course, is to settle upon an episode in which the idea arises naturally but vividly from action and situation. Such an episode in *Julius Caesar* is the one in which Brutus resolves to exalt not only the mission but the tactics of conspiracy: having accepted republicanism as an honorable end, he sets out to dignify assassination, the means, by lifting it to a level of rite and ceremony.[2] In II i, as Cassius urges the killing of Antony as a necessary accompaniment to the death of Caesar, Brutus declares that 'such a course will seem too bloody . . ., / To cut the head off and then hack the limbs'. With this thought a sense of purpose comes over him: 'Let's be sacrificers, but not butchers, Caius.' Here his conflict seems to be resolved, and for the first time he is more than a reluctant presence among the conspirators as he expands the theme which ends his hesitation and frees his moral imagination:

> We all stand up against the spirit of Caesar,
> And in the spirit of men there is no blood;
> Oh, that we then could come by Caesar's spirit,
> And not dismember Caesar! But, alas,
> Caesar must bleed for it! And, gentle friends,
> Let's kill him boldly, but not wrathfully;
> Let's carve him as a dish fit for the gods,
> Not hew him as a carcass fit for hounds.

This proposed conversion of bloodshed to ritual is the manner in which an abstract Brutus will be presented in terms of concrete art. From the suggestion of Plutarch that Brutus' first error lay in sparing Antony, Shakespeare moves to the image of Antony as a limb of Caesar, a limb not to be hacked because hacking is no part of ceremonial sacrifice. From Plutarch's description of Brutus as high-minded, gentle and disinterested, Shakespeare proceeds to the Brutus of symbolic action. Gentleness and disinterestedness become embodied in the act of 'unwrathful' blood sacrifice. High-mindedness becomes objectified in ceremonial observance.

A skeptical reader may ask why the episode just described is any more significant than a number of others such as Brutus' scene with Portia or his quarrel with Cassius. If more significant, it is so only because of its relation to a thematic design. I agree, moreover, that Shakespeare gains his effects by variety; as a recognition, in fact, of his complexity I hope to show that the structure of *Julius Caesar* is marked by references both varied and apt to Brutus' sacrificial rite, and that this process includes expository preparation in earlier scenes, emphasis upon 'mock-ceremony' in both earlier and later scenes, and repeated comment by Antony upon butchery under the guise of sacrifice – ironical comment which takes final form in the parley before Philippi.

Derived in large measure from Plutarch, but never mechanically or unselectively, the theme of incantation and ritual is thus prominent throughout *Julius Caesar*, and this is no less true at the beginning than during the crucial episodes of Acts II and III. In the opening scene of the play we are confronted with a Roman populace rebuked by Marullus for ceremonial idolatry of Caesar:

> And do you now put on your best attire?
> And do you now cull out a holiday?
> And do you now strew flowers in his way
> That comes in triumph over Pompey's blood?

For this transgression Marullus prescribes a counter-observance by the citizens in immediate expiation of their folly:

> Run to your houses, fall upon your knees,
> Pray to the gods to intermit this plague
> That needs must light on this ingratitude.

To which Flavius adds:

> Go, go, good countrymen, and for this fault,
> Assemble all the poor men of your sort;
> Draw them to Tiber banks, and weep your tears
> Into the channel, till the lowest stream
> Do kiss the most exalted shores of all.

And after committing the populace to these rites of atonement for their festal celebration of Caesar, the two tribunes themselves leave to remove the devotional symbols set up for his welcoming. 'Go you . . . towards the Capitol;/ This way will I. Disrobe the images/ If you do find them decked with ceremonies./ . . . let no images/ Be hung with Caesar's trophies.' It is the hope of Flavius that these disenchantments will make Caesar 'fly an ordinary pitch, / Who else would soar above the view of men'.

Act I, scene ii is equally unusual in carrying the theme of ritual. It is apparent that Shakespeare had a wide choice of means for staging the entry of Caesar and his retinue; yet he selects an entry based upon Plutarch's description of the 'feast Lupercalia' in which the rite of touching or striking barren women by runners of the course is made prominent. Caesar, moreover, after ordering Calpurnia to be so touched by Antony, commands: 'Set on; and leave no ceremony out.' It can be said, in fact, that the whole of this scene is written with ceremonial observance as a background. Its beginning, already described, is followed by a touch of solemnity in the soothsayer's words; next comes its main expository function, the sounding of Brutus by Cassius, and throughout this interchange come at intervals the shouts and flourishes of a symbolic spectacle. When the scene is again varied by a formal re-entry and exit of Caesar's train, Casca remains behind to make a mockery of the rite which has loomed so large from off-stage. Significantly, in Casca's travesty of the ceremonial crown-offering and of the token offering by Caesar of his throat for cutting, Shakespeare has added a satirical note which does not appear in Plutarch.

The process, then, in each of the two opening episodes has been the bringing of serious ritual into great prominence, and of subjecting it to satirical treatment. In the first scene the tribunes denounce the punctilio planned for Caesar's entry, send the idolatrous crowd to rites of purification, and set off themselves to desecrate the devotional images. In the second scene a multiple emphasis of ceremony is capped by Casca's satire which twists the crown ritual into imbecile mummery. At this point, and in conformity with the mood set by Casca, occurs Cassius' mockery in soliloquy of Brutus:

> Well, Brutus, thou art noble; yet I see
> Thy honorable mettle may be wrought
> From that it is dispos'd; therefore it is meet
> That noble minds keep ever with their likes;
> For who so firm that cannot be seduc'd?

The next scene (I iii) is packed with omens and supernatural portents, a note which is carried directly into II i where Brutus, on receiving the mysterious papers which have been left to prompt his action, remarks,

> The exhalations whizzing in the air
> Give so much light that I may read by them.

Appropriately, the letters read under this weird glow evoke his
first real commitment to the 'cause':

> O Rome, I make thee promise,
> If the redress will follow, thou receivest
> Thy full petition at the hand of Brutus!

Now appear his lines on the interim 'between the acting of a
dreadful thing/ And the first motion' in which 'the state of man/
Like to a little kingdom, suffers then/ The nature of a insurrection'. This conventional symbolizing of political convulsion by
inward insurrection is followed by the soliloquy on conspiracy:

> O, then by day
> Where wilt thou find a cavern dark enough
> To mask thy monstrous visage? Seek none, Conspiracy!
> Hide it in smiles and affability.

The conflict within Brutus thus becomes clear in this scene.
First, the participant in revolution suffers revolution within
himself; then the hater of conspiracy and lover of plain dealing
must call upon Conspiracy to hide in smiling courtesy.

We have now reached the critical point (II i 154 ff) to which
attention was first called, an outward presentation of Brutus'
crisis through his acceptance of an assassin's role upon condition
that the assassins become sacrificers. Already a theme well established in preceding scenes, the idea of ritual is again made
prominent. As the soliloquy on conspiracy closes, the plotters
gather, and the issue becomes the taking of an oath. Brutus
rejects this as an idle ceremony unsuited to men joined in the
honesty of a cause and turns now to the prospect of Caesar's
death. This time, however, honorable men do need ceremony,
ceremony which will purify the violent act of all taint of butchery
and raise it to the level of sacrifice. But although Brutus has
steadied himself with a formula his conflict is still unresolved,
for as he sets his course he 'unconsciously' reveals the evasion
which Antony later will amplify: to transmute political killing

into ritual is to cloak it with appearances. We began with Brutus' passage on carving Caesar as a dish for the gods; these are the lines which complete it:

> And let our hearts, as subtle masters do,
> Stir up their servants to an act of rage,
> And after seem to chide 'em. This shall make
> Our purpose necessary and not envious;
> Which so appearing to the common eyes,
> We shall be called purgers, not murderers.

The contradiction is interesting. In an anticlimax, Brutus has ended his great invocation to ritual with a note on practical politics: our hearts shall stir us and afterward seem to chide us; we shall thus 'appear' to the citizenry as purgers, not murderers.

Shakespeare never presents Brutus as a demagogue, but there are ironical traces of the politician in him which suggest Covell's adverse picture of Roman liberators.[3] It is curious, in fact, that although Brutus is commonly thought to be unconcerned over public favor, he expresses clear concern for it in the passage just quoted and in III i 244–51, where he sanctions Antony's funeral speech only if Antony agrees to tell the crowd that he speaks by generous permission, and only if he agrees to utter no evil of the conspiracy. Nor is Brutus' speech in the Forum wholly the nonpolitical performance it is supposed to be; certainly Shakespeare's Roman citizens are the best judges of it, and they react tempestuously. Although compressed, it scarcely discloses aloofness or an avoidance of popular emotive themes.

Act II, scene ii now shifts to the house of Caesar, but the emphasis on ritual continues as before. With dramatic irony, in view of Brutus' recent lines on sacrificial murder, Caesar commands, 'Go bid the priests do present sacrifice.' Calpurnia who has 'never stood on ceremonies' (omens) is now terrified by them. News comes that the augurers, plucking the entrails of an offering, have failed to find a heart. Calpurnia has dreamed that smiling Romans have laved their hands in blood running from Caesar's statue, and Decius Brutus gives this its favorable interpretation which sends Caesar to his death.

The vivid assassination scene carries out Brutus' ritual prescription in dramatic detail, for the killing is staged with a formalized approach, ending in kneeling, by one conspirator after
another until the victim is surrounded. This is met by a series of
retorts from Caesar ending in 'Hence! Wilt thou lift up Olympus',
and the 'sacrifice' is climaxed with his 'Et tu Brute!' The conspirators ceremonially bathe their hands in Caesar's blood, and
Brutus pronounces upon 'this our lofty scene' with the prophecy
that it 'shall be acted over/ In states unborn and accents yet
unknown!'

The mockery in counterritual now begins as a servant of
Antony enters (III i 121) and confronts Brutus:

> Thus, Brutus, did my master bid me kneel,
> Thus did Mark Antony bid me fall down;
> And being prostrate, thus he bade me say:
> Brutus is noble, wise, valiant, and honest.

Here a threefold repetition, 'kneel', 'fall down', and 'being prostrate', brings the ceremonial irony close to satire. Following
this worship of the new idol by his messenger, Antony appears
in person and with dramatic timing offers himself as a victim.
In one speech he evokes both the holy scene which the conspirators so desired and the savagery which underlay it:

> Now, whilst your purpled hands do reek and smoke,
> Fulfill your pleasure. Live a thousand years,
> I shall not find myself so apt to die;
> No place will please me so, no mean of death,
> As here by Caesar, and by you cut off.

The murder scene is thus hallowed by Antony in a manner which
quite reverses its sanctification by the conspirators. Brutus, forbearing, attempts to mollify Antony with his cherished theme of
purgation:

> Our hearts you see not. They are pitiful,
> And pity to the general wrong of Rome –
> As fire drives out fire, so pity pity –
> Hath done this deed on Caesar.

Antony's response is again one of counterceremony, the shaking
of hands in formal sequence which serves to make each conspirator stand alone and unprotected by the rite of blood which had
united him with the others. The assassins had agreed as a token
of solidarity that each of them should stab Caesar. Antony seems
to allude to this:

> Let each man render me his bloody hand.
> First, Marcus Brutus, will I shake with you;
> Now, Caius Cassius, do I take your hand;
> Now, Decius Brutus, yours; now yours, Metellus;
> Yours, Cinna; and, my valiant Casca, yours;
> Though last, not least in love yours, good Trebonius.
> Gentlemen all – alas what shall I say?

It is then that Antony, addressing the body of Caesar, suddenly
delivers his first profanation of the ritual sacrifice:

> Here wast thou bay'd, brave hart;
> Here didst thou fall; and here thy hunters stand,
> Sign'd in thy spoil, and crimson'd in thy lethe.

And lest the allusion escape, Shakespeare continues Antony's
inversion of Brutus' ceremonial formula: the dish carved for the
gods is doubly transformed into the carcass hewn for hounds
with further hunting metaphors of Caesar as a hart in the forest
and as 'a deer strucken by many princes'. Brutus agrees to give
reasons why Caesar was dangerous, 'or else were this a savage
spectacle', and the stage is set for what may be called the play's
chief counterritual. Only Brutus, who planned the rite of sacrifice, could with such apt irony arrange the 'true rites' and 'ceremonies' which are to doom the conspiracy.

> I will myself into the pulpit first
> And show the reason of our Caesar's death.
> What Antony shall speak, I will protest
> He speaks by leave and by permission,
> And that we are contented Caesar shall
> Have all true rites and lawful ceremonies.

But exactly after the manner of his speech announcing the ritual

sacrifice (II i) Brutus concludes again on a note of policy: 'It
shall advantage more than do us wrong.'

Next follows Antony *solus* rendering his prophecy of 'domestic
fury and fierce civil strife' symbolized in Caesar's ghost which will

> Cry 'Havoc', and let slip the dogs of war,
> That this foul deed shall smell above the earth.

The passage is similar in utterance, function, and dramatic
placement to Carlisle's prophecy on the deposition of Richard
II, and for that reason it is to be taken seriously as a choric
interpretation of Caesar's death. Significantly, the beginning
lines again deride Brutus' erstwhile phrase, 'sacrificers but not
butchers':

> O, pardon me, thou bleeding piece of earth,
> That I am meek and gentle with these butchers!

It is unnecessary to elaborate upon the Forum scene; Antony's
oration follows the speech of Brutus with consequences familiar
to all readers. But there is an element in Antony's turning of the
tables which is just as remarkable as the well-known irony of his
references to 'honourable men'. If we remember that Shakespeare
has emphasized ritual at various planes of seriousness and of
derision, the conclusion of Antony's speech to the populace will
link itself with the previous theme. For here Antony re-enacts the
death of Caesar in a ritual of his own, one intended to show that
the original 'lofty scene' presented a base carnage. Holding
Caesar's bloody mantle as a talisman, he reproduces *seriatim* the
sacrificial strokes, but he does so in terms of the 'rent' Casca
made and the 'cursed steel' that Brutus plucked away with the
blood of Caesar following it. Again, each conspirator had struck
individually at Caesar and had symbolically involved himself
with the others; for the second time Antony reminds us of this
ritual bond by recounting each stroke, and his recreation of the
rite becomes a mockery of it. Brutus' transformation of blood
into the heady wine of sacrifice is reversed both in substance and
in ceremony.

For the 'realists' among the conspirators what has occurred can be summed up in the bare action of the play: the killing of Caesar has been accomplished, but the fruits of it have been spoiled by Brutus' insistence that Antony live and that he speak at Caesar's funeral. 'The which', as North's Plutarch has it, 'marred all'. With reference to Brutus, however, something much more significant has been enacted; the 'insurrection', the contradiction, within him has taken outward form in his attempt to purify assassination through ceremony. This act, not to be found in Plutarch,* symbolizes the 'Elizabethan' Brutus

* A reference at this point to Plutarch will serve both to clarify my meaning and to allay some natural doubts concerning the dramatist's intention. While it is true that the ritual murder of Caesar is Shakespeare's own contribution, the expository preparation for it in Act I comes from an episode in Plutarch in which Antony concludes the Lupercalian rites by offering a laurel crown twice to Caesar, and in which the tribunes are described as desecrating ritual offerings (*Shakespeare's Plutarch*, ed. Tucker Brooke (1909) I 92-3; see also II 19-20). Hence we have basic ritual materials for Shakespeare's first two scenes present in one convenient block of his source which also offered a convenient beginning for the play. Does this prevent us from attaching significance to the unusual presence of ritual elements in the exposition scenes? I believe it does not, for two reasons. First, the choice of source material by a dramatist is itself significant; Shakespeare could have started the play with other episodes in Plutarch or with scenes of his own invention. Secondly, it is immaterial whether he began *Julius Caesar* with this episode in his source and, because of its wealth of ritual detail, was led to the theme of ritualized assassination, or whether he began with the theme and chose source materials for exposition which agreed with it. In either case the same remarkable unity between earlier and later parts of the play would have been achieved, and it is this unity which is important. Guesses about its origin in the playwright's composition are profitless. We do know that Shakespeare's Brutus plans the killing of Caesar as ritual, while Plutarch presents it as the very opposite of this. Plutarch's description of the assassination emphasizes, in fact, resemblance to the hunting down of an animal, the very effect Brutus seeks explicitly to avoid in the 'carcass-hounds' figure, and the one which Antony magnifies in his counteremphasis of imagery drawn from hunting. North notes it thus: 'Caesar turned him nowhere but he was stricken at by some . . . and was hacked and mangled among them, as a wild beast taken of hunters.' (*Shakespeare's Plutarch*, I 101-2.)

compelled by honor to join with conspirators but required by conscience to reject Conspiracy.

We have followed the ritual theme in *Julius Caesar* from early scenes to the point of Antony's oration, at which it is completely defined. There remains, however, a terminal appearance of the theme in the first scene of Act v. The ultimate clash between the idealism of Brutus and Antony's contempt for it comes during the parley on the eve of Philippi, at which Antony again drives home the old issue of ceremonial imposture. Brutus has observed that his enemy wisely threats before he stings; the reply is Antony's last disposition of the sacrificial rite:

> Villains, you did not so when your vile daggers
> Hack'd one another in the sides of Caesar,
> You show'd your teeth like apes, and fawn'd like hounds,
> And bow'd like bondmen, kissing Caesar's feet;
> Whilst damned Casca, like a cur, behind
> Struck Caesar on the neck.

Antony invokes the 'hacking' which Brutus earlier forswore, and he again inverts the cherished formula of sacrifice: once more the dish carved for gods becomes the carcass hewn for hounds. Over the body of Caesar he had previously employed the hunting-hound figure ('Here wast thou bay'd, brave hart'); the apes, the hounds, and the cur of these lines complete his vengeful irony of metaphor.

What, finally, is to be inferred from Antony's concluding passage on 'the noblest Roman of them all'? Commonly found there is a broad vindication of Brutus which would deny an ironical interpretation. When Antony's elegiac speech is read plainly, however, its meaning is quite limited: it declares simply that Brutus was the only conspirator untouched by envy, and that, in intention, he acted 'in a general honest thought/ And common good to all'. The Elizabethan view of Brutus as tragically misguided is thus consistent with Antony's pronouncement that he was the only disinterested member of the conspiracy. But Brutus is not to be summed up in an epitaph; as the impersonal member of a conspiracy motivated largely by personal ends, he sought in a complex way to resolve his contradiction by depersonalizing, ritualizing, the means.

Shakespeare's achievement, however, is not confined to the characterization of a major figure, for we have seen that the ceremonial motive extends beyond the personality of Brutus into the structure of the play. Exposition stressing the idea of ritual observance leads to the episode in which Brutus formulates the 'sacrifice', and clear resolution of the idea follows in event and commentary. Structural craftsmanship thus supplements characterization and the two combine, as in *Richard II*, to state the political philosophy implicit in the play.

Source: *Unity in Shakespearian Tragedy* (1956).

NOTES

1. See the discussion in J. E. Phillips's *The State in Shakespeare's Greek and Roman Plays* (New York, 1940) pp. 172 ff. Mr Phillips quotes at length from such typical spokesmen as Sir Thomas Elyot and Thomas Craig. His analysis of *Julius Caesar* on this basis is also illuminating. See also the present author's *The Populace in Shakespeare* (New York, 1949) p. 147, for a condemnation by William Covell of Romans who aroused civil dissension by covering their purposes 'with the fine terms of a common good, of the freedom of the people, of justice . . .'. The parallel with Brutus is a very close one, and Covell, moreover, explicitly avows a topical relation of such Roman history to the civil tensions of Elizabethan England.

2. My article on the ritual theme in *Julius Caesar* (*PMLA*, LXVI 765 ff) appeared in 1951 as an early draft of this chapter. Some of my principal observations have been repeated by Ernest Schanzer in a recent essay ('The Tragedy of Shakespeare's Brutus', in *Journal of English Literary History* (March 1955) pp. 1 ff; see pp. 6–8).

3. See the reference and quotation in note 1.

Virgil K. Whitaker

BRUTUS AND THE TRAGEDY
OF MORAL CHOICE (1953)

BRUTUS is the first of Shakespeare's superb tragic figures who fail through false moral choice.

In attempting to dramatize a moral choice, Shakespeare was breaking new ground, just as he had done in trying to show the development of Hal from hellion to worthy king. But this time he had adequate precedent, which he used. . . . I do not mean to assert that Shakespeare knew and used one of the moralities, but rather that a living dramatic tradition leads from them to him. There is a similar progress in dramatic technique from the moralities through *Faustus* to *Julius Caesar*. The moralities were fundamentally allegories of moral choice. In *The Castle of Perseverance*,[1] for example, mankind enters describing his birth 'this night'. He is attended by a good and a bad angel, who debate for control of him. He yields to the bad angel and accepts the seven deadly sins. But Shrift and Penance win him back to the Castle of Perseverance, which is assaulted by Pride, Wrath, and Envy, who conduct a running debate with the virtues Meekness, Patience, and Charity until they are beaten back. The subsequent action, in which all ends happily and virtuously, need not concern us. Enough has been said to show several things. A conflict is presumed to go on in the soul of any man confronted with a choice between moral conduct and temptation. This conflict is presented in the form of a debate between good and bad angels and between virtues and vices, who personify and externalize the *psychomachia* which descended to Christian ethics from Plato and Aristotle. This concept of morality is implicit in the New Testament word for sin, *hamartia* ('missing the mark'), which is, incidentally, the term used by Aristotle for the tragic hero's flaw. The psychology involved was formulated in Christian terms, I believe, by Augustine in his *De Libero Arbitrio*, and from him it descended to subsequent thinkers, among them Hooker. To return to drama, the next important step in the treatment of this 'war of the soul' was taken by Marlowe, who attempted in *Faustus* to present the spiritual biography of a scholar driven by the sin of despair to ultimate damnation. The good and evil angels still appear, but the good angel states sound doctrine, which Faustus does not understand. It is likely, therefore, that the angels are now intended to present the struggle between God and Satan for the soul of man rather than to externalize moral tension. Marlowe keeps within the mind of his hero the conflict that leads to false choice. He presents it in a long soliloquy. Since Shakespeare probably borrowed his technique in *Julius Caesar* from this soliloquy, it is worth examining.

Faustus is presented in his study. After rejecting philosophy, physic, and law as pursuits, he turns to divinity.

> When all is done, Divinitie is best.
> *Jeromes* Bible, *Faustus*, view it well.
> *Stipendium peccati mors est*: ha, *Stipendium*, &c.
> The reward of sinne is death: thats hard.
> *Si peccasse negamus, fallimur, & nulla est in nobis veritas.*
> If we say that we have no sinne,
> We deceive our selves, and theres no truth in us.
> Why then belike
> We must sinne, and so consequently die.
> I, we must die an everlasting death:
> What doctrine call you this, *Che sera, sera*,
> What wil be, shall be? Divinitie, adieu,
> These Metaphisickes of Magicians,
> And Negromantike bookes are heavenly:
> Lines, circles, sceanes, letters and characters:
> I, these are those that *Faustus* most desires. (II 65–80)

In choosing magic in preference to divinity and therefore committing his soul to Lucifer, Faustus of course sins, though not irreparably as he imagines. Marlowe presents him as making this wrong choice because of fallacious reasoning based upon culpable ignorance. He ignores the grace and mercy of God, and his ultimate destruction comes about because he continues to despair of God's mercy. This emphasis upon the danger of despair was, of course, a medieval and Renaissance commonplace. In *The Faerie Queene* Despair personified urges upon Red Cross exactly the same arguments that Faustus uses, and Una, in her only outburst of anger, exposes their falsity: 'In heavenly mercies has thou not a part?' (I ix 53). Marlowe has a subtler way of implying the same fallacy. As a basis of his reasoning, Faustus quotes part of two key texts, which the audience undoubtedly knew. But they also knew the rest of the texts, which Faustus does not quote. Completing his quotations exposes his error. 'The reward of sin is death, (but the gift of God is eternal life, through Jesus Christ our Lord' – Romans VI 23). If we say that we have no sin, we deceive ourselves, and there is no truth in us. (If we confess our sins, he is faithful and just to forgive us our sins, and to cleanse us from all unrighteousness' – I John I 8–9.)[2] From Faustus' false choice in this passage, and from his failure to correct it, resulted his final descent to Hell.

Shakespeare presents Brutus' false choice in a famous soliloquy (II i 10–34) that has been a puzzle to scholars.[3] But it does not seem to me particularly difficult if Marlowe's technique and Shakespeare's political views are kept in mind. Like Marlowe, Shakespeare expected his audience to detect a fallacy in reasoning. Many other writers of his time expected the same thing, including Spenser, Chapman,* and Milton. A very instructive essay could be written, in fact, on the use of the logical fallacy by Renaissance authors as an expository device, and on the resulting confusion of modern readers less trained in dialectic. But Shakespeare was unable to place such clear signposts within Brutus' soliloquy as Marlowe had provided for Faustus; so he warned the audience in advance. Cassius plies Brutus with suggestions throughout a scene which is punctuated by shouts as Caesar is being offered

---

* With *Faustus* and *Julius Caesar*, cf. *Bussy D'Ambois*, where the initial exposition of Bussy's character depends on the fact that he states sound moral doctrine in his opening soliloquy (I i 1–33) and then violates these principles as soon as Monsieur offers him gold.

the crown offstage; then he concludes with a soliloquy in which
he explains how he proposes to win Brutus over to his scheme:

> Well, Brutus, thou art noble; yet, I see,
> Thy honorable metal may be wrought
> From that it is dispos'd: therefore it is meet
> That noble minds keep ever with their likes;
> For who so firm that cannot be seduc'd?
> Caesar doth bear me hard, but he loves Brutus.
> If I were Brutus now and he were Cassius,
> He should not humour me. I will this night,
> In several hands, in at his windows throw,
> As if they came from several citizens,
> Writings all tending to the great opinion
> That Rome holds of his name; wherein obscurely
> Caesar's ambition shall be glanced at;
> And after this let Caesar seat him sure,
> For we will shake him, or worse days endure.
>
> (I ii 312–26)

In short, Brutus is noble but proud of his reputation as a descend-
ant of the Brutus who expelled the last kings of Rome, and pride
is the most insidious of the passions that spring from man's
sensible appetite. Upon that vanity Cassius proposes to work
by throwing into Brutus' window messages purporting to come
from various citizens. By the time of Brutus' soliloquy his
scheme is taking effect.

As numerous writers upon Shakespeare and poetic drama have
reminded us, quite rightly, his technique is one of suggestion
rather than of complete representation. There was no need for
him to portray the entire mental struggle leading up to a crucial
choice, but he did have to imply how it came about convincingly
enough to stimulate the imagination of his audience. He might
attempt to parallel all stages of the inner conflict. That he did in
Othello, with somewhat doubtful success. Or he might present
the climax of the struggle, giving only a hint of what had gone
before. This is his method in *Julius Caesar*, as it is in *Macbeth*
and, with variations, in *King Lear*. The first line of Brutus'
soliloquy resumes an interrupted process of cogitation. 'It must

be by his death.' Two assumptions are implicit in this remark. Caesar can be prevented from being king only by killing him, and killing a ruler is justified only if he is a tyrant. The former was axiomatic to anyone with a knowledge either of English history or of Machiavelli, and it is explicit in Brutus' first words. The latter should have been clear to the audience, since Cassius had just harped throughout the preceding scene on the weakness of those who submit to tyrants. It is clearly implied by the reasoning throughout the soliloquy. Having established his premises, Brutus continues:

> It must be by his death; and for my part,
> I know no personal cause to spurn at him
> But for the general. He would be crown'd:
> How that might change his nature, there's the question.
> It is the bright day that brings forth the adder,
> And that craves wary walking. Crown him? That –
> And then, I grant, we put a sting in him
> That at his will he may do danger with.
> Th' abuse of greatness is when it disjoins
> Remorse from power; and, to speak truth of Caesar,
> I have not known when his affections sway'd
> More than his reason. But 'tis a common proof
> That lowliness is young Ambition's ladder,
> Whereto the climber-upward turns his face;
> But when he once attains the upmost round,
> He then unto the ladder turns his back,
> Looks in the clouds, scorning the base degrees
> By which he did ascend. So Caesar may;
> Then, lest he may, prevent. And, since the quarrel
> Will bear no colour for the thing he is,
> Fashion it thus: that what he is, augmented,
> Would run to these and these extremities;
> And therefore think him as a serpent's egg
> Which, hatch'd, would, as his kind, grow mischievous,
> And kill him in the shell.   (II i 10–34)

His meaning is somewhat as follows. I have no personal grievance; so, if I act, it must be for the Roman people. The question that I must answer is whether crowning Caesar might change his nature. If we crown him, we give him the power to do great harm. But he will do harm and abuse his greatness only if he uses power without remorse (that is, without a moral sense). But, to speak truthfully, Caesar has never let his affections win control over his reason (in other words, he has never shown any inclination to irrational and immoral conduct). But it is common experience that humility is merely the ladder to ambition (ambition was for the Elizabethans a vice). Once the climber has achieved his ambition, he scorns the humility by which he ascended. Caesar may do so; therefore anticipate him. And, *since his present conduct gives no warrant whatever* for concluding that he will be a tyrant and therefore for killing him, assume that, once he gains absolute power, he will proceed to extremities; and kill him to prevent what he may become, as one would destroy a serpent's egg because a serpent is, by nature, dangerous.

Shakespeare has done his best to make the fallacies in the reasoning obvious. Brutus says explicitly that he has no evidence to support the conclusion that Caesar will become immoral and that he must kill on an assumption without basis; he ends by remarking that one destroys a serpent's egg because it is the 'kind' (nature) of a serpent to be poisonous, but he has opened by observing that Caesar will be a tyrant only if crowning him changes his nature. His error in assuming that he is acting for the Roman people is proved by later events.

I take it that Brutus' doubling back upon his previous reasoning, as he does in the last seven lines, is intended by Shakespeare to suggest that his mind is still not made up at the end of the soliloquy. But there follows an appeal to his fatal weakness. Lucius re-enters with another letter. Logic yields to pride, and reason becomes the tool of appetite. Brutus resolves upon action, and Caesar's doom is sealed. But Brutus has one further revelation to make. The process of choice has been agonizing:

> Since Cassius first did whet me against Caesar,
> I have not slept.
> Between the acting of a dreadful thing
> And the first motion, all the interim is
> Like a phantasma or a hideous dream.

> The Genius and the mortal instruments
> Are then in council; and the state of a man,
> Like to a little kingdom, suffers then
> The nature of an insurrection.   (II i 61–9)

To make assurance doubly sure, Shakespeare, through Brutus, points out that an insurrection has occurred: passion has overturned reason. But this agony in retrospect is a little unconvincing. In *Othello* and *Macbeth* Shakespeare showed, during the choice itself, the full agony that his heroes suffered.

From Brutus' decision followed action. As a result of the killing of Caesar chaos engulfed all Rome, and discord and then death overwhelmed Brutus and Cassius themselves.

This kind of scene was new to Shakespeare and indeed, so far as I know, to all drama except for *Faustus*. A choice that involves moral issues is, of course, fundamental to most serious action. It underlies Antigone's defiance of Creon or Bolingbroke's deposition of Richard II. What was new was the attempt to make the act of choice an important part of the play and to work it out in detail according to accepted psychological theory. Shakespeare motivates his action by a formal scene of moral choice.

In comparison with the chronicle plays just preceding it and even with the comedies contemporary with it, *Julius Caesar* is remarkable as being the first Shakespearean play in which the motivation is really adequate and in which we become acquainted with the characters through their mental processes as well as through their actions. There are a few loose ends such as Brutus' unexplained and very imprudent departure before Antony's funeral oration. But Brutus nearly always has reasons for what he does, and those reasons, whether sound or unsound, reveal his character and carry forward the action of the play. The same generalization might be made about both Caesar and Cassius. This change has been accomplished partly by concentration upon a smaller body of events and especially by giving a new importance to the soliloquy in the structure of the play. In fact, if the preceding analysis of Shakespeare's thinking is sound, the interpretation of the play as a whole turns upon the three key soliloquies by Cassius, Brutus, and Antony, and upon Antony's conventional summary speech over Brutus' body. Antony, in fact, is a little torn between his roles as dramatist's mouthpiece and as practical politician, and we are in danger of underestimating the significance of his soliloquy because we assign it only to the politician. For the same reason critics have generally overlooked the parallels between his funeral oration and Brutus' soliloquy. He actually uses the same evidence that Brutus mentions, and the people accept his conclusion as logical – which it is. In fact, Shakespeare failed to make his meaning as clear in this play as it is in *Lear* or *Antony and Cleopatra* or *Coriolanus*. Antony is too involved in the action to be an effective guide to the audience, and there is no chorus character to underscore the folly of the hero as do Kent and the Fool or Enobarbus or Menenius Agrippa. Perhaps Shakespeare also relied too heavily upon character contrast. For Cassius seems constantly to be used as a foil to Brutus, illustrating by contrast both the latter's virtue and his lack of worldly wisdom. Tassin writes that Shakespeare 'seems much to have admired this vigorous, impulsive, and generous man'.[4] So it seems in the final scenes of the play, but not in those before Brutus joins the conspiracy, where Cassius is motivated by envy. I suspect, therefore, that Cassius is the beneficiary, not of Shakespeare's affection but of his artistic design. He was trying primarily to illustrate Brutus' weaknesses by contrasting them in the final scenes with Cassius' practical ability and his generosity, just as in the early scenes and in Antony's final summary he used the dishonesty of Cassius' motives to emphasize Brutus' nobility.

The play is less clear than the later tragedies in another respect. *Othello, Macbeth,* and *Lear* not only confess that they have sinned but also recognize in specific terms the weakness that led them to err. Brutus acknowledges the might of Caesar before he dies, but he never sees how his own pride has helped to make that might effective.

Despite these defects, which Shakespeare learned to remedy, he showed magnificent control in working out his ideas by a slight manipulation of Plutarch's material. The same skill is illustrated by the play's easy command of a good deal of learning. Details from a variety of minor sources have been employed so

skillfully that one is unconscious of their intrusion. In addition
to those already mentioned, an interesting echo of one of
Montaigne's essays has been found in the last part of Brutus'
oration,[5] although like all the suggested examples of Montaigne's
influence before *The Tempest*, it is only close enough to be tan-
talizing but not to be indubitable. The rhetoric from Shakespeare's
school days is used with extraordinary effectiveness both in
fashioning the orations and in creating a style that 'counterfeited
that brief compendious manner of speech of the Lacedaemonians'
to which Plutarch says that Brutus was addicted.[6] Whether
Brutus' style also reflects the Stoic prose becoming fashionable in
reaction against Ciceronianism there is no way of telling. In
addition to handling the omens accurately in terms of the best
contemporary learning, Shakespeare was careful to distinguish
between their influence and men's free will. Cassius' famous
lines are absolutely sound:

> Men at some time are masters of their fates;
> The fault, dear Brutus, is not in our stars,
> But in ourselves, that we are underlings.
>
> (I ii 139–41)

Cassius also delivers a string of Renaissance commonplaces on
death (I iii 91–7) that remind one vaguely of Donne's sonnet
'Death, be not proud'. Finally, it is probable that Shakespeare
intended to characterize Cassius as a melancholy malcontent of
the type much discussed at the time and familiar enough in drama.
Plutarch applies Caesar's remark that he feared 'lean and whitely-
faced fellows' (which is given in the lives of both Caesar and
Brutus) to Brutus and Cassius jointly, but Shakespeare applies
it only to Cassius and adds details that were appropriate to the
malcontent (cf. I ii 194–210).[7]

   But the significance of *Julius Caesar* for the development of
Shakespeare's thought lies not in these details but in its use of a
formula which appears in all the great tragedies except *Hamlet* –
– a formula for tragedy of moral choice, which is somewhat as
follows. During the dramatic exposition three things are accomplished. The dilemma facing the hero is explained, as in *Julius*

Caesar, or a situation is developed which will confront the hero with the necessity of making a fundamental choice, as in the remaining plays. A character is presented who for his own reasons wishes the hero to make a false choice. He may be the antagonist, as are Iago and, in a sense, the tribunes in *Coriolanus* and Goneril and Regan in *Lear*; or he may be a collaborator like Cassius, Lady Macbeth, or Cleopatra. This character explains, generally in a soliloquy, the weakness that predisposes the hero to make a false choice (in *Antony and Cleopatra* this function is given to Philo in the opening speech). As the next step, in violation of all probability the actual choice is made in a single scene, the most improbable of all being that in which Othello enters speaking of his devotion to Desdemona and exits resolved to murder her. The false moral choice then leads to a decisive act, and from that act results the hero's downfall. Every hero except Brutus recognizes and states explicitly the full extent of his error.

That the hero's downfall results from irrationality Shakespeare is at pains to make clear. One or more characters repeatedly point out the folly of the hero's ways. In *Julius Caesar* Cassius and Antony both do so, as we have noted; in *Othello* Iago and Emilia (at the end of the play); in *King Lear* Kent, Goneril and Regan, and the Fool; in *Macbeth* Banquo; in *Antony and Cleopatra* Enobarbus; in *Coriolanus* Menenius Agrippa and Volumnia. One of these figures – Antony, Emilia, Banquo, Kent, Enobarbus, and Volumnia – stigmatizes the choice itself as false either when it is made or shortly thereafter. It is also interesting that, as we move from concern with the individual in *Othello* to *Macbeth*, which emphasizes the individual but presents the social order, to *Lear*, which considers both social and universal order, the scene of moral choice moves forward. In *Othello* it is Act III, scene iii, the climax of the play; in *Macbeth*, Act I, scene vii; in *Lear*, Act I, scene i, which telescopes exposition of the false choice, decisive act, and explanation of character weaknesses into the opening scene, so that the entire play may be devoted to consequences. There is, furthermore, a technical development in these tragedies paralleling that in the early chronicles. The plays up through *Macbeth* depend heavily on self-revelation through soliloquies and asides; *Antony and Cleopatra* and *Coriolanus* are almost free of these devices. *Antony and Cleopatra* is carelessly put together in other respects, but *Coriolanus*, though lacking power to grip the audience, is one of Shakespeare's most carefully constructed plays. This formula that was worked out in *Julius Caesar*, and even the elaborate use of self-revelation, grew out of the system of ideas to which Shakespeare was to give expression in *Troilus and Cressida*. It enabled the tragedies to absorb the learning which was too much for *Troilus and Cressida* and to achieve a perfect fusion of thought and action.

SOURCE: *Shakespeare's Use of Learning* (1953).

NOTES

1. Reprinted in part in J. Q. Adams, *Chief Pre-Shakespearian Dramas* (Cambridge, Mass., 1924) pp. 265–87; the entire text appears in *The Macro Plays*, ed. F. J. Furnivall and A. W. Pollard (1904) pp. 76–186.

2. Cf. M. Mahood, *Poetry and Humanism* (1950) p. 69.

3. Note H. B. Charlton's sound reading of the soliloquy (*Shakespearian Tragedy* (1948) p. 77).

4. A. de V. Tassin, 'Julius Caesar', ii. *Shakespearian Studies by Members of the Department of English and Comparative Literature at Columbia University* (New York, 1916) p. 268.

5. *Julius Caesar*, ed. T. S. Dorsch (Arden Shakespeare, 1955) III ii 27.

6. *Four Lives from North's Plutarch*, ed. R. H. Carr (1906) p. 113.

7. Cf. G. B. Harrison, 'An Essay on Elizabethan Melancholy', in Nicholas Breton *Melancholike Humours* (1929) pp. 64–7.

Ernest Schanzer

THE TRAGEDY OF BRUTUS (1963)

LET us take a look at Brutus and the nature of his tragedy. While Shakespeare's Caesar, Cassius, and Antony owe little to their prototypes in Plutarch, his Brutus is substantially Plutarch's Brutus. Yet, even here, for all that makes him a dramatic character as distinct from a copy-book hero, his divided mind, his self-deception, his final tragic disillusion, Shakespeare received no hints from Plutarch.

It is a mistake to see Brutus as the unworldly scholar, blind to political realities, devoid of a knowledge of life, called from his books to assume a task for which he was not fitted. This view was dear to Romantic critics, who liked to present this phantom Brutus as Shakespeare's first sketch in preparation for their phantom Hamlet. Shakespeare depicts Brutus as a bad judge of character, but as by no means devoid of political shrewdness and practical wisdom.* For instance, in Plutarch it is Antony who suggests that Caesar's 'body should be honourably buried, and not in hugger mugger, lest the people might thereby take occasion to be worse offended if they did otherwise'.[1] Shakespeare transfers the argument to Brutus, making him declare:

> What Antony shall speak, I will protest
> He speaks by leave and by permission;
> And that we are contented Caesar shall
> Have all true rites and lawful ceremonies.
> It shall advantage more than do us wrong.
>
> (III i 239–43)

---

* This combination is not unique in the play. It is found again in Antony: witness his remark about Cassius (I ii 196–7).

That Shakespeare regarded the argument as by no means 'fatuous', as one commentator calls it, but as shrewd, practical politics
is shown by his putting a variation of it a year or two later into
the mouth of his arch-politician Claudius:

> the people muddied,
> Thick and unwholesome in their thoughts and whispers
> For good Polonius' death; and we have done but greenly
> In hugger-mugger to inter him.   (*Hamlet*, IV v 78–81)

(The 'hugger-mugger' suggests that Shakespeare had that very
passage from Plutarch at the back of his mind when writing
these lines, a striking example of how North's more vivid idioms
were garnered up in the poet's memory, to be brought out when
some similarity of situation recalled them.) Brutus's advice is in
itself sound enough and would have justified itself with anyone
but Antony, whom he so fatally misjudges.

Again, I cannot agree with commentators who speak of
Brutus's oration as an example of his political naïveté, of the
scholar's inability to understand the common people or to
present his case effectually. It seems to me, on the contrary, an
extremely shrewd and highly effective piece of oratory. In his
soliloquy Brutus could find nothing with which to reproach
Caesar except his desire for the crown. The murder is in his eyes
purely preventive, designed to protect the commonwealth from
the kind of person Caesar is likely to become upon the acquisition
of greater power. To win the support of a mob clamouring for
satisfaction with no better arguments to justify the murder of
their hero is clearly no simple matter. How does Brutus achieve
it? He begins by subtly, unobtrusively, flattering his audience.
The very fact that he does not talk down to them, will not speak
their language, as Antony does, is a compliment to their intelligence. And even if they cannot quite follow him in his clipped,
carefully patterned sentences, they can at least make out that the
noble Brutus asks them to respect his honour, to censure him in
their wisdom, to be his judges. Nothing could be more flattering
except his next suggestion, that among them there may be a dear
friend of Caesar's. Then comes the assertion, true as we know it

to be, but therefore none the less effective, that only a superior love of his country made him slay his dearest friend. Still no charge has been brought against Caesar. Then suddenly the question is sprung on them: 'Had you rather Caesar were living, and die all slaves, than that Caesar were dead, to live all free men?' That the alternative may be quite unreal will not occur to the people under the influence of Brutus's oratory. At last an accusation is made, but one of the vaguest kind: Caesar was ambitious. And at once, before they have time to ask for evidence, there follows the series of rhetorical questions which so ingeniously forestall any objections from his audience:

Who is here so base that would be a bondman? If any, speak; for him have I offended. Who is here so rude that would not be a Roman? If any, speak; for him have I offended. Who is here so vile that will not love his country? If any, speak; for him have I offended. I pause for a reply.

Nothing could be more skilful. He has brought only the vaguest charge against Caesar and yet effectively blocked all further questions from the crowd, shown himself the saviour of his country, and gained the love and admiration of the people. The speech is kept as short as possible, so that detailed accusations would seem out of place, and, in closing, he hurriedly refers the people for facts to the records in the Capitol, with a final display of fairmindedness:

The question of his death is enroll'd in the Capitol; his glory not extenuated wherein he was worthy; nor his offences enforc'd, for which he suffered death.

Brutus ends with a parting glance at the benefits the people will derive from Caesar's death, and with an expression of his willingness to die for his country. The whole speech is as shrewdly contrived and, as the response of the people shows, quite as effective as Antony's. And Brutus has the far more difficult task: that of defending the murder of 'the foremost man of all this world' on a charge which he cannot substantiate. All that Antony needs to do is to discredit the allegation of Caesar's ambition in order to nullify Brutus's entire argument. The fact that all that Brutus says no doubt appears to him strictly true and is sincerely felt in no way lessens the great skill of the speech.

At other times, too, in the play Brutus does not show himself devoid of practical wisdom. The reasons he gives for marching to Philippi may be mistaken, but they certainly show no lack of an eye for the expedient and politic. Altogether, I think we must banish the myth of the unpractical dreamer from our image of Shakespeare's Brutus.[2]

It would seem that just as in Hamlet Shakespeare wished to represent the Renaissance ideal of the encyclopaedic man, the 'uomo universale', in Brutus he wished to represent the ideal of the harmonious man, whose gentleness, courtesy, and love of music all bear witness to his 'well-tempered' nature. It is to this quality in him that Antony pays his final tribute:

> His life was gentle; and the elements
> So mix'd in him that Nature might stand up
> And say to all the world 'This was a man!'

Yet both Hamlet and Brutus are depicted from their first appearance as wrenched from their ordinary selves, steeped in melancholy, so that their normal nature is largely veiled from us, and is glimpsed chiefly through the tribute of others, an Antony or an Ophelia. Brutus, the harmonious man, is ironically shown to us throughout the first half of the play as rent by discordant emotions, and later, in the quarrel-scene, 'like sweet bells jangled, out of tune and harsh'. Of the civil war in Brutus, resulting from the conflict between personal and public loyalties, we learn upon his first appearance, when he speaks to Cassius of 'poor Brutus with himself at war', and of his being vexed of late 'with passions of some difference' (i.e. with conflicting emotions). It is echoed and amplified by the tempests that precede the assassination and which appear to Casca to spring from 'civil strife in heaven' (I iii II). And finally, in fulfilment of Antony's terrible prophecy, the civil war spreads from microcosm and macrocosm to the body politic, finding its culmination at Philippi and its reflection even in the quarrel-scene. Brutus's inner struggle continues until the assassination, taking on a nightmare quality, and somewhat altering its nature. For while the earlier struggle seems caused mainly by rival loyalties, by warring principles, after Brutus's decision to murder Caesar is reached it is the deed itself, now revealed to his imagination in all its stark horror, that causes his feelings to rebel against the decision which his intellect has made. This, I take it, is the meaning of the much disputed

> Between the acting of a dreadful thing
> And the first motion, all the interim is
> Like a phantaşma or a hideous dream.
> The Genius and the mortal instruments
> Are then in council; and the state of man,
> Like to a little kingdom, suffers then
> The nature of an insurrection. (II i 63–9)

While his mind considers the various possible ways of carrying out the murder (pictured as a council meeting between man's presiding genius, his intellect, and the mortal instruments, the means of bringing about the death), his instincts and passions are in revolt against the decision of their ruler. Insurrection has taken the place of Civil War within him. His gentle, frank, and generous nature is in revolt not only against the deed itself, but against the whole conspiracy, with all the secrecy and deceitfulness it entails. This is how he greets the announcement of the arrival of his fellow-conspirators:

> They are the faction. O conspiracy,
> Sham'st thou to show thy dang'rous brow by night,
> When evils are most free? O, then by day
> Where wilt thou find a cavern dark enough
> To mask thy monstrous visage? Seek none, conspiracy;
> Hide it in smiles and affability!
> For if thou path, thy native semblance on,
> Not Erebus itself were dim enough
> To hide thee from prevention.

To save himself from these nightmare realizations he plunges headlong into self-delusion. In his soliloquy he had acquitted Caesar of any kind of tyrannical behaviour:

> and to speak truth of Caesar,
> I have not known when his affections sway'd
> More than his reason.

A little later, in the company of the conspirators, he tries to persuade himself that Caesar is already a full-blown tyrant.[3]

> No, not an oath. If not the face of men,
> The sufferance of our souls, the time's abuse,
> If these be motives weak, break off betimes,
> And every man hence to his idle bed.
> So let high-sighted tyranny range on,
> Till each man drop by lottery.   (II i 114–19)

Caesar here is no longer the serpent's egg of Brutus's soliloquy, nor Flavius's young hawk whose growing feathers must be plucked betimes (1 i 73–6), but a full-grown falcon, scouring for prey. Plutarch, as we saw, could not make up his mind whether Caesar at the end of his life was a tyrant or not, asserting now the one and then the other. Shakespeare embodies these self-contradictions in Brutus, but gives them a psychological basis in his need for the comforts of self-delusion.

Like Othello, Brutus tries to free himself both from the burden of guilt and from the physical horror of the murder by adopting a ritualistic and aesthetic attitude towards it.[4]

> Let's kill him boldly, but not wrathfully;
> Let's carve him as a dish fit for the gods,
> Not hew him as a carcase fit for hounds.
>   (II i 172–4)

Both these 'honourable murderers' picture the deed as an act of sacrifice. 'Let us be sacrificers, but not butchers, Caius.' It is not a husband murdering his wife, not a friend murdering his 'best lover' and benefactor; they are 'purgers, not murderers'. 'It is the cause, it is the cause, my soul.' Caesar must be killed beautifully, ceremonially.

The ritualistic bathing of their hands in Caesar's blood, suggested by Brutus after the murder, carries this further, and, incidentally, fulfils Calpurnia's prophetic dream.

> Stoop, Romans, stoop,
> And let us bathe our hands in Caesar's blood
> Up to the elbows, and besmear our swords.
>
> (III i 106–8)

But, ironically, the action suggests another ritual, far removed
from that which Brutus has in mind, the custom of huntsmen
at the kill to steep their hands in the blood of their victim. It
is to this bloody rite that Antony refers.

> Here wast thou bay'd, brave hart;
> Here didst thou fall; and here thy hunters stand,
> Sign'd in thy spoil, and crimson'd in thy Lethe.*

Whereas Brutus pictures to himself the murder as a ceremonial
slaying of the sacrificial beast on the altar of the commonweal,
Antony sees it as the bloody slaughter of the noble stag, the
King of the Forest, for the sake of the spoil. For under cover
of his metaphor Antony can dare to accuse the conspirators to
their faces of killing Caesar for the sake of booty, the basic
meaning of 'spoil'.† But fearing he has gone too far he at once
insinuates a piece of flattery, as is his practice throughout this
scene:

> How like a deer strucken by many princes
> Dost thou here lie!

From Antony's soliloquy we realize that even the hunting-
metaphor was a form of flattery.

> O, pardon me, thou bleeding piece of earth,
> That I am meek and gentle with these butchers!

* Whether we accept Capell's explanation of 'lethe' as 'a term used
by hunters to signify the blood shed by a deer at its fall' – and I can
find no evidence to support it – or take it to mean 'stream of death'
and hence 'life-blood', does not much affect the force of the image.

† According to C. T. Onions (*A Shakespeare Glossary*, 1951), 'spoil'
means '(in hunting) capture of the quarry and division of rewards to
the hounds, (hence) slaughter, massacre'.

It is an ironic comment on Brutus's illusions and his 'Let us be sacrificers, but not butchers, Caius'. The assassination turns into something very different from a ritual slaying. Plutarch mentions that 'divers of the conspirators did hurt themselves striking one body with so many blows'.[5] Shakespeare makes Antony allude to this during the 'flyting' on the battle-field, when he speaks of how the conspirators' 'vile daggers / Hack'd one another in the sides of Caesar' (v i 39–40). It is not a very pretty picture. Nor does the reality of Caesar's body 'marr'd with traitors' bear much relation to Brutus's aesthetic vision. Disconcerting to it is also the conspirators' flattery of Caesar, which makes him speak of Metellus' 'spaniel-fawning' and threaten to spurn him like a cur out of his way. It is not as priests officiating at a sacrifice that the conspirators are here seen, not even as huntsmen, but as hounds that fawn upon their victim before tearing it to pieces. It is to this image that Antony returns on the battle-field, when he accuses them of having 'fawned like hounds',

> Whilst damned Casca, like a cur, behind
> Struck Caesar on the neck.

On one other occasion Antony uses a metaphor from the hunt. In his soliloquy he envisages the war of revenge as a savage hunting-scene in which this time the conspirators are the quarry, no quarter is given, and Caesar's ghost acts as the chief huntsman:

> And Caesar's spirit, ranging for revenge,
> With Até by his side come hot from hell,
> Shall in these confines with a monarch's voice
> Cry 'Havoc!' and let slip the dogs of war.

> (III i 271–4)

This whole complex of hunting-metaphors was presumably set off in the poet's mind by Plutarch's description of Caesar as 'hacked and mangled among them, as a wild beast taken of hunters'.[6]

The need for self-delusion, which drives Brutus to depict Caesar as a dangerous tyrant and to visualize his murder as a sacrificial rite, makes him afterwards try to persuade himself

that they have done a benefit not only to their country but to
Caesar himself. He eagerly takes up Casca's

> Why, he that cuts off twenty years of life
> Cuts off so many years of fearing death,

exclaiming,

> Grant that, and then is death a benefit.
> So are we Caesar's friends, that have abridg'd
> His time of fearing death.   (III i 104–6)

In his soliloquy we find Brutus engaged in a more subtle form
of self-deception in the attempt to still his inner conflict. We are
not here watching an act of choice. The choice has already been
made, as the opening line makes us realize: 'It must be by his
death'. How Brutus arrived at this absolute 'must' we are never
shown. It would seem that Shakespeare wishes us to feel that the
decision had nothing to do with reason and logic, that he has
somehow fallen victim to Cassius's rhetoric without being able
to accept his arguments or share his motives. What we are watching in the soliloquy is Brutus's attempt to defend his decision
before the court of his conscience. The rhythm of the verse, the
disjointed sentences, the wording in such lines as

> And since the quarrel
> Will bear no colour for the thing he is,
> Fashion it thus –   (II i 28–30)

all bring out the anxious groping for some plausible justification
of the deed. Caesar's desire for the crown does not in itself appear
sufficient cause to Brutus. Shakespeare's Brutus is by no means a
doctrinaire republican, in contrast to Plutarch's Brutus, who
reproaches Cicero for favouring Octavius, declaring, 'For our
predecessors would never abide to be subject to any Master, how
gentle or mild soever they were'.[7] Brutus's opposition to kingship rests on his fears of the corrupting effect of the power it
bestows, not on the nature of its office. 'Th' abuse of greatness is,
when it disjoins / Remorse from power' (II i 18–19). It is startling
to find Brutus in the remainder of the soliloquy speaking of Caesar

as if he were still at the beginning of his career, to hear him talk of 'the bright day that brings forth the adder', of 'young ambition's ladder', of Caesar as a serpent's egg. Like the reference to his 'lowliness' it is absurdly out of keeping with the picture of Caesar as the ageing Colossus that we are given in the course of the play. It would seem that, finding nothing in the mere fact of kingship, nor anything in Caesar's past behaviour to justify the assassination, Brutus deludes himself by vastly exaggerating the gap that separates the present from the future Caesar, the dictator from the king. Once this position is taken up, Brutus has no difficulty in advancing a logical argument for the assassination, and in this he is aided by his metaphor. It suggests the justification for the preventive murder, since it implies that, just as the adder, once hatched, is a menace that can no longer be controlled, so Caesar, once crowned, would be out of reach of the assassins' daggers. He must therefore be destroyed while he is still accessible, even though there is the possibility that the egg may hatch not a serpent but a dove. The argument is quite cogent and contains no confusion, as some commentators have claimed. But it is founded on self-deception.

By thus putting the justification for the murder on a pragmatic basis Brutus lays the foundation for his later tragedy. Had he been a doctrinaire republican and murdered Caesar to save the republic from kingship he would have been safe, if not from inner conflict, at least from tragic disillusion. For his purpose would have been accomplished. But by justifying the deed to himself and others on the grounds of 'pity to the general wrong of Rome' (III i 171), the wrong that Caesar may have committed in the future, he puts himself at the mercy of events. For it is only by establishing a government under which the people suffer less wrong than they would have done under Caesar's rule that the murder can, to Brutus, be justified. And what are the consequences as they are depicted in the play? They are adumbrated in Antony's prophecy: 'Domestic fury and fierce civil strife / Shall cumber all the parts of Italy. . . . All pity chok'd with custom of fell deeds . . .' (III i 264 ff.). It is a grim, ironic comment on Brutus's words in the same scene:

> And pity to the general wrong of Rome,
> As fire drives out fire, so pity pity,
> Hath done this deed on Caesar.   (III i 171–3)

In the succeeding scenes we find Antony translating his prophecy into fact. We see the domestic fury unchained by him
tearing the harmless Cinna to pieces, and in the following scene
observe, in all its cold-blooded ruthlessness, the régime that
has been set up in Rome in the place of Caesar's. The blood-bath
of the triumvirs contrasts with Caesar's scrupulous and unselfish
administration of justice of which we had glimpses in his 'What
touches us ourself shall be last serv'd' (III i 8), and his behaviour
over the repeal of Cimber's banishment. News reaches Brutus
that seventy senators have been put to death. His wife has committed suicide. And, to cap it all, his cause has been tarnished by
Cassius's malpractices. Instead of benefiting his country, Brutus
has, from the best of motives and the highest of principles,
plunged it into ruin. The two elements which Aristotle thought
necessary for the profoundest tragedy, *peripeteia* and *anagnorisis*,
an ironic turn of events which makes an action have the very
opposite effect of that intended, and the realization of this by the
agent, are thus seen to be fundamental to our play. They are
found, in varying degrees of prominence, in all of Shakespeare's
mature tragedies.

SOURCE: *Shakespeare's Problem Plays* (1963).

NOTES

1. 'Brutus', in *Shakespeare's Plutarch*, ed. Tucker Brooke (1909)
pp. 136–7.

2. In this view of Brutus I am supported by Brents Stirling (*Unity
in Shakespearian Tragedy* (New York, 1956) p. 47); by Adrien Bonjour (*The Structure of Julius Caesar* (Liverpool, 1958) p. 20); and above
all by Maria Wickert, who, in a valuable article, provides further
evidence against the view that Shakespeare wanted us to regard Brutus's

oration as deficient in skill ('Antikes Gedankengut in Shakespeares *Julius Caesar*', in *Shakespeare Jahrbuch*, LXXXII/LXXXIII (1948) 10–24).

3. This element of self-delusion has already been pointed out by Sir Mark Hunter, in *Royal Society of Literature: Essays by Divers Hands*, X (1931) 136 ff, and by J. I. M. Stewart, *Character and Motive in Shakespeare* (1949) pp. 51 ff.

4. This point has also been made by Brents Stirling, who brings out the pervasive presence of elements of ritual and ceremony throughout the play (*Unity in Shakespearian Tragedy*, ch. 4).

5. 'Caesar', in *Shakespeare's Plutarch*, p. 102.

6. Ibid., pp. 101–2.

7. 'Brutus', in *Shakespeare's Plutarch*, p. 141.

Mark Hunter

BRUTUS AND THE POLITICAL CONTEXT (1931)

OVER Shakespeare's imagination the career and personality of Julius Caesar exercised an extraordinary fascination. This has many times been noted. 'There is no other historical character', says one critic, 'who is so repeatedly alluded to throughout the plays.' Many of these allusions are trifling enough, and witness merely to the frequency with which the thought of Julius Caesar recurred to the poet's mind. Others are remarkable, not only as illustrating Shakespeare's conception of Caesar's transcendent greatness, but because, though not inappropriate to the dramatic situation in which they occur, they have no striking propriety in respect of the characters in whose mouths they are put. Thus it is the little Prince in *Richard III* who says of such an incident in Caesar's life as his (supposed) building the Tower of London, that even if it were not registered –

> Methinks the truth should live from age to age,
> As 'twere retayl'd to all posteritie,
> Euen to the generall all-ending day.
>
> .   .   .
>
> Death makes no Conquest of this Conqueror.

In a late play it is Cloten, a person not inclined to 'love the highest when he sees it', who exclaims,

> There be many Caesars
> Ere such another Julius;

and in a very early play Queen Margaret recalls the act of Brutus and the other conspirators as a deed standing out in all history as the arch-type of political crime. Among allusions of another kind there is no need to be reminded of Horatio's reference in *Hamlet* to the portents which foretold that crime,

> In the most high and palmy state of Rome,
> A little ere the mightiest Julius fell,

or of the tributes in the present play to 'the foremost man of all
the world' (from an opponent) and 'the Noblest man that ever
lived in the Tide of Times' spoken by an adherent, but in a
soliloquy right at the centre of the play, and with a direct bearing
on the tragedy's central theme.

The recollection of the notes of admiring appreciation scattered throughout the plays, prompts, and has often prompted, the
question, Why did Shakespeare in his play of *Julius Caesar*
represent the great soldier and statesman as a figure theatrically of
secondary importance, and in other respects not conspicuously
heroic? The question may be diversely answered, but, in part,
the assumption underlying it is itself open to question. A critic,
analysing the text, may doubtless make out a case, especially if
he emphasises what is said about Caesar by persons who 'bear
him hard'. Put the tragedy, however, to the true test, the test of
the stage – the impression created in the minds of those sitting
at the play – and the personality of Julius moves before us as
something right royal; a character, not indeed immune from
calumnious stroke, but sufficiently great to render the impas-
sioned eulogy of Antony and the calm tribute of Brutus not inconsistent with what we have actually heard and seen of the
object of their praise. If a contrast is felt, then someone has
blundered. It may be the player or the producer; I do not think
it is the playwright.

Nevertheless, theatrically (I use the term in no disparagement)
Caesar's is a minor part. So much is certain; and equally certain
is it that Shakespeare, in spite of the hold Caesar had over his
imagination, when he came to write a play about him, made no
attempt to portray the mightiest Julius 'in his huge and proper
life'. Many solutions might be offered of this simple puzzle, if
puzzle it be, but one will suffice. The life of Caesar did not afford
the stuff out of which an effective play can be constructed. Hence
it is not the life, but the death of Julius, which is the central and
all-controlling theme of the tragedy; the death of Caesar, the

circumstances leading to, attending and resulting from it; how also several persons, greatly endowed, but not quite rising to fully tragic dimensions, were affected by it. There is truth, therefore, in the old gibe that in the play of *Julius Caesar* the eponymous hero is brought upon the stage merely to be killed.

The personal interest in this play, the appeal of individual character, is not concentrated, as it is in the normally constructed tragedies, on one dominating figure which overshadows all the rest. It is distributed. This feature illustrates the affinity of which I spoke between the Roman plays and the histories; for in a history play, as conceived by Shakespeare, the single hero, a Hamlet, a Lear, a Macbeth, is not essential. From the point of view of the theatre – a point of view which should not be in conflict with any other legitimate line of approach – there is in *Julius Caesar* no bright particular star dimming the glory of all his fellows in the firmament. The varying choice of famous actor-managers, for so long as we have record of them, favouring now Brutus, now Cassius, and now again Antony, is significant; for on the stage no one of these characters dominates the action throughout. The first Act of the tragedy is Cassius' Act; the second is Brutus'; the third is Antony's; and in the fourth and fifth Cassius and Brutus together make a joint tragic appeal. The varying preferences of the actor-managers in this matter are indeed more instructive than the unanimity (almost) with which the commentators, partly misled by a false chronology, and also (quite naturally and profitably) absorbed in questions 'from the purpose of playing', have sought the central theme of the tragedy of *Julius Caesar* in a spiritual struggle in the soul of a single outstanding character – Brutus. But Brutus, of whom I shall have more to say presently, is not the centre and soul of the play. Apart from the obvious significance of the title, there is an objection, very simple and obvious also, which militates against the critical assumption that Brutus is the hero of the tragedy. In the first scene of each of the great normal tragedies, the leading personage, if not brought directly on the stage, is introduced so prominently in the dialogue, as to leave the audience in no doubt as to the character on behalf of whom their interest and sympathies will principally be engaged. In the opening scene of *Julius Caesar* Brutus is not so much as mentioned; everything that is said or done has reference to Caesar.

The opening scene of a Shakespeare play has always a peculiar significance (I do not say the feature is distinguishing), not merely in virtue of its providing a convenient and effective starting-point for what is to follow, but as furnishing a clue to the play's theme, or particular complexion, and to the nature of the action in which story and character will develop. The situation presented in the first scene of *Julius Caesar* is distinctly a political situation; and it is accordingly against a background of politics that the action is cast. In the lesser personages individual character is shown as almost entirely determined, in the greater figures, as directly influenced, by the bias of political conceptions. The political issue treated in the play is vividly brought out in the same first scene. The conflict has its centre in the imperial sway of Julius, under which the masses of the people repose quietly in a 'pathetic contentment' (to use a now famous phrase), from which it would seem they ought to be disturbed –

You Blockes, you stones, you worse than senseless thinges:
. . . knew you not Pompey?

The republican oligarchs are represented in the scene in the persons of the two politicians, Flavius and Marullus, enemies of Caesar. These eloquent gentlemen do not appear again in the play; there is later just one brief mention of them; but they serve their turn, and their words and actions make clear the kind of political principles which form the entire stock-in-trade of the lesser members of the aristocratic conspiracy, and even of the nobler protagonists, Brutus and Cassius. The people are represented by certain commoners, afterwards styled plebeians – a term by which Shakespeare evidently understood merely the lower social orders. Their spokesmen are a worthy carpenter and a cobbler distinguished by his rude wit and genial independence of character.

Fortunately I need not dwell at any length on Shakespeare's treatment of the common people, politically considered, or on his appreciation of their qualities of heart and head. The old critical view that the poet regarded the common people as wholly foolish and despicable, that he brought 'citizens' on the stage merely to ridicule them, has been refuted, I think once for all, by Professor Chambers in his memorable essay, 'The Expression of Ideas, particularly Political Ideas . . . in Shakespeare'.

What I desire to stress in this place is the contrast presented in the play between the visible facts of the 'condition of the People', and the facts as they take shape in the imagination of the politicians. The worthy commoners have come out in their best attire to see Caesar and rejoice in his triumph. Unlike the Plebeian in *Coriolanus*, they have no grievance. They seem to be quite happy, and fairly prosperous; only eager, like the good fellows they are, 'to get themselves into more work'. There is no sign that they feel themselves to be victims of any sort of oppression, and evidently the notion that there is anything unworthy in acquiescence in a rule that is merely righteous (we have Brutus' testimony that it is righteous) is a political conception far beyond them. Comparisons of the relative merits of good government and self-government would be meaningless to them. They do not trouble their heads about political theories at all. They are not 'politically minded', but they genuinely admire their country's great ones, and are hero-worshippers to a man. They rejoice at Caesar's good fortune, as later they will weep over his dead body; and when for a moment they are carried away by the noble presence of Brutus (they do not follow his arguments) their sole impulse is to make the uncompromising republican a king.

To the oligarchs, Flavius and Marullus, such subservience is an offence. They will have no holiday-making over Caesar's triumph. The great man must be boycotted, and a general fast strictly observed:

> Runne to your houses, fall upon your knees,
> Pray to the Gods to intermit the plague
> That needs must light on this ingratitude.

Not that in their detestation of tyranny the noble senators have any respect for, or fellow-feeling with, the People. These are 'idle creatures', 'blocks and stones', 'mechanicals' who should not stir abroad without the badge of their lowly professions; vulgar, to be driven from the streets. To Casca, a patriot 'swift in execution of any bold and noble enterprise', the populace are just the tag-rag, the rabblement, owners of chopt hands, sweaty night-caps, and other malodorous properties.

Brutus, it is true, does not, and could not, speak like this; nor indeed could the noble Cassius; but, Brutus excepted, there is no sign anywhere that the enemies of the Dictator, though they have all the political catch-words at command – Liberty, Freedom, Enfranchisement, a place in the commonwealth for everybody – care one jot for the welfare of any one outside their own order.

They have a certain political ideal, shared by Brutus with the least worthy of his confederates, and the ideal rings out clear in the concluding verses of the opening scene. At first, apparently, the complaint of Flavius and Marullus against the common folk is just that the people have ceased to shout for the faction they themselves favour. When they are left to themselves –

> These growing feathers, pluckt from Caesar's wing,
> Will make him flye an ordinary pitch,
> Who else would soare above the view of men,
> And keepe us all in seruile fearefulnesse.

There it is; just repudiation of the principle of the rule of the single person, the rule, which, to Shakespeare, was the norm of all manner of earthly power. 'Now is it Rome indeed,' cried Cassius,

> Now is it Rome indeed, and Roome enough,
> When there is in it but one only man,
> O! you and I have heard our Fathers say,
> There was a *Brutus* once, that would have brook't
> The eternall Diuell to keepe his State in Rome
> As easily as a King.

Some ten years later than the composition of this play, Shakespeare, in *Antony and Cleopatra*, put the same political doctrine into a speech of the younger Pompey:

> What was't
> That mou'd pale Cassius to conspire? And what
> Made the all-honor'd, honest Romaine Brutus,
> With the arm'd rest, Courtiers of beauteous freedome,
> To drench the Capitall, but that they would
> Have one man but a man.

And, in answer to these heroics, we have the quiet comment of Caesar himself when, speaking of Cassius, he says,

> Such men as he be never at heart's ease
> Whiles they behold a greater than themselves,
> And therefore are they very dangerous.

To Brutus, at one point, it would almost seem that the forbidden thing was not so much the actual fact of kingship as the name and symbol of royal rule. Brutus, indeed, to his credit, was not completely satisfied with the bare repudiation of kingship as such; he wanted confirmation of the traditional belief in some pretext of injuries or oppression as an invariable concomitant of monarchic rule; and he finds what he seeks, with the help of a most accommodating imagination, which grows, like jealousy, by what it feeds on.

That strange soliloquy of Brutus 'in his orchard' has puzzled commentators. 'What character', asked Coleridge, 'did Shakespeare mean his Brutus to be?' The puzzle ceases, however, when we recognise that the Brutus of Shakespeare is, for all his studious habits, no profound or subtle thinker, that he has no coherent political philosophy, and is not the 'ideal Republican' Swinburne imagined him to be. Shakespeare, perhaps, was not much interested in 'ideal republicans', but he was greatly interested in a nobly-natured mistaken man, such as he pictured Brutus; a man who, in Dowden's phrase, was 'studious of self-perfection', but who, just because his motives were so unblemished and his reasons so confused, was terribly liable to go astray. 'It must be by his death,' Brutus begins. That, by Cassius' persuasion, seems settled; and Brutus goes on to find justification for the deed which he now feels to be a duty laid on him. He has 'no personal cause to spurn at' Caesar, and the absence of personal grievance seems to go some way to warrant the act. One should murder on principle, and Caesar must be killed, not to serve any selfish end, 'but for the generall'; that is to say, for our jolly friends the carpenter and the shoemaker, who would be vastly astonished to learn that Caesar had to be slaughtered for their advantage. Brutus, however, makes an attempt to be honest with himself:

> Th' abuse of Greatnesse, is, when it disioynes
> Remorse from Power.

Note, it is the abuse, not greatness itself, that Brutus boggles at; but the cobbler and his fellows so far have not suffered from the abuse; for then follows a tribute, the highest that could well be paid, to the calm wisdom and impartial justice of Caesar's rule –

> To speak truth of Caesar,
> I have not knowne, when his Affections sway'd
> More than his Reason.

'The quarrel', he confesses, 'will beare no colour for the thing he is'; that is, on its merits there is no case; but we may 'fashion it thus'. Caesar wishes to be crowned (though, to be sure, that is just Casca's suspicion about him); and that *might* (still a mere possibility) 'change his nature'; and so to avoid a hypothetic disaster, let us –

> thinke him as a Serpent's egge,
> Which hatch'd, would as his kinde grow mischievous;
> And kill him in the shell.

Highly curious reasoning, in seeking to analyse which we have perhaps (to use a phrase of Johnson's), 'wasted criticism on unresisting imbecility'. But that precisely is how the account now stands. Brutus, in allowing his eyes even slightly to glance at reality, has for the moment proved false to the republican faith that is in him. We shall forget it presently, as Brutus himself sublimely forgets. A very little while after this self-communing we hear Brutus, carried away by self-engendered emotion, passionately exhorting his confederates:

Brutus. Give me your hands all ouer, one by one,
Cassius. And let vs sweare our Resolution.
Brutus. No, not an Oath: if not the Face of men,

– (the pleasant countenances of the holiday-making artisans, for instance) –

> if not the Face of men,
> The sufferance of our Soules, the Times Abuse;
> If these be Motiues weake, breake off betimes,
> And every man hence, to his idle bed:
> So let high-sighted Tyranny range on,
> Till each man drops by Lottery.

So short a space has been needed to convert, in Brutus' mind, greatness that has never been abused, and impulse never uncontrolled by reason, into a high-sighted tyranny under which no man's life is safe.

From this pinnacle of patriotic fervour Brutus never afterwards descends. It is all hallucination, of course, but it has come to have the sanction of a religious faith. No argument is needed to establish it. When he addresses the people Brutus simply asserts that Caesar had to be slain because he was ambitious; if they ask for proof, they must have 'respect to his honour', and take his word for it that it is so. And so when the spell of Brutus' presence is withdrawn, Antony has an easy task; for Antony *does* deal in argument, such as his hearers can appreciate; he bases his arguments on facts well known to them; so that in a little the honour of Brutus seems to rest on foundations as frail as does the ambition of Caesar; and the work of the conspirators is undone. In Brutus, however, the process of self-deception goes on. Before Philippi he has brought himself to believe that Caesar, the ruler whose justice Brutus himself had confessed to be beyond reproach, had been righteously struck down 'for supporting robbers' –

> Did not great *Iulius* bleede for Iustice sake?
> What Villaine touch'd his body, that did stab,
> And not for Iustice? What? Shall one of Vs,
> That strucke the Formost man of all this World,
> But for supporting Robbers. . . .

And so on. And again, when the cause is lost, Brutus takes comfort in the thought that he will –

> have glory by this loosing day
> More than *Octauius*, and *Marke Antony*,
> By this vile Conquest shall attaine vnto.

Such, in Shakespeare, is Brutus the politician; and the strange inconsistencies cannot be charged to the playwright's account. They are of the texture of Brutus' nature. Noble-hearted and sincere beyond question, he is intellectually dishonest. Fanatic as he is, he has never schooled himself to face facts. Placed on a pedestal by adoring friends, he accepts the position a little too complacently. His self-righteousness renders him incapable of recognising the possibility that he himself, in opinion or conduct, can ever be in the wrong. He is (so he imagines) 'Arm'd so strong in honesty' that censure passes by him 'as the idle winde' which he 'respects not'. And while he is himself inconsistent, even so does he suffer his associates, unreproved, to speak and act in glaring contradiction of the pure and lofty protestations with which he is always ready. Cassius can pour into his ear, unchecked, dispraise of Caesar, inspired plainly by mere envy and spite. Caius Ligarius is welcomed as a confederate in an enterprise, pronounced to be free from all taint of personal malice, on the ground that he bears Caesar a grudge. One need not recall the treachery of Decius and Trebonius, evil means to an evil end, but approved by Brutus. His own conduct, apart from the capital crime, is sometimes at strange variance with principles simultaneously professed. We remember in what high terms Brutus denounces corruption . . . the itching palm, the fingers contaminated with base bribes, the 'mighty space of our large Honors' sold 'for so much, trash, as may be grasped thus'. 'I myself,' he exclaims –

> had rather Coine my Heart,
> And drop my Blood for Drachmaes, then to wring
> From the hard hand of Peazants, their vile trash
> By any indirection. . . .

Splendid sentiments, and no doubt inspired by conscious rectitude. We forget for the moment – we are intended to forget – that Brutus' indignation is due not only to hatred of extortion, but to resentment because (as he asserts) Cassius has refused him a share of the 'vile trash' so indirectly obtained.

Then there is that curious passage in the last Act (the wording somewhat confused in North; the meaning worse-confounded in Shakespeare) in which Brutus in one breath declares suicide 'cowardly and vile', and in the next assures Cassius that he 'bears so great a mind' that if the worst comes to the worst, he will fall by his own hand. In the end, however he may have judged Cato, he kills himself, with no word to suggest a suspicion that the deed is other than entirely glorious. Pathetically inconsistent to the last; for, as his 'tongue ends his liues History', we do not know how he judges of it; whether it has, or has not all been in vain.

> Night hangs upon mine eyes, my Bones would rest
> That have but labour'd to attain this houre.

He believes he will have glory; and one clear gain he can record –

> Countrymen,
> My heart doth ioy, that yet in all my life,
> I found no man, but he was true to me.

A wholly beautiful thought!

We do not remember, we are not intended at the moment to remember, that of these true friends Caesar was one, and not the least; we do not reflect that with all the talk of loving where he slew, of sacrificing a victim not butchering a man, no word of simple human compunction for his monstrous ingratitude has ever escaped Brutus' lips. There is no irony in all this. Shakespeare, I think, has no dealings with irony, as it is now sometimes understood; it is not the *vanity* of false political aspirations and visionary aims which asks emotional response; it is 'the pity of it'. Even the befogged and wholly mischievous politician in Brutus demands and receives pity; but he would not be the compellingly human figure Shakespeare has made him, were he not shown at moments when life really matters, when the aspirations of politicians, worthy and unworthy, fade into nothingness.

It would be an impertinence to dwell on this side of the picture at any length. It has been so often done and done so well – all the tenderness and beauty of the relations between Brutus and his noble wife; the gentleness which, even when he is 'sick of many griefs', will not suffer him to waken a sleeping boy; the deep sincerity of the love which, even in perversity, binds him to Cassius; the sad solemnity of their farewell –

> For euer, and for euer, farewell *Cassius*,
> If we do meete againe, why we shall smile;
> If not, why then this parting was well made;

and the profundity of grief revealed in the final tribute spoken over Cassius dead, the slowly reiterated words, which linger and fall heavily, like a passing bell, on the ear:

> Friends, I owe mo tears
> To this dead man, then you shall see me pay,
> I shall find time, Cassius: I shall find time.

SOURCE: *Royal Society of Literature: Essays by Divers Hands*, x (1931).

John Anson

CAESAR'S STOIC PRIDE
(1966)

THE decade of the fifteen-nineties, when *Julius Caesar* was written, marks the rise of Neo-Stoicism in England.[1] In 1594, Sir John Stradling issued his translation of Justus Lipsius' *Two Bookes of Constancie*, and, four years later, Du Vair's *The Moral Philosophie of the Stoicks* appeared in an English version by the Oxford scholar Thomas James. The doctrine of self-sufficient impassivity advanced by their works, although it derives from a long and varied classical tradition, became associated in its more popular redactions principally with Seneca and the ancient Romans. Chapman's 'Senecal' hero Clermont is ranked by the Guise 'past the reaches of this age, / ... with the best of th'ancient Romanes' (*The Revenge of Bussy D'Ambois*, II i), and Shakespeare's Stoic Horatio, seizing the cup that has just poisoned Gertrude and Claudius, proclaims, 'I am more an antique Roman than a Dane' (v ii 352).[2] Thus, for the Elizabethans, Neo-Stoicism resuscitated a distinctly Roman ethos: to be a Stoic meant, in effect, to be a Roman, to emulate Brutus or Cato[3] and follow the counsel of Seneca, 'ferre mortalia, nec perturbari his, quae vitare nostrae potestatis non est'.[4]

To many, of course, this Roman creed of constancy, however its authors sought to align it with Christian teaching, seemed, in its blanket condemnation of all emotion, to do a violence to both human nature and conscience. For Browne and Bacon, as for Jonson in *Bartholomew Fair*, whose Adam comforts himself in the stocks with Latin *sententiae*,[5] there was something absurd in the Stoic pose of indifference that claimed to rise above all natural vulnerability. 'The Stoics that condemn passion,' wrote Browne in *Religio Medici*, 'and command a man to laugh in Phalaris his bull, could not endure without a groan a fit of the

Stone or Colick.'[6] For Marston, by contrast, there was a deeper
perception of pathos in the collapse of Roman composure under
the weight of adversity:

> Man will breake out, despight philosophie.
> Why, all this while I ha but plaid a part,
> Like to some boy, that actes a tragedie,
> Speakes burly words, and raves out passion;
> But, when he thinks upon his infant weaknesse,
> He droopes his eye. I spake more than a god.
> Yet am lesse than a man.
> I am the miserablest sowle that breathes.[7]

With rare psychological insight, the plaint of Pandolfo reveals
the radical terror that Stoic assertion pretended to stifle. For moral
incisiveness, however, nothing surpasses the character of the
Senecan hero sketched years before by Erasmus in *The Praise of
Folly*:

'tis agreed of all hands that our passions belong to Folly; inasmuch
as we judge a wise man from a fool by this, that the one is ordered
by them, the other by reason; and therefore the Stoics remove
from a wise man all disturbances of mind as so many diseases.
But these passions do not only the office of a tutor to such as are
making towards the port of wisdom, but are in every exercise of
virtue as it were spurs and incentives, nay and encouragers to
well doing; which though that great Stoic Seneca most strongly
denies, and takes from a wise man all affections whatever, yet in
doing that he leaves him not so much as a man but rather a new
kind of god that was never yet nor ever like to be. Nay, to speak
plainer, he sets up a stony semblance of a man, void of all sense
and common feeling of humanity. And much good to them with
this wise man of theirs; let them enjoy him to themselves, love
him without competitors, and live with him in Plato's commonwealth, the country of ideas or Tantalus' orchards. For who
would not shun and startle at such a man, as at some unnatural
accident spirit? A man dead to all sense of nature and common
affections, and no more moved with love or pity than if he were a
flint or rock; whose censure nothing escapes; that commits no
errors himself, but has a lynx's eyes upon others; measures everything by an exact line, and forgives nothing; pleases himself

with himself only; the only rich, the only wise, the only free man, and only king; in brief, the only man that is everything, but in his own single judgment only; that cares not for the friendship of any man, being himself a friend to no man; makes no doubt to make the gods stoop to him, and condemns and laughs at the whole actions of our life? And yet such a beast is this their perfect wise man.[8]

The picture painted by Folly of the Stoic sage as a marble simulacrum unmoved by love or pity exaggerates like a cartoon the most unnatural distortions in the posture of Roman virtue, but the doubt becomes clear, that constancy will turn to hardness and self-reliance to pride.*

When one turns to Shakespeare, then, writing in 1599, it is hardly surprising to find him producing a Roman play that reflects the current discussion of Neo-Stoic ethics. In fact, I believe it is possible to approach *Julius Caesar* as a drama exploring just the moral petrification Erasmus diagnosed as the illness of Senecal man. As a first step, it seems convenient to look at Caesar, because he embodies in little the condition of Rome at large. Typically, as the leading figure of his society, he constitutes a microcosmic reflection of it; his values represent communal values in general, and their limits mark the limits of an entire culture. Judging from the pronouncement he makes at his highest hour, the quality Caesar most prizes is just that Constancy upon which Lipsius dilates:

> I could be well mov'd, if I were as you;
> If I could pray to move, prayers would move me;
> But I am constant as the Northern Star,
> Of whose true-fix'd and resting quality
> There is no fellow in the firmament.

* In all fairness to the Stoics, it should be pointed out that Lipsius, for example, carefully distinguishes constancy from forwardness, '*Which is a certaine hardnesse of a stubberne mind proceeding from pride or vaine glorie*', whereas 'constancie is PATIENCE, and lowliness of mind, which is, *A voluntarie sufferance without grudging of all things whatsoeuer can happen to, or in a man.*' (*Two Bookes of Constancie*, ed. Kirk, p. 79.)

> The skies are painted with unnumb'red sparks,
> They are all fire, and every one doth shine;
> But there's but one in all doth hold his place.
> So in the world: 'Tis furnish'd well with men,
> And men are flesh and blood, and apprehensive;
> Yet in the number I do know but one
> That unassailable holds on his rank,
> Unshak'd of motion; and that I am he,
> Let me a little show it, even in this —
> That I was constant Cimber should be banish'd
> And constant do remain to keep him so.   (III i 58–73)

Whatever its accuracy as self-evaluation, Caesar's boast reveals at least the ideal of greatness to which, presumably, he and his hearers alike subscribe. To appreciate just how Stoic this ideal is, one need only compare it with Lipsius' own ventilations:

Thou seest then (*Lipsius*) that INCONSTANCY is the companion of OPINION, & that the propertie of it is to bee soone chaunged, and to wish that vndone, which a litle before it caused to be done. But CONSTANCIE is a mate alwayes matched with reason. Vnto this therefore I do earnestlie exhort thee. Why flyest thou to these vaine outward things? This is onelie that faire beautifull *Helena* which will present vnto thee a wholesome cup of counterpoyson, wherewith thou shalt expell the memorie of all cares and sorrowes, and whereof when thou hast once taken a taste, being firmelie setled against all casualties, bearing thy selfe vpright in all misfortunes, neither puffed vp nor pressed downe with either fortune, thou maist challenge to thy selfe that great title, the neerest that man can haue to God, *To be immooueable.*[9]

Clearly, not only the values but the language itself, the tone and vocabulary of Caesar's declamation, belong to the commonplaces of the Stoic revival. Fixed, unassailable, godlike, Caesar claims for himself a position of moral supremacy in a social order.

What finally invalidates this claim is not so much its untruth, for, as Dorsch points out, Caesar's heroic stature is virtually assumed in the drama,[10] and flattery and pride only serve to intensify his Senecan 'confidence' (II ii 49); rather, its failure lies deeper within its very assumptions, in a falsification of values upon which the claim is constructed. From a world of men who are 'flesh and blood, and apprehensive', Caesar boasts that he stands apart in an isolation conceived not as the result but the source and quintessence of his greatness. To ensconce himself thus unassailably from humanity, however, he dissevers himself perforce from his own flesh and blood as well:

> These couchings and these lowly courtesies
> Might fire the blood of ordinary men
> And turn preordinance and first decree
> Into the law of children. Be not fond
> To think that Caesar bears such rebel blood
> That will be thaw'd from the true quality
> With that which melteth fools – I mean, sweet words,
> Low-crooked curtsies, and base spaniel fawning.
>
> (III i 36–42)

Unthawed, unmelting, Caesar achieves his greatness through the express disowning of his human kind-ness, through the disavowal, above all, of fear and pity, the specifically tragic emotions which mark the awareness of frailty respectively in oneself and in others. Even his indifference to death, which constitutes the ultimate expression of his Stoic nobility, only obfuscates in the very fact of mortality all its moral significance:

> Cowards die many times before their deaths;
> The valiant never taste of death but once.
> Of all the wonders that I yet have heard,
> It seems to me most strange that men should fear,
> Seeing that death, a necessary end,
> Will come when it will come. (II ii 32–7)

The point, which Caesar misses, is not that the valiant die once, but that they die as well, that hero and coward alike fall equally subject to death, in the face of which all aspiration seems so much dust and illusion. This is the lesson of mortality, whose tragic irony it is Antony's gift to rescue from Caesar's ruin:

> O mighty Caesar! dost thou lie so low?
> Are all thy conquests, glories, triumphs, spoils,
> Shrunk to this little measure? (III i 148–50)

> The evil that men do lives after them;
> The good is oft interred with their bones.
>
> (III ii 81–2)

To appreciate fully the distortions in Caesar's position, however, there is nothing more revealing than comparing his ideal with Henry the Fifth's, the Stoic image of greatness with the Christian's, which Shakespeare had just treated. For Henry, greatness remains inescapably twinned with humanity in a union whose uneasy balance it is his constant struggle to maintain. Never to forget his underlying vulnerability even in the midst of performing the rites of power Henry comes to recognize as the 'hard condition' exacted of sovereignty. Thus, as he passes among his troops on the eve of Agincourt, disguised, appropriately, in the cloak of his own subaltern, he tries to remind his men of the Monarch's 'human conditions', that the king knows fear and doubt as well as other mortals.

Henry, the Christian monarch, then, perceives his greatness as an essentially social and ritualistic *persona* behind which there stands another private, corporeal being. Together they form the whole man, and it is Henry's achievement to reach a position from which he can oversee them both. By contrast, Caesar acknowledges only his public identity, so that, though he too is wakened by portents of his mortality, he recognizes no fear but continues 'always Caesar' (I ii 212), to himself a third person emptied of the voice of soliloquy. At the root of his attitude lies a denial of the physical body that stands in diametric opposition to Henry's affirmation of the senses; in accord with Stoic doctrine, Caesar regards corporeal nature as something external and antithetic to what Lipsius eulogizes as inner spiritual fire:

First you are not ignorant that man consisteth of two parts, Soule and Body. That being the nobler part, resembleth the nature of a spirit and fire: This more base is compared to the earth. These two are ioyned together, but yet with a iarring concord, as I may say, neither doe they easily agree, especially when controuersie ariseth about souerainty & subiection. For either of them would bear sway, and chiefly that part which ought not. The earth aduanceth it selfe aboue the fire, and the dirty nature aboue that which is diuine. Herehence arise in man dissentions, stirs, & a continual conflict of these parts iarring together. The captains are, REASON and OPINION. That fighteth for the soule, being in the soule: This for, and in the body. Reason hath her offspring from heauen, yea from God: and *Seneca* gaue it a singular commendation, saying *That there was hidden in man parte of the diuine spirit.* . . . For, you are deceiued if you think al the soul to be *Right reason*, but that only which is vniforme, simple, without mixture, seperate from al filth or corruption: and in one word, as much as is pure & heauenlie. For albeit the soul be infected and a litle corrupted with the filth of the bodie and contagion of the senses: yet it retayneth some reliks of his first ofspring, and is not without certaine cleare sparks of that pure fiery nature from when it proceeded.[11]

The concept of a pure and ethereal inner fire that grows corrupt from mixture with lower terrestrial matter recalls at once the imagery of Caesar's own speeches and helps to clarify the dilemma of his position; for just as to conserve in its essence this spiritual fire one must lock it up like the germ of flame in a flint, so to preserve inviolate the 'spark' of his individuality, Caesar, paradoxically, cannot allow his blood to be melted; to guard the flame within him he becomes cold and insensate.

While to the modern this formulation sounds like verbal double talk, it rests, in fact, upon a physiological doctrine that underlies both the imagery and action of the entire drama. Briefly, according to the Elizabethans, the faculties of motion and emotion belong to the sensitive soul and have their seat in the heart, which is regularly described as king and commander of the body. Upon advice from the brain, which houses the cognitive powers and acts in the role of chancellor and privy-counsellor,* the heart dilates or contracts, thus disposing the

* Robert Burton, *The Anatomy of Melancholy*, ed. Floyd Dell and Paul Jordan-Smith (New York, 1957) p. 131, writes: 'Of the *noble* there be three principal parts, to which all the rest belong, and whom they serve, *brain, heart, liver*; according to whose site, three regions, on a threefold division, is made of the whole body. As first of the *head*, in which the animal organs are contained, and brain itself, which by his nerves give sense and motion to the rest, and is (as it were) a Privy

humors and passions, and, ultimately, all behavior. As Robert
Burton describes it:

Of this region the principal part is the *Heart*, which is the seat
and fountain of life, of heat, of spirits, of pulse, and respiration;
the Sun of our body, the King and sole commander of it: the
seat and organ of all passions and affections; (it lives first, and
dies last, in all creatures); of a pyramidical form, and not much
unlike a pineapple; a part worthy of admiration, that can yield
such variety of affections, by whose motion it is dilated or con-
tracted, to stir and command the humours in the body: as in
sorrow, melancholy; in anger, choler; in joy, to send the blood
outwardly; in sorrow, to call it in; moving the humours, as horses
do a chariot. This *heart*, though it be one sole member, yet it
may be divided into two creeks *right* and *left*. . . . *The left creek*
hath the form of a *cone*, & is the seat of life, which, as a torch
doth oil, draws blood into it, begetting of it spirits and fire; and,
as fire in a torch, so are spirits in the blood.[12]

What I would like to suggest is that this anatomy of the heart can
serve as an anatomy of the drama as well. In the first place, it
reveals that to be immovable, to feel no pity, and to keep one's
blood from being fired all involve the same physiological process, inhibition of the operation of the heart. By implication,
since what the heart commands at the center the hand performs
at the periphery as the outward organ *par excellence* of feeling
and moving, inhibition of the heart results in narcosis of the hand
and means that the body grows increasingly 'out of touch'. Thus,
at his first appearance during the Lupercalia, Caesar requests the
'quick spirited' Antony (I ii 29) 'to touch Calphurnia' because
'the barren, touched in this holy chase, / Shake off their sterile
curse' (I ii 7-9). Subsequently, his repressive morality finds
expression in his refusal to hear Artemidorus' petition: 'What
touches us ourself shall be last serv'd' (III i 8). To be touched for
Caesar would mean: (1) to have physical contact and sensation,

---

Counsellor, and Chancellor, to the *Heart*. The second region is the
chest or middle *belly*, in which the *Heart* as King keeps his Court, and
by his arteries communicates life to the whole body.'

(2) to feel pity, (3) to be kindled like touchwood, all the very activities against which he has closed his heart.*

Organically, Caesar's dissociation of hand and heart reveals itself in his attack of the falling sickness, when, from his loathing to lay his fingers off the crown, he sinks into insensibility:

I saw Mark Antony offer him a crown – yet 'twas not a crown neither, 'twas one of these coronets – and, as I told you, he put it by once; but for all that, to my thinking, he would fain have had it. Then he offered it to him again; then he put it by again; but to my thinking he was loath to lay his fingers off it. And then he offered it the third time. He put it the third time by; and still as he refus'd it, the rabblement hooted, and clapp'd their chopt hands, and threw up their sweaty nightcaps, and uttered such a deal of stinking breath because Caesar refus'd the crown that it had, almost, chok'd Caesar; for he swoonded and fell down at it. (I ii 237–50)

In this incident, which is specifically denied in the source, and, in fact, in his whole presentation of Caesar's illness, Shakespeare, I believe, is attempting to represent the pathologic constrictive-ness of Stoic morality. According to Plutarch, in order to palliate an angry remark that escaped him when he was forced by the populace to refuse the title of king, Caesar cleverly invented an epileptic seizure to use as his excuse. In turning this feigned attack into a real occurrence, however, Shakespeare has made Caesar's falling into the symptom of his pride, the traumatic manifestation of his thwarted ambition. For, while Casca, with his usual literal-mindedness, offers the epidemiological explana-tion that the fit was caught from the stinking breath of the popu-lace, the disease, as Cassius suggests when he quips that Rome has the falling sickness (I ii 257–8), easily can be viewed in an allegorical perspective, and, in fact, as Oswei Temkin has pointed out in his history of epilepsy, there was a tradition of doing so.

* For 'touch' meaning 'excite pity' consider Cassius' condolence on the death of Portia, 'O insupportable and touching loss!' (IV iii 151); for the meaning 'to enkindle', 'The nimble gunner/With linstock now the devilish cannon touches' (*Henry V*, III, Prologue, 32–3).

Commenting on Jesus' exorcism of the epileptic boy related in
Matthew xvii, Mark ix, and Luke ix, Theophilus and Bede, for
instance, suggest that the evil demon is described as deaf and
dumb because it will neither hear nor confess the Word of God.[13]
Shakespeare, be it noted, has included, without historical basis,
both symptoms of deafness (I ii 213) and dumbness (I ii 255)
and exhibited Caesar putting Flavius and Marullus 'to silence'
(I ii 289) and refusing to hear the word of the soothsayer which,
according to Plutarch, was offered long before.[14] Moreover, in
view of the fact that epilepsy was called 'little apoplexy',[15] the
following dialogue between Falstaff and the Lord Chief Justice
offers an interesting parallel both to Caesar's deafness and to his
refusal to hear:

> *Falstaff.* And I hear, moreover, his Highness is fall'n into this
> same whoreson apoplexy.
> *Justice.* Well, God mend him. I pray you let me speak with
> you.
> *Falstaff.* This apoplexy, as I take it, is a kind of lethargy, an't
> please your lordship; a kind of sleeping in the blood a
> whoreson tingling.
> *Justice.* What tell you me of it? Be it as it is.
> *Falstaff.* It hath it original from much grief, from study and
> perturbation of the brain. I have read the cause of his
> effects in Galen. It is a kind of deafness.
> *Justice.* I think you are fall'n into the disease, for you hear not
> what I say to you.
> *Falstaff.* Very well, my lord, very well. Rather an't please you,
> it is the disease of not list'ning, the malady of not
> marking that I am troubled withal.   (I ii 122–40)

In *The Ancrene Riwle*, the falling sickness of the sparrow, probably
connected with the falling of the sparrow in Matthew x 29, is
held up as a lesson to the anchoress that humiliation and con-
trition are necessary evils to keep the flesh from becoming too
proud:

The sparrow hath yet another property which is very good for
an anchoress, although it is hated: that is, the falling sickness. For

it is very necessary that an anchoress of holy and highly pious life have the falling sickness. I do not mean the sickness which is commonly so called; but that which I call falling sickness is an infirmity of the body, or temptation of carnal frailty, by which she seems to herself to fall down from her holy and exalted piety. She would otherwise grow presumptuous, or have too good an opinion of herself, and so come to nothing.[16]

In Shakespeare's own day, a similar moralization of epilepsy was offered by the famous zoologist Aldrovandi in his *Monstrorum Historia*:

This affliction must beyond doubt be likened to the disease of pride which in truth can be called a sacred disease, since it triumphs over saintly and perfect men. Likewise, epilepsy is called a damage, so to say, of the upper regions, and not without reason since it has cast down the highest angels. For we read in Holy Script: The Lord has destroyed the seats of proud princes. Thus the affliction of pride is generated when the bad humors of an empty little glory are carried to the ventricles of the mind. . . . For then every process of correct function is impeded and the soul falls headlong from the state of grace; and so the tremor of despair, the stridor of wrath and perturbation, the froth of malediction, and the distortion of the face, namely, the ugliness of a bad habit, are brought about.[17]

Thus, starting with the New Testament, there grew up a tradition of allegorizing the various symptoms of epilepsy and seeing in its characteristic swooning and insensibility the signs of an obdurate pride. Applied to Caesar, this kind of interpretation seems particularly compelling because his symptoms stand so closely allied to his moral attitudes. His striving to achieve a Stoic impassivity beyond emotional feeling psychosomatically, as it were, deadens his bodily feelings as well. Again, to quote Burton:

All Philosophers impute the miseries of the body to the soul, that should have governed it better by command of reason, and hath not done it. The Stoicks are altogether of opinion (as Lipsius & Piccolomineus record) that a wise man shold be without all manner of passions and perturbations whatsoever, as Seneca reports of Cato, the Greeks of Socrates, and Jo. Aubanus of a nation in Africa, so free from passions, or rather so stupid, that, if they be wounded with a sword, they will only look back. Lactantius will exclude *fear from a wise man*: others except all, some the greatest passions. But let them dispute how they will, set down in theses, give precepts to the contrary; we find that of Lemnius true by common experience; *no mortal man is free from these perturbations*; or if he be so, sure he is either a god or a block.[18]

Just so, by excluding the passions, repressing the sensitive soul, and disjoining the operational nexus of hand and heart, does Caesar begin to emerge as a kind of godlike block, a marble monster, who, in his will to remain untouchable, threatens to occupy the whole space of the living world:

> Why, man, he doth bestride the narrow world
> Like a Colossus, and we petty men
> Walk under his huge legs and peep about
> To find ourselves dishonourable graves.   (I ii 135–8)

Whatever his intentions, Cassius' image seems to capture Caesar's essence, embracing the dissident opinions of characters and critics alike; now a god, now a block, Caesar emerges precisely a colossus, and, as such, the incarnation of Stoic man.

SOURCE: *Shakespeare Studies*, II (1966).

NOTES

1. My discussion of Neo-Stoicism is indebted to the excellent summary of the subject in Herschel Baker's *The Image of Man: A Study of the Idea of Human Dignity in Classic Antiquity, The Middle Ages and the Renaissance* (New York, 1961) pp. 301–12.

2. Hiram Haydn, *The Counter-Renaissance* (New York, 1960) pp. 624 ff, discusses Horatio as a Stoic.

3. In *The Revenge of Bussy D'Ambois*, the Guise commends Clermont as a revived Brutus, and in *Caesar and Pompey* Cato becomes one of his model Stoics.

4. Seneca 241a, quoted in Justus Lipsius, *Two Bookes of Constancie*, Englished by Sir John Stradling, ed. Rudolph Kirk (New Brunswick, 1939) p. 105.

5. *Bartholomew Fair*, IV iv, where Adam is mocked as 'a Stoic i' the stocks'.

6. Sir Thomas Browne, *The Religio Medici and Other Writings*, Everyman's Library (1956) p. 60. In *Much Ado*, Leonato is clearly making the same point about the Stoics when he says: 'I pray thee peace. I will be flesh and blood;/For there was never yet philosopher/That could endure the toothache patiently,/However they have writ the style of gods,/And made a push at chance and sufferance' (v i 34–8).

7. *The Works of John Marston*, ed. J. O. Halliwell (1856): *Antonio's Revenge*, IV v.

8. Desiderius Erasmus, *The Praise of Folly*, trans. John Wilson (1668; Ann Arbor, 1958) pp. 46–7.

9. Lipsius, *Two Bookes of Constancie*, p. 83.

10. *Julius Caesar*, ed. T. S. Dorsch (Arden Shakespeare, 1955) p. xxix.

11. Lipsius, *Two Bookes of Constancie*, pp. 80–1.

12. Burton, *Anatomy of Melancholy*, ed. Dell and Jordan-Smith, pp. 133–4.

13. Quoted in O. Temkin, *The Falling Sickness* (Baltimore, 1945) p. 168.

14. *Narrative and Dramatic Sources of Shakespeare*, ed. G. Bullough (London and New York, 1964) v 83.

15. Temkin, *Falling Sickness*, p. 126.

16. Quoted in Temkin, p. 169, from the translation by Morton (1853).

17. Quoted and translated by Temkin, p. 168.

18. Burton, *Anatomy of Melancholy*, ed. Dell and Jordan-Smith, p. 218.

Some longer footnotes have been omitted. P.U.

John Palmer

THE CHARACTER OF CAESAR
(1945)

A short analysis of the character of Caesar, as unfolded by the dramatist, will ... serve as a bridge to carry us over from the first three to the last two Acts of the play.

In making this analysis it is essential to grasp a fundamental difference between Shakespeare's method and that of most other dramatists. It is, indeed, more than a difference of method, for it stands at the heart of his genius. The ordinary way of presenting a dramatic hero upon the stage is to build him up feature by feature. He is seen performing actions, and is heard to utter speeches, which reveal his essential traits, and the author is careful to ensure that these traits are consistent. The character is shown to be brave or cowardly, generous or mean, kindly or cruel, simple or sophisticated, and he is allowed to act or speak only in accordance with his primary qualities. Such dramatic characters are easily grasped. They have both simplicity and coherence, being the result of deliberate selection and logical arrangement. Every piece of information about them afforded by the dramatist is in keeping. We are never puzzled by their conduct; nor are we moved to protest that this sort of person would not behave in that sort of way.

Shakespeare frequently goes to the opposite extreme. He has his characters alive and fully-formed in his mind. He takes for granted their primary qualities, which emerge, as it were, by accident. These characters are more than a sum of the traits which they exhibit. They do not come alive, feature by feature. They spring upon the stage in full career. They are not constructed; they enter upon the scene, men and women, rounded and complete in the imagination of the author, who assumes that his audience will recognise them for what they are as soon as they appear. They walk in upon us, each of them 'in his habit as he lived'. Shakespeare can thus exhibit them, if he chooses, behaving as men and women do, at odds with themselves, betraying inconsistencies and contradictions which no other dramatist has dared to permit in an equal degree. Taking the reality of Hamlet or Falstaff for granted, he can allow them to act out of character without destroying our belief in them but, on the contrary, increasing our sense of their human veracity. Hamlet, irresolute in action, courteous by nature and humane in disposition, surprises but in no way disconcerts us when he leads an attack upon a pirate ship, is gross with Ophelia or brutal in his references to the dead Polonius. Falstaff, a trained soldier of courage and resource, who at Shrewsbury leads his men into the thick of the battle where they are 'peppered', can yet find discretion the better part of valour and be exposed to ridicule as the man who ran away at Gadshill. Commentators on Shakespeare are puzzled by such inconsistencies and some critics have egregiously discovered them to be faults. But in no respect is Shakespeare's genius more manifest than in allowing his characters to act in ways which, at first sight and to the strictly logical mind, seem at variance with their essential qualities. It is worth noting that such apparent contradictions become more frequent as Shakespeare grows creatively more absolute. They are less notable in his political than in his comic characters and in his tragic characters they become master-strokes of delineation.

The political character of Caesar as presented by Shakespeare, which has been condemned by many as a slight, negligent and impertinent libel upon a great man, may with advantage be considered in the light of this tendency to take essential qualities for granted and to dwell upon traits in seeming contradiction with them. Caesar's greatness is assumed throughout the play. It fills the mind of the dramatist and is communicated to his audience in phrases that fall from his pen whenever Caesar is mentioned, even by his enemies. This Caesar has got the start of the majestic world. He bestrides it like a Colossus. His fall is heralded by a 'strange impatience of the heavens' and by portentous things which shake the minds of the stoutest of the

Romans. Cassius, meeting Casca in the storm, names to him a man 'most like this dreadful night, prodigious grown and fearful'. Caesar is about to die and 'all the sway of earth shakes like a thing infirm'.

The essential greatness of Caesar being thus assumed, Shakespeare is free to exhibit in him human weaknesses apparently inconsistent with it. There are many advantages in this method of presentation. It gives reality to Caesar, the man; it suggests that Caesar's spirit is mightier than his person, a suggestion which is essential to the unity of the play; it enables the dramatist to present him in flesh and blood without reducing in stature the men who murder him; finally, it permits the audience to sympathise with Brutus just sufficiently to give poignancy to the disaster which overtakes him.

This last point is of major dramatic importance. The play could not easily have risen to the level of tragedy if Caesar had been portrayed consistently in full majesty. The conspiracy must then have inevitably impressed the audience as no more than a stupid plot contrived by a group of self-seeking politicians under the leadership of a misguided political crank. Such, in effect, it was, but the skilful dramatist, if he is to retain the sympathetic attention of his audience, will not obtrude the fact, but allow it to become fully apparent only at the close.

The infirmities of Caesar are not inventions of the dramatist. They are in part historical and in part derived from Plutarch's delight in the foibles of great men and his tendency to find such foibles more pronounced in his Roman heroes than in the heroes of his native Greece. They are, moreover, infirmities which in a greater or less degree are inseparable from political success and the exercise of power. Caesar, like other men of destiny, is superstitious. Caesar, like other exalted personages, refers to himself in the third person. Caesar, like other men whose position requires them to assume superhuman qualities, claims to be impervious to fear or argument and determined to enforce his will, even though he knows himself to be in the wrong. These are traits common to all dictators.

Caesar's entry into the play at once establishes the key of this imperial symphony. He comes upon the stage, a great crowd following. He calls Calpurnia to his side. 'Peace, ho! Caesar speaks.' The crowd is hushed to silence and awaits the oracle:

Caesar. Calpurnia!
Calpurnia. Here, my lord.
Caesar. Stand you directly in Antonius' way,
    When he doth run his course. Antonius!
Antony. Caesar, my lord?
Caesar. Forget not, in your speed, Antonius,
    To touch Calpurnia; for our elders say,
    The barren, touchèd in this holy chase,
    Shake off their sterile curse.
Antony. I shall remember:
    When Caesar says 'Do this,' it is perform'd.

All Rome is bent to hear this Caesar. O lame and impotent conclusion! The first words that fall from his lips show faith in an old wives' tale. Caesar is himself half ashamed of his credulity. The belief that Calpurnia's infertility can be cured by the touch of a runner in the feast of Lupercal he attributes, not to himself, but to 'our elders'. There may be something in it, but Caesar does not commit himself.

The procession moves on, but the crowd is hushed a second time. A soothsayer has cried to Caesar.

Caesar.   Ha! Who calls?
Casca. Bid every noise be still: peace yet again!
Caesar. Who is it in the press that calls on me?
    I hear a tongue, shriller than all the music,
    Cry 'Caesar!' Speak; Caesar is turn'd to hear.
Soothsayer. Beware the ides of March.
Caesar.   What man is that?
Brutus. A soothsayer bids you beware the ides of March.
Caesar. Set him before me; let me see his face.
Casca. Fellow, come from the throng; look upon Caesar.
Caesar. What say'st thou to me now? Speak once again.
Soothsayer. Beware the ides of March.
Caesar. He is a dreamer; let us leave him: pass.

This first brief scene prefigures all the traits whereby Shakespeare is to present the mighty Caesar in flesh and blood. They will be deepened and enlivened as the play proceeds, but very little of substance will be added. Here, announced from the start, is a superstition cautious of revealing itself; an acquired habit, which has become second nature, of regarding himself as already a legendary person; a repudiation in himself of foibles which expose him to ridicule or, indeed, of any qualities which render him merely human. He dismisses the soothsayer as a dreamer, but nevertheless remembers his warning. He collaborates, as it were, in his own deification. *Peace, ho! Caesar speaks. . . . When Caesar says 'Do this', it is performed. . . . Bid every noise be still: peace yet again.* To such a chorus which endues with solemnity his least word or whim, Caesar, as though he were referring to some remote Olympian figure, himself supplies the grave antiphony: *'Caesar is turned to hear'*: and he bids the soothsayer *'Look upon Caesar'*, as though inviting an inspection of his divinity. He is living up to that legend of himself which every successful political figure is sooner or later driven to create.

But Shakespeare is careful not to leave us under the impression that this prodigious person, who has come to regard himself as a public institution, has entirely lost his humanity. Shakespeare, in fact, seems positively to delight in contrasting the man with his façade. What could be more shrewd, timely or alert than Caesar's famous description of Cassius? Caesar, however, even as he gives this signal proof of a genial and lively perception, must instantly remember that he is Caesar. Cassius is a man to be feared, but Caesar, being Caesar, can fear nothing:

> Let me have men about me that are fat;
> Sleek-headed men and such as sleep o' nights:
> Yond Cassius has a lean and hungry look;
> He thinks too much: such men are dangerous.

> Would he were fatter! But I fear him not:
> Yet if my name were liable to fear,
> I do not know the man I should avoid
> So soon as that spare Cassius. He reads much;

He is a great observer, and he looks
Quite through the deeds of men; he loves no plays,
As thou dost, Antony; he hears no music;
Seldom he smiles, and smiles in such a sort
As if he mock'd himself, and scorn'd his spirit
That could be moved to smile at any thing.
Such men as he be never at heart's ease
Whiles they behold a greater than themselves,
And therefore are they very dangerous.
I rather tell thee what is to be fear'd
Than what I fear; for always I am Caesar.

The domestic scene in which Calpurnia tries to dissuade Caesar from going to the Capitol, presents this same mischievous contrast of the natural man with the public figure. Caesar has had a bad night. Nor heaven nor earth has been at peace. Calpurnia has thrice cried out in her sleep. Caesar is thoroughly and humanly upset. He sends a servant off to the priests, ordering them to do present sacrifice and report on their success. Calpurnia enters:

Calpurnia. What mean you, Caesar? think you to walk forth?
    You shall not stir out of your house to-day.
Caesar. Caesar shall forth; the things that threaten'd me
    Ne'er look'd but on my back; when they shall see
    The face of Caesar, they are vanishèd.

Caesar, in the first person, is troubled, but Caesar in the third person cannot admit it. Calpurnia, however, sticks to her guns. She has had bad dreams and heard fearful accounts of horrid sights seen by the watch. Caesar, again protesting his immunity from fear, argues himself into a stolid defiance of omens in which he partially believes:

Caesar.   What can be avoided
    Whose end is purpos'd by the mighty gods?
    Yet Caesar shall go forth; for these predictions
    Are to the world in general as to Caesar.
Calpurnia. When beggars die, there are no comets seen;
    The heavens themselves blaze forth the death of princes.

> *Caesar.* Cowards die many times before their deaths;
>   The valiant never taste of death but once.
>   Of all the wonders that I yet have heard,
>   It seems to me most strange that men should fear;
>   Seeing that death, a necessary end,
>   Will come when it will come.

The servant comes to report the result of his errand to the priests. Caesar's adjurations, addressed to himself, grow more eloquent as the portents become more fearful. He lashes himself into an ecstasy of divine assurance:

> *Caesar.* What say the augurers?
> *Servant.* They would not have you to stir forth to-day.
>   Plucking the entrails of an offering forth,
>   They could not find a heart within the beast.
> *Caesar.* The gods do this in shame of cowardice:
>   Caesar should be a beast without a heart,
>   If he should stay at home to-day for fear.
>   No, Caesar shall not: danger knows full well
>   That Caesar is more dangerous than he:
>   We are two lions litter'd in one day,
>   And I the elder and more terrible:
>   And Caesar shall go forth.

But mark what follows:

> *Calpurnia.*   Alas! my lord,
>   Your wisdom is consumed in confidence.
>   Do not go forth to-day: call it my fear
>   That keeps you in the house, and not your own.
>   We'll send Mark Antony to the senate-house;
>   And he shall say you are not well to-day:
>   Let me, upon my knee, prevail in this.
> *Caesar.* Mark Antony shall say I am not well;
>   And, for thy humour, I will stay at home.

There is no prettier stroke of character in the play. Caesar has declared himself immovable. But Calpurnia, knowing her lord, offers him a way out and the natural man grasps it with an eagerness which shows how empty were the protestations of the demigod. 'Call it *my* fear that keeps you in the house', suggests the tactful wife, and Caesar complies immediately.

From the entry of Decius, who comes to bring Caesar to the senate-house, to the moment when Caesar invites the conspirators to take wine with him, Shakespeare continues to contrast the human with the legendary figure.

Decius, in his colloquy with Caesar, presents an attitude typical of the public servant who is accustomed to deal with persons in high office. He knows Caesar to be great, but refuses to be impressed. He is the junior minister or high official who seeks compensation for accepting the supremacy of an abler man by indulging a humorous perspicacity at his expense and airing an intimate acquaintance with his foibles. He is the courtier, inwardly proud of his access to august circles, who nevertheless affects a smiling disparagement of the privilege. He is the man who lives for a ribbon, but professes amusement at having to wear it. He will inform you that His Excellency is peevish this morning, having eaten or drunk unwisely the night before; that His Worship grows every day more difficult to manage and is every day more easily misled. He is the man to whom the absurdities of public life are very tolerable, provided they can be successfully exploited and at the same time afford him opportunities for the exercise of a small wit at the expense of a great man. He is the universal valet to whom no one is ever a hero. He sounds an echo, through the ages, of pleasantries exchanged in antechambers, lobbies, corridors or other purlieus where little people attend their masters. He is that familiar creature of the alcove who is always ready to claim that he can drop the right word into the right ear at the right moment.

It was Cassius, discussing ways and means with Brutus in his orchard, who first raised the question: What if Caesar should decide not to attend the meeting of the senate?

> For he is superstitious grown of late,
> Quite from the main opinion he held once
> Of fantasy, of dreams, and ceremonies:
> It may be, these apparent prodigies,
> The unaccustom'd terror of this night,

> And the persuasion of his augurers,
> May hold him from the Capitol to-day.

Decius jumps at the occasion. This is just his line of country:

> Never fear that: if he be so resolved,
> I can o'ersway him; for he loves to hear
> That unicorns may be betray'd with trees,
> And bears with glasses, elephants with holes,
> Lions with toils, and men with flatterers;
>
> Let me work;
> For I can give his humour the true bent,
> And I will bring him to the Capitol.

He catches Caesar in one of his majestic attitudes:

> *Decius.* Caesar, all hail! good morrow, worthy Caesar:
>   I come to fetch you to the senate-house.
> *Caesar.* And you are come in very happy time,
>   To bear my greeting to the senators,
>   And tell them that I will not come to-day:
>   Cannot, is false, and that I dare not, falser:
>   I will not come to-day: tell them so, Decius.
> *Calpurnia.* Say he is sick.
> *Caesar.*   Shall Caesar send a lie?
>   Have I in conquest stretch'd mine arm so far,
>   To be afeard to tell greybeards the truth?
>   Decius, go tell them Caesar will not come.

Decius is outwardly respectful but inwardly amused. With deference he suggests that Caesar's message may be found ridiculous:

> Most mighty Caesar, let me know some cause,
> Lest I be laugh'd at when I tell them so.

Caesar condescends to explain. Calpurnia has dreamed that his statue spouted blood and that many lusty Romans came smiling and bathed their hands in it. Decius, not in the least deceived by Caesar's pretence that he is staying at home to please his wife, sets out to show that the dream is not a bad but a good omen:

> This dream is all amiss interpreted;
> It was a vision fair and fortunate:
> Your statue spouting blood in many pipes,
> In which so many smiling Romans bathed,
> Signifies that from you great Rome shall suck
> Reviving blood, and that great men shall press
> For tinctures, stains, relics, and cognizance.
> This by Calpurnia's dream is signified.

Caesar accepts this interpretation and Decius presses his advantage. He speaks now to the small Caesar whom he claims to know so well. He can address this Caesar in a spirit of mockery which he hardly troubles to conceal – promise him a bauble, declare openly that people may laugh at him or throw doubt upon his courage:

> The senate have concluded
> To give this day a crown to mighty Caesar.
> If you shall send them word you will not come,
> Their minds may change. Besides, it were a mock
> Apt to be render'd, for some one to say
> 'Break up the senate till another time,
> When Caesar's wife shall meet with better dreams.'
> If Caesar hide himself, shall not they whisper
> 'Lo, Caesar is afraid'?

Decius has successfully performed his mission and Caesar makes ready to accompany him. At this moment Brutus enters with the conspirators. The short passage in which Caesar greets them brings him suddenly to life again. He has a word for everyone and it is the right word. This is the real Caesar, courteous and accessible, who has it in him to win hearts and to command respect:

> Caius Ligarius,
> Caesar was ne'er so much your enemy
> As that same ague which has made you lean.
>
> See! Antony, that revels long o'nights,
> Is notwithstanding up. Good morrow, Antony.

> Bid them prepare within:
> I am to blame to be thus waited for.
> Now, Cinna; now, Metellus; what, Trebonius!
> I have an hour's talk in store for you;
> Remember that you call on me to-day:
> Be near me, that I may remember you.

The scene concludes with Caesar's invitation to take wine with him.

Henceforth Caesar, the man, is lost in Caesar's effigy. To Artemidorus, who intercepts him on his way to the senate-house and entreats him to read first a scroll that touches him nearly, he grandly replies: 'What touches us ourself shall be last served.' To Metellus Cimber, who petitions on his knees that his banished brother may be recalled, he yet more grandly answers:

> I must prevent thee, Cimber.
> These couchings and these lowly courtesies
> Might fire the blood of ordinary men,
> And turn pre-ordinance and first decree
> Into the law of children. Be not fond,
> To think that Caesar bears such rebel blood
> That will be thaw'd from the true quality
> With that which melteth fools; I mean, sweet words,
> Low crookèd court'sies and base spaniel-fawning.

Brutus and Casca join in Cimber's petition and Caesar pays his last egregious tribute to Caesar:

> But I am constant as the northern star,
> Of whose true-fix'd and resting quality
> There is no fellow in the firmament.
> The skies are painted with unnumber'd sparks,
> They are all fire and every one doth shine,
> But there's but one in all doth hold his place:
> So, in the world; 'tis furnish'd well with men,
> And men are flesh and blood, and apprehensive;
> Yet in the number I do know but one
> That unassailable holds on his rank,
> Unshaked of motion.

Caesar's most famous observation in this scene has, however, yet to be heard. It has a curious history. But for a celebrated gibe at Shakespeare for writing it, the line would have been lost to posterity. A contemporary critic, in declaring it to be nonsense, preserved the true reading of the text.

Here a longer parenthesis than usual is justified. Ben Jonson, for he, of course, was the critic who performed this service for us, let slip his censure at the end of a famous paragraph in the 'Discoveries':

Many times he (Shakespeare) fell into those things could not escape laughter: as when he said, in the person of Caesar, one speaking to him, 'Caesar, thou dost me wrong': he replied, 'Caesar did never wrong but with just cause', and such like, which were ridiculous.

Jonson was not quoting from an imperfect memory at random. He was obviously citing an instance well known to his readers and at which he had frequently mocked in conversation with his friends.

And so we come to the heart of this small mystery. The words quoted by Jonson are nowhere to be found in any printed text of the play. The corresponding passage in the folio text, in which Caesar finally rejects the appeal of Metellus Cimber for the recall of his brother, contains neither Cimber's protest, 'Caesar, thou dost me wrong,' nor Caesar's reply, 'Caesar did never wrong but with just cause.' The folio text gives to Caesar at the conclusion of the speech in which he rejects Cimber's appeal a comparatively tame remark which, in the circumstances, is dramatically irrelevant:

Know, Caesar doth not wrong, nor without cause
Will he be satisfied.

There can be no reasonable doubt of the true reading. Jonson's version is dramatic, significant and in character. The folio version is insipid, superfluous and out of character not only with Shakespeare's presentation of Caesar as a whole but with the particular scene which is taking place. Caesar has just insisted that nothing

will move him from his purpose. Was he likely to conclude upon
a *non-sequitur* which suggests that he might be satisfied if cause
were shown?

Jonson has been accused by some critics of deliberately mis-
reporting his friend in order to hold him up to ridicule or of
carelessly misquoting the words from memory. Others, like
Gifford, accept Jonson's words as correct but defend them half-
heartedly. Gifford trounces the folio reading in which, he says,
there is no congruity, the poetry being as 'mean as the sense',
but he says of Jonson's version: 'The fact seems to be that this
verse, which closely borders on absurdity without being absolutely absurd, escaped the poet in the heat of composition and,
being unluckily one of those quaint slips which are readily
remembered, became a jocular and familiar phrase of the day.'

But what are we to say of the devoted editors of the first folio
who, because this quaint slip had become a jocular and familiar
phrase of the day, piously amended it so that posterity might
not poke fun at their master? Had it not been for Jonson's faithful record of what he actually heard in the theatre, the folio
rendering would have stood without a rival and one of the most
natural and telling lines of the tragedy would have been lost
forever – as who knows how many have not been lost in other
plays.

Caesar did never wrong but with just cause – it is Shakespeare's
finishing touch to the portrait of a dictator. It is the last, if it be
not also the first, assumption of the man who lives for power that
the wrong he does is right. So simple and constant a trait of the
man who esteems himself a leader needs no elucidation. Shakespeare's line is not one of those quaint slips of disorderly genius
with which he is so often credited. Still less is it in any way
absurd, except to minds grown mad with method.

Ave et vale Caesar! We take farewell of his human infirmities
and of the false grandeur into which he was betrayed. Henceforth
we have to do with that other Caesar, mourned by Antony:

> Thou art the ruins of the noblest man
> That ever livèd in the tide of times;

who still lives in the spirit and who will determine the further
progress of the tragedy. The last two Acts of the play depict the
inexorable fulfilment of Antony's prophetic oration over his
body in the senate-house:

> Domestic fury and fierce civil strife
> Shall cumber all the parts of Italy;
> Blood and destruction shall be so in use,
> And dreadful objects so familiar,
> That mothers shall but smile when they behold
> Their infants quarter'd with the hands of war;
> All pity choked with custom of fell deeds:
> And Caesar's spirit, ranging for revenge,
> With Atè by his side come hot from hell,
> Shall in these confines with a monarch's voice
> Cry 'Havoc', and let slip the dogs of war.

Antony here announces the dominant theme of the play and
exhibits Caesar as a link between the two sections.

Source: *Political Characters of Shakespeare* (1945).

Harley Granville-Barker

MARK ANTONY (1927)

> There is a tide in the affairs of men,
> Which, taken at the flood, leads on to fortune. . . .

MARK ANTONY cannot always talk so wisely, but he takes the tide that Brutus loses. He is a born opportunist, and we see him best in the light of his great opportunity. He stands contrasted with both Cassius and Brutus, with the man whom his fellows respect the more for his aloofness, and with such a rasping colleague as Cassius must be. Antony is, above all things, a good sort.

Shakespeare keeps him in ambush throughout the first part of the play. Up to the time when he faces the triumphant conspirators he speaks just thirty-three words. But there have already been no less than seven separate references to him, all significant. And this careful preparation culminates as significantly in the pregnant message he sends by his servant from the house to which it seems he has fled, bewildered by the catastrophe of Caesar's death. Yet, as we listen, it is not the message of a very bewildered man. Antony, so far, is certainly – in what we might fancy would be his own lingo – a dark horse. And, though we may father him on Plutarch, to English eyes there can be no more typically English figure than the sportsman turned statesman, but a sportsman still. Such men range up and down our history. Antony is something besides, however, that we used to flatter ourselves was not quite so English. He can be, when occasion serves, the perfect demagogue. Nor has Shakespeare any illusions as to what the harsher needs of politics may convert your sportsman once he is out to kill. The conspirators are fair game doubtless. But Lepidus, a little later, will be the carted stag.

> A barren-spirited fellow; one that feeds
> On abject orts and imitations,
> Which, out of use and staled by other men,
> Begin his fashion: do not talk of him
> But as a property . . .

to serve the jovial Antony's turn! This is your good sort, your sportsman, your popular orator, stripped very bare.

The servant's entrance with Antony's message, checking the conspirators' triumph, significant in its insignificance, is the turning point of the play.* But Shakespeare plucks further advantage from it. It allows him to bring Antony out of ambush completely effective and in double guise; the message foreshadows him as politician, a minute later we see him grieving deeply for his friend's death. There is, of course, nothing incompatible in the two aspects of the man, but the double impression is all-important. He must impress us as uncalculatingly abandoned to his feelings, risking his very life to vent them. For a part of his strength lies in impulse; he can abandon himself to his feelings, as Brutus the philosopher cannot. Moreover, this bold simplicity is his safe-conduct now. Were the conspirators not impressed by it, did it not seem to obliterate his politic side, they might well and wisely take him at his word and finish with him then and there. And at the back of his mind Antony has this registered clearly enough. It must be with something of the sportsman's — and the artist's — happy recklessness that he flings the temptation at them:

> Live a thousand years,
> I shall not find myself so apt to die:
> No place will please me so, no mean of death,
> As here by Cæsar, and by you cut off,
> The choice and master spirits of this age.

He means it; but he knows, as he says it, that there is no better way of turning the sword of a so flattered choice and master spirit aside. It is this politic, shadowed aspect of Antony that is to

* As Moulton demonstrates in an admirable passage. [See p. 36 of the present volume. P.U.]

be their undoing; so Shakespeare is concerned to keep it clear at the back of our minds too. Therefore he impresses it on us first by the servant's speech, and Antony himself is free a little later to win us and the conspirators both.

Not that the politician does not begin to peep pretty soon. He tactfully ignores the cynicism of Cassius,

> Your voice shall be as strong as any man's
> In the disposing of new dignities.

But by Brutus' reiterated protest that Caesar was killed in wise kindness what realist, what ironist – and Antony is both – would not be tempted?

> I doubt not of your wisdom.
> Let each man render me his bloody hand. . . .

And, in bitter irony, he caps their ritual with his own. It is the ritual of friendship, but of such a friendship as the blood of Caesar, murdered by his friends, may best cement. To Brutus the place of honour in the compact; to each red-handed devotee his due; and last, but by no means least, in Antony's love shall be Trebonius who drew him away while the deed was done. And so to the final, most fitting apostrophe:

> Gentlemen all!

Emotion subsided, the politician plays a good game. They shall never be able to say he approved their deed; but he is waiting, please, for those convincing reasons that Caesar was dangerous. He even lets slip a friendly warning to Cassius that the prospect is not quite clear. Then, with yet more disarming frankness, comes the challenging request to Brutus to let him speak in the market place. As he makes it, a well-calculated request! For how can Brutus refuse, how admit a doubt that the Roman people will not approve this hard service done them? Still, that there may be no doubt at all, Brutus will first explain everything to his fellow-citizens himself, lucidly and calmly. When reason has made sure of her sway, the emotional, the 'gamesome', Antony may do homage to his friend.

> Be it so;
> I do desire no more

responds Antony, all docility and humility, all gravity – though if ever a smile could sharpen words, it could give a grim edge to these. So they leave him with dead Caesar.

In this contest thus opened between the man of high argument and the instinctive politician, between principle (mistaken or not) and opportunism, we must remember that Antony can be by no means confident of success. He foresees chaos. He knows, if these bemused patriots do not, that it takes more than correct republican doctrines to replace a great man. But as to this Roman mob – this citizenry, save the mark! – whoever knows which way it will turn? The odds are on the whole against him. Still he'll try his luck; Octavius, though, had better keep safely out of the way meanwhile. All his senses are sharpened by emergency. Before ever Octavius' servant can speak he has recognized the fellow and guessed the errand. Shakespeare shows us his mind at its swift work, its purposes shaping.

> Passion, I see, is catching, for mine eyes,
> Seeing those beads of sorrow stand in thine,
> Began to water

– from which it follows that if the sight of Caesar's body can so move the man and the man's tears so move him, why, his own passion may move his hearers in the market place presently to some purpose. His imagination, once it takes fire, flashes its way along, not by reason's slow process though in reason's terms.*

* How many modern actors upon their picture stage, with its curtain to close a scene for them pat upon some triumphant top note, have brought this one to its end twenty lines earlier upon the familiar, tremendous, breathless apostrophe (did Shakespeare ever pen such another sentence?) that begins,
> Woe to the hand that shed this costly blood!
> Over thy wounds now do I prophesy. . . .
But to how untimely an end! The mechanism of Shakespeare's theatre forbade such effects. Caesar's body is lying on the main stage, and must

To what he is to move his hearers we know. The famous speech is a triumph of histrionics, for though the actor of Antony must move us with it also – and he can scarcely fail to – Shakespeare has set him the further, harder and far more important task of showing us an Antony the mob never see, of making him clear to us, moreover, even while we are stirred by his eloquence, of making clear to us just by what it is we are stirred. It would, after all, be pretty poor playwriting and acting which could achieve no more than a plain piece of mob oratory, however gorgeous; a pretty poor compliment to an audience to ask of it no subtler response than the mob's. But to show us, and never for a moment to let slip from our sight, the complete and complex Antony, impulsive and calculating, warm-hearted and callous, aristocrat, sportsman and demagogue, that will be for the actor an achievement indeed; and the playwright has given him all the material for it.

Shakespeare himself knows, no one better, what mere histrionics may amount to. He has been accused of showing in a later play (but unjustly, I hold) his too great contempt for the mob; he might then have felt something deeper than contempt for the man who could move the mob by such means; he may even have thought Brutus made the better speech. Antony, to be sure, is more than an actor; for one thing he writes his own part as he goes along. But he gathers the ideas for it as he goes too, with no greater care for their worth than the actor need have so long as they are effective at the moment. He lives abundantly in the present, his response to its call is unerring. He risks the future. How does the great oration end?

> Mischief, thou are afoot;
> Take thou what course thou wilt!

---

be removed, and it will take at least two people to carry it. Here is one reason for the arrival of Octavius' servant. But as ever with Shakespeare, and with any artist worth his salt, limitation is turned to advantage. If dead Caesar is to be the mainspring of the play's further action, what more forceful way could be found of making this plain than, for a finish to the scene, to state the new theme of Octavius' coming, Caesar's kin and successor?

A wicked child, one would say, that has whipped up his fellow-children to a riot of folly and violence. That is one side of him. But the moment after he is off, brisk, cool and businesslike, to play the next move in the game with that very cool customer, Octavius.

He has had no tiresome principles to consult or to expound.

> I only speak right on. . . .

he boasts;

> I tell you that which you yourselves do know.

An admirable maxim for popular orators and popular writers too! There is nothing aloof, nothing superior about Antony. He may show a savage contempt for this man or that; he has a sort of liking for men in the mass. He is, in fact, the common man made perfect in his commonness; yet he is perceptive of himself as of his fellows, and, even so, content.

What follows upon his eloquent mourning for Caesar? When the chaos in Rome has subsided he ropes his 'merry fortune' into harness. It is not a very pleasant colloquy with which the fourth Act opens.

> *Antony.* These many then shall die; their names are pricked.
> *Octavius.* Your brother too must die; consent you, Lepidus?
> *Lepidus.* I do consent.
> *Octavius.*   Prick him down, Antony.
> *Lepidus.* Upon condition Publius shall not live,
>   Who is your sister's son, Mark Antony.
> *Antony.* He shall not live; look, with a spot I damn him.

The conspirators have, of course, little right to complain. But four lines later we learn that Lepidus himself, when his two friends have had their use of him, is to fare not much better than his brother – than the brother he has himself just given so callously to death! Can he complain either, then? This is the sort of beneficence the benevolent Brutus has let loose on the world.

But Antony finishes the play in fine form; victorious in battle, politicly magnanimous to a prisoner or two, and ready with a resounding tribute to Brutus, now that he lies dead. Not in quite such fine form, though; for the shadow of that most unsportsmanlike young man Octavius is already moving visibly to his eclipse.

These, then, are the three men among whom Shakespeare divides this dramatic realm; the idealist, the egoist, the opportunist. The contrast between them must be kept clear in the acting by all that the actors do and are, for upon its tension the living structure of the play depends. And, it goes without saying, they must be shown to us as fellow creatures, not as abstractions from a dead past. For so Shakespeare saw them; and, if he missed something of the mind of the Roman, yet these three stand with sufficient truth for the sum of the human forces, which in any age, and in ours as in his, hold the world in dispute.

SOURCE: *Prefaces to King Lear, Cymbeline and Julius Caesar* (1963).

J. Dover Wilson

BEN JONSON AND
JULIUS CAESAR (1949)

IF we neglect *Titus Andronicus* as pseudo-classical, and only his by adoption and not by grace (of which it has little enough), *Julius Caesar* was Shakespeare's earliest attempt to try his fortune in the perilous arena of Roman tragedy. And a very bold attempt it was, made by a man equipped with but 'small Latin', under the keenly censorious eye of a learned friend alert for every slip or sign of weakness, to say nothing of a learned enemy, as many suppose Chapman to have been.

When the play was produced in the autumn of 1599 the friendship was probably little more than a year old; for in 1598 Ben Jonson's *Every Man in his Humour* had been performed by the Chamberlain's Company, with Shakespeare taking part; and it was Shakespeare who, according to a story which Rowe reports, had 'by a remarkable piece of humanity and good nature' introduced the still comparatively unknown dramatist to his fellow-actors and induced them to accept the play.[1] 'After this', Rowe continues, 'they were professed friends, though I don't know whether the other ever made him an equal return of gentleness and sincerity.' Rowe appears to have momentarily forgotten the magnificent *laudatio* which Jonson wrote for the posthumous edition of his 'beloved' friend's plays; but it cannot be denied that his immediate 'return' was rather sincere than gentle. In his next play, *Every Man out of his Humour*, performed in 1599, once again by Shakespeare's fellows, he mocks, not necessarily ill-naturedly, at two passages from *Julius Caesar*. First, in Act III scene iv, a couple of coxcombs, Clove and Orange, talk 'fustian' philosophy together in the hearing of others to 'make 'hem believe we are great scholars'; one of their scraps of spurious

Aristotelianism being 'Reason long since is fled to animals, you know', which is a patent fling at Antony's

> O judgment! thou art fled to brutish beasts,
> And men have lost their reason;

and, whether of malice prepense, or as I prefer to think because he missed Shakespeare's point, quoted out of its context as a serious 'philosophical' (that is to say scientific) observation. But Shakespeare was as learned as Jonson or anyone else in the science of his day and put it to better use in his plays than most dramatists. Antony's exclamation makes excellent sense when taken in its context and considered in relation to beast-lore. The best commentary on it is Hamlet's exclamation in the first soliloquy:

> O God! a beast, that wants discourse of reason,
> Would have mourned longer.

This proves that Shakespeare was well aware of the Aristotelian doctrine which ascribed the God-given faculty of reason and judgment to man alone·* but shows him equally aware that, despite this doctrine, beasts seemed capable of compassion, which was generally regarded as one of the highest manifestations of reason. For as Anne remarks to the inhuman Richard Crookback:

> No beast so fierce but knows some touch of pity.†

It is just this paradox, this contradiction between scientific theory and a matter of common observation, that Antony has in mind, since like Hamlet and Lady Anne he too is referring to compassion. The passage begins:

> You all did love him once, not without cause.
> What cause withholds you then to mourn for him?

---

* Cf. *Hamlet*, IV v 83–5:
>   . . . poor Ophelia,
> Divided from herself and her fair judgement,
> Without the which we are pictures or mere beasts.

† *Richard III*, I ii 71. See also *Henry VIII*, II iii 10; *Titus*, II iii 151; *Winter's Tale*, II iii 186–9.

The exclamation follows naturally thereafter; and is itself followed by a moment or two's silence as Antony gives way to grief; while, when later he succeeds in moving the crowd to compassion, he returns to the same theme:

> O, now you weep and I perceive you feel
> The dint of pity: these are gracious drops.

But Jonson ignored all this, took the words out of their context and held them up to ridicule as 'fustian philosophy'. Yet it is not to be supposed that Shakespeare was without his defenders, even if he did not defend himself in one of those 'wit-combats' Fuller speaks of. And that the passage became the talk of the town is suggested by an echo of Jonson's gibe which appears in an anonymous play *The Wisdom of Dr Dodipoll* (pub. 1600), and runs 'then reason's fled to animals, I see'.[2]

Aristotelian psychology being long since out of date, this first of Jonson's jests is more obscure to us than it would have been to his contemporaries. His second no one can miss. In Act v scene vi of the same play, when Sir Puntarvolo, after beating the scurrilous Carlo Buffone to put him 'out of his humour', proceeds to seal up his lips with wax, the victim's last pitiful cry is 'Et tu Brute!' which he addresses to his friend Macilente who treacherously holds the candle for the execution of Puntarvolo's vengeance. And that the use of this tag was at once a good stage joke and a thrust at Shakespeare's ignorance is suggested by Dr Simpson, who notes that 'Jonson', who knew his Suetonius, would be aware that what the dying Caesar said was something different',[3] and something moreover in Greek not in Latin.

Yet while Ben could mock at Shakespeare's history and 'philosophy' he was not above picking up a 'philosophical' crumb of the latter from under his table. When Shakespeare makes Antony say of the dead Brutus:

> His life was gentle, and the elements
> So mixed in him that Nature might stand up
> And say to all the world 'This was a man!' –

he drew upon the Galenic physiology, still orthodox in his day, which, based upon the notion that the life of man doth, as Sir Toby puts it, 'consist of the four elements' (viz. earth, water, air and fire), declared that health, bodily and spiritual, depended upon a balance between them. Jonson avails himself of the same conception in the following description of Crites, a character in *Cynthia's Revels* (acted 1600), wherein he draws a picture of his ideal man and does not hesitate to give him features strongly reminiscent of his own:

A creature of a most perfect and divine temper. One in whom the humours and elements are peaceably met, without emulation of precedency: he is neither too fantastically melancholy, too slowly phlegmatic, too lightly sanguine, or too rashly choleric, but in all so composed and ordered, as it is clear Nature went about some full work, she did more than make a man when she made him.*

A commonplace of the age, implying no borrowing from either side, it may be said, while it may be argued that so far from the initial impetus coming from Shakespeare the lines just quoted from *Julius Caesar* were probably themselves inspired by *Every Man in his Humour*. Yet even if this last be true the wording of the eulogy on Crites is so similar to that of Antony's on Brutus, that an echo can hardly be questioned. And while Jonson echoed Shakespeare, Drayton in turn echoed both in the following stanza from the 1603 edition of *The Barons' Wars* in praise of Mortimer:

> He was a man, then boldly dare to say,
> In whose rich soul the virtues well did suit,
> In whom, so mixed, the elements all lay
> That none to one could soveraignty impute,
> As all did govern, yet all did obey;
> He of a temper was so absolute
> 　　As that it seemed, when Nature him began,
> 　　She meant to show all that might be in man.†

* *Cynthia's Revels*, II iii 123 ff. I quote from *Ben Jonson*, ed. Herford and Simpson, IV 74, modernizing the spelling.

† Canto III, stanza 40. In her notes on this Mrs Tillotson cites *Julius Caesar*, V v 85–7, and adds: 'the lines are not in *Mortimeriados* [1596],

Here lines 4 and 5 clearly derive from Jonson's 'without emulation of precedency', while 'so mixed, the elements', a form of words Jonson does not use, seems with equal probability to point back to Shakespeare.

Finally, there is yet a fourth passage in *Julius Caesar* associated with Jonson and better known for being so than any of those already cited; a passage interesting, moreover, as affording in the opinion of many the only known instance in the Folio of an alteration made in deference to literary criticism. It forms the concluding portions of Caesar's speech rejecting the petition of the kneeling Metellus Cimber just before the assassination and runs as follows in the text as it has come down to us:

> Thy brother by decree is banished:
> If thou dost bend and pray and fawn for him,
> I spurn thee like a cur out of my way.
> Know Caesar doth not wrong, nor without cause
> Will he be satisfied.

And here is Jonson's comment which forms part of his reply, first printed in *Discoveries* (1640), to the players' boast that Shakespeare 'never blotted out line':

His wit was in his own power; would the rule of it had been so too. Many times he fell into those things could not escape laughter: as when he said in the person of Caesar, one speaking to him: 'Caesar thou dost me wrong' – he replied: 'Caesar did never wrong, but with just cause', and such like, which were ridiculous. [4]

As thus quoted Caesar's words, though undoubtedly referring to the same situation, correspond with those of the Folio text neither in phrase nor in meaning. We are therefore faced with an alternative: either, as Steevens who first drew attention to the

---

so there can be no doubt that Drayton is the imitator, and the verse is in fact nearer to its model in 1619 than in 1603. His collaboration in the lost play *Caesars Fall* in 1602 may have made him especially familiar with Shakespeare's play.' (*The Works of Michael Drayton* (1941) v 67.) She does not notice the link with *Cynthia's Revels*.

criticism supposed, Jonson 'quoted the line unfaithfully' in order to ridicule Shakespeare, or, as Tyrwhitt suggested in reply to Steevens, 'the players or perhaps Shakespeare himself, overawed by so great an authority, withdrew the words in question'.[5] Steevens's explanation has found favour with good critics like Aldis Wright[6] and Mark Hunter,[7] who agree that but for Jonson's comment 'no one would have suspected any corruption in the passage', a contention I find difficult to rebut, though some feel that the last line and a half in the Folio version follow those before with a certain inconsequence. Yet I am confident that Tyrwhitt offers the true interpretation and for three reasons.

First, any idea that Jonson invented out of sheer malice the line he criticizes seems to me quite incredible. Even if we accept in full and without question Drummond's well-known description of him as 'a contemner and scorner of others, given rather to lose a friend than a jest',[8] that only means that he enjoyed retailing scandal or making unkind jokes at his friends' expense, not that he would go to the length first of concocting an absurdity and then of falsely attributing it to a fellow-dramatist in order to lampoon him. Such a piece of mean treachery is irreconcilable both with what we know of Jonson's frank if splenetic character and with the admiration and affection which breathe from the lines to Shakespeare already spoken of. As for the other two reasons, they would be valid whatever views we hold about him, since they are inescapable inferences from indisputable dates.

The criticism, I have said, is to be found in Jonson's *Discoveries*, a posthumous publication but compiled for the most part between 1626 and his death in 1637,[9] that is to say after the publication of the First Folio in 1623. Is it really conceivable that Jonson proposed to pass this absurdity off as Shakespeare's when the story could be checked and confuted by a simple reference to the printed text, a text moreover for which he had himself written two sets of commendatory verses? To do so would be to court instant exposure as a lying traducer, an exposure the more certain that, as he was aware, the dead Shakespeare had energetic partisans among literary men. One of these was

Leonard Digges, who, having in his lines for the First Folio
named *Julius Caesar* as unequalled among contemporary dramas,
made the point still more explicit in an expanded version of
these, printed a generation later, as follows:

> So I have seen, when *Caesar* would appear,
> And on the stage at half-sword parley were
> Brutus and Cassius, oh how the audience
> Were ravished, with what wonder they went thence;
> When some new day they would not brooke a line
> Of tedious, though well-laboured, *Catiline*;[10]

and so on, comparing play with play of the two authors and ever
in Jonson's disfavour. This appeared in 1640, when Jonson too
was dead; but it shows what some had long thought, and what
Jonson must have known they thought.

The third reason is, I think, more cogent still. That the line as
quoted in *Discoveries* was, at least in general tenor, well known to
the theatre public is proved by its appearance in one of Jonson's
plays; and, as with 'O judgment, thou art fled to brutish beasts',
he puts it in the mouth of a character to raise a laugh. The play is
The Staple of News, first acted 'by His Majesty's Servants' in
1626 and the allusion, which occurs in the Induction, is thus
printed in the 1631 text:[11]

> EXPECTATION. *I can doe that too, if I haue cause.*
> PROLOGUE.   *Cry you mercy*, you neuer did wrong, but with
>   iust cause.

The difference of type shows that a quotation was intended, and
there can be no doubt that the audience was expected to recognize
it as such. It must have been a pretty familiar quotation too,
since source and author are not even hinted at. And yet in 1626
Julius Caesar was already twenty-seven years old. The lines cited
above from Digges explain the mystery. *Julius Caesar* retained
its hold on the affections of playgoers long after its original
production; and though our very imperfect theatrical records
give no trace of a revival at the beginning of Charles I's reign,
the allusion in *The Staple of News* is itself strong evidence that in

1626 Caesar's words were fresh in mind, that is to say had been recently heard on the stage; the same stage, for both plays belonged to the King's men. In face of all this, to contend that

> Caesar did never wrong, but with just cause

was a distortion of Shakespeare's meaning on Jonson's part not merely does wrong to Jonson's memory, it does a wrong for which no cause whatever can be shown. In other words, Shakespeare must have written what Jonson reports or something very like it, and what he wrote must have remained in the prompt-book and been spoken by the player taking Caesar's part at least three years after the other version had appeared in the First Folio.

It remains to inquire why the change was made, what precisely the change was, and who made it. None of these questions can of course be answered with absolute certainty, but one or two probabilities may be ventilated. As to the last, some have jumped to the conclusion that the change was made by Jonson himself, whose commendatory verses in the Folio suggest that he might have had a hand in the preparation of its text. If this means that *Julius Caesar*, in copy or proof, was passed on to him for correction as a classical expert, the supposition is disproved by the presence in the revised text of many other features which he would have considered solecisms and have amended, a glaring instance being the Italian form given to some of the Latin names. If, on the other hand, it means that the scribe who prepared the copy for the printer made the change at Jonson's instigation or in deference to his condemnation of the passage, that seems very probable, and is as far as we are likely to get with the answers to the first and the third questions. It is even possible that he asked Jonson to rewrite it for him, since it is hard to believe that a mere scribe invented the Folio reading. Tyrwhitt, it is true, suggested in 1766 that what originally stood in Shakespeare's manuscript was:

> Know, Caesar doth not wrong, but with just cause;
> Nor without cause will he be satisfied;

a reconstruction which ingeniously combines the meaning that

Jonson recollected with the words of the Folio text; and if this be right then any scribe might have made the change by simply deleting four words. Tyrwhitt's solution, however, involves two difficulties: first, it implies that Jonson's verbal memory, well known for its accuracy, was less precise than usual; secondly, the line as he recollected it is so manifestly superior to the line and a half of Tyrwhitt's reconstruction that it is hard to believe the recollection anything but exact.

The first critic to bring out this last point, as far as I know, was the late John Palmer in 1945. He noted that the words

Nor without cause will he be satisfied,

which belong to the text both of Tyrwhitt and of the Folio, and imply that Caesar 'might be satisfied if cause were shown', make a very lame conclusion to a speech the whole tenor of which is that the decree of banishment is irrevocable, and seems quite inconsistent with 'constant as the northern star' in the speech that follows. On the other hand, Jonson's single line,

Caesar did never wrong, but with just cause,

is 'dramatic, significant and in character'. Its very isolation and abruptness give it just that hint of menace and air of inflexible finality which the end of such a speech demands. 'It is Shakespeare's finishing touch to the portrait of a dictator. It is the last, if it be not also the first, assumption of the man who lives for power that the wrong he does is right.'[12] I am of course aware that 'wrong' does not necessarily mean wrongdoing in Shakespeare, though Jonson evidently assumed it did, and that the line might be interpreted 'Caesar never punished a man unjustly'. The sense Palmer places upon it seems, however, the more likely because dramatically the richer; or Shakespeare, as often elsewhere, may have deliberately used an ambiguous word to allow his audience a choice of meanings. Anyhow, in neither case is the meaning the least 'ridiculous'. As with 'O judgment, thou art fled to brutish beasts', Jonson has taken the passage as a logical or philosophical proposition without reference to context or character.

And that, I think, explains a point which Palmer has not squarely faced: the protest 'Caesar, thou dost me wrong' which Jonson reports as the occasion of Caesar's contemptuous reply. Some critics have given it to Metellus Cimber and made the dialogue run:

> *Caesar.* . . . I spurn thee like a cur out of my way.
> *Metellus.* Caesar, thou dost me wrong.
> *Caesar.* Caesar did never wrong but with just cause
> *Metellus.* Is there no voice. . . .

But that, by associating 'wrong' with 'spurn' etc., would empty Caesar's line of its larger dramatic significance, to say nothing of degrading it from its position as an exceedingly effective close to the preceding speech. Moreover, as Aldis Wright objects, 'for Metellus to interrupt Caesar with the petulant exclamation . . . is out of character with the tone of his speeches before and after, which is that of abject flattery'. Take it how you will, such a protest cannot be fitted into the context. Yet what is there surprising in this? Is it inconsistent to suppose that Jonson's memory, so clear as to Caesar's 'ridiculous' words, was vague about the dramatic occasion on which they are used? His highly critical intelligence, prejudiced against the play directly he learnt that Shakespeare was attempting a theme so far, as he considered, out of his element, seized upon anything he could quote or laugh at as absurdities and paid little or no attention to the context, in which he was not interested. In the *Discoveries*, however, some kind of peg for the quotation was necessary and what he supplied was harmless and good enough for the purpose.

That we should have four instances of Jonson criticizing this one play, and that the criticisms should extend over a period of twenty-five years or more, suggest something of an *idée fixe*. It was Sidney Lee's belief that the famous 'purge' which according to *The Return from Parnassus* Shakespeare had administered to Jonson was the writing of *Julius Caesar* in which he 'proved his command of topics . . . peculiarly suited to Jonson's classicised vein and had in fact outrun his churlish comrade on his own ground'.[13] However that may be, a play on such a theme by one who was no scholar could hardly have been anything but a standing offence in his eyes. That it brought throngs to the theatre would not surprise him; he knew the 'barbarism' of the London public. And when it continued to do so after he had shown in *Sejanus* and *Catiline* how plays on classical themes, based on the original historical sources not on some English translation of a French translation of Plutarch's *Lives*, ought to be written, he could console himself with

> Art hath an enemy called Ignorance.*

But when the players insisted on praising their Shakespeare for the wrong things he was bound to speak out. That he 'never blotted out line' was the man's weakness; how much better the plays might have been had 'he blotted a thousand', as anyone who knew his Horace[14] could have told them. And this, he protested, and honestly protested, was not malevolence on his part but sound criticism. Even to speak of it as 'ridiculously patronising'[15] is unfair. After all, did not Matthew Arnold criticize Wordsworth and Shelley and Keats in much the same fashion and much the same spirit? Poets are apt to misapprehend each other, especially when they belong to the same period. The very brightness of their genius blinds them to the peculiar excellences of a genius differing from their own. Certainly Jonson quite failed to understand Shakespeare; his praise of him in the First Folio proves that. He even missed the point of the passages he picked out for laughter or censure in *Julius Caesar*. Misunderstanding, however, does not quite account for all. There was rancour in the cup; the unconscious realization by a proud spirit of another's superiority. Jonson won a great place for himself, a great following, and he deserved them.[16] But it was his fate to live from beginning to end of his career in the shadow of one by whom his genius was

> rebuked, as it is said
> Mark Antony's was by Caesar.

SOURCE: *Shakespeare Survey 2* (1949).

* *Every Man out of his Humour*, Induction, I ii 9.

NOTES

1. Rowe does not mention the title of the play in question, but it can hardly have been any but *Every Man in his Humour*. See *Ben Jonson*, ed. C. H. Herford and P. and E. Simpson (1925–52) I 18.

2. First noted by E. Koeppel in *Shakespeare Jahrbuch*, XLIII (1907) 210.

3. *Notes and Queries*, 11 Feb. 1899.

4. *Ben Jonson*, VIII 583–4 (spelling modernized).

5. See James Boswell's *Life of Malone* (1821) XII 75–6.

6. *Julius Caesar* (Clarendon Press series), note on III i 47–8.

7. *Julius Caesar*, ed. App. D. This edition ('The College Classics', Madras, 1900), though little known in England, contains a full and interesting commentary, in which the editor's friend Dr Percy Simpson had a large share.

8. See *Ben Jonson*, I 151.

9. Ibid., I 104.

10. From *Poems: written by Wil. Shakespeare Gent*, 1640 (reprinted in E. K. Chambers, *William Shakespeare* (1930) II 232–4), in which 'Catilines' is misprinted for 'Catiline'. Again I modernize the spelling.

11. *Ben Jonson*, VI 280.

12. John Palmer, *Political Characters of Shakespeare* (1943) pp. 44–6. Alfred Harbage (*As They Liked It* (1947) p. 83), who also accepts Jonson's version, finds a less sinister meaning in it. He cites 'Bassanio's plea to Shylock's judge, "To do a great right, do a little wrong" ', and notes that Shakespeare constantly uses the moral dilemma in an experimental or provocative way.

13. *Life of Shakespeare* (1916) pp. 353–4.

14. See *De Arte Poetica*, II 291–4.

15. *Julius Caesar*, ed. Hunter, p. 390.

16. I do not think these concluding remarks are inconsistent with G. E. Bentley's monumental *Shakespeare and Jonson: Their Reputations in the Seventeenth Century Compared*, 2 vols. (Chicago, 1945), or with his inaugural address, *The Swan of Avon and the Bricklayer of Westminster* (Princeton University), which came to hand after this article was already in type.

SELECT BIBLIOGRAPHY

BOOKS

Adrien Bonjour, *The Structure of Julius Caesar* (Liverpool U.P., 1958). Particularly valuable on the relationship of characterisation to structure in the play as a whole.

B. R. Breyer, 'A New Look at *Julius Caesar*', in *Essays in Honor of Walter Clyde Curry* (Tennessee U.P., 1954). A somewhat unconvincing attempt to prove that the meaning of the play is 'existentialist despair'; but a good counterweight to those who hold that Brutus in his context is *obviously* wrong.

Maurice Charney, *Shakespeare's Roman Plays: the Function of Imagery in the Drama* (Harvard U.P., 1961).

T. S. Dorsch, introduction to the New Arden edition of *Julius Caesar* (Methuen and Harvard U.P., 1955).

New Variorum edition of *Julius Caesar*, ed. H. H. Furness, Jr (J. B. Lippincott & Co., 1913). Contains excerpts from much of the pre-1900 criticism of the play.

Vernon Hall, Jr, '*Julius Caesar*: a Play without Political Bias', in *Studies in the English Renaissance Drama*, ed. J. W. Bennett, O. Cargill and V. Hall (New York U.P., 1959; Peter Owen, 1961). Argues that Shakespeare's main purpose was to exhibit the grandeur that was Rome.

G. Wilson Knight, 'The Torch of Life: an Essay on *Julius Caesar*', in *The Imperial Theme* (3rd edition, Methuen and Barnes & Noble, 1961). On the imagery. Perceptive in places but not as good as the succeeding chapter, parts of which are reprinted in the present volume. 'Brutus and Macbeth', in *The Wheel of Fire* (4th edition, Methuen and Barnes & Noble, 1962).

T. R. Lounsbury, *Shakespeare and Voltaire* (David Nutt, 1902).

An informative volume, which treats the *Julius Caesar* episode at some length.

M. W. MacCallum, *Shakespeare's Roman Plays and their Background* (Macmillan, 1910; 2nd edition, Macmillan, 1964). A standard work, which retains its value, though it now seems rather slow-moving.

Shakespeare Survey 10, ed. Allardyce Nicoll (Cambridge U.P., 1957). The special theme of this volume is the Roman plays. The survey of criticism from 1900 to 1956 by J. C. Maxwell includes work on *Julius Caesar*; and the articles by T. J. B. Spencer on 'Shakespeare and the Elizabethan Romans' and by W. M. Merchant on 'Classical Costume' are also specially relevant to *Julius Caesar*.

Norman Sanders, introduction to the New Penguin edition of *Julius Caesar* (Penguin, 1967). This edition also contains a section on 'Further Reading'.

Ernest Schanzer, introduction to *Shakespeare's Appian* (Liverpool U.P., 1956) pp. xix–xxiii. What Antony's Forum speech owes to Appian.

A. C. Sprague, *Shakespeare and the Actors* (Harvard U.P., 1945) pp. 319–26. Describes some of the stage-business used in performances of *Julius Caesar*.

Algernon De Vivier Tassin, '*Julius Caesar*', in *Shakespearian Studies by Members of the Department of English . . . at Columbia University* (Columbia U.P., 1916). Mainly concerned with the play's relation to its sources. There are good pages on Cassius.

J. A. K. Thomson, *Shakespeare and the Classics* (Allen & Unwin and Barnes & Noble, 1952) pp. 242–50. Comment on *Julius Caesar* and Plutarch.

D. A. Traversi, *Shakespeare: the Roman Plays* (Hollis & Carter and Stanford U.P., 1963) pp. 21–75. Contains a detailed commentary on *Julius Caesar* in the style which Mr Traversi has made his own.

J. Dover Wilson, introduction to his edition of *Julius Caesar* (Cambridge U.P., 1949).

ARTICLES

Leonard F. Dean, '*Julius Caesar* and Modern Criticism', originally published in the *English Journal* (Oct. 1961) and included in the Signet edition of *Julius Caesar*, ed. W. and B. Rosen (New English Library, 1963). A brief, selective review.

Marvin Felheim, 'The Problem of Time in *Julius Caesar*', in *Huntington Library Quarterly*, XIII (1949–50). A highly technical study.

R. A. Foakes, 'An Approach to *Julius Caesar*', in *Shakespeare Quarterly*, V (1954) 259–70. Reprinted in the Signet edition of the play.

Robert Ornstein, 'Seneca and the Political Drama of *Julius Caesar*', in *Journal of English and Germanic Philology*, LVII (1958) 51–6.

Irving Ribner, 'Political Issues in *Julius Caesar*', in *Journal of English and Germanic Philology*, LVI (1957). A somewhat willed attempt to measure everything in the play by 'Renaissance principles', supposed universally held.

W. D. Smith, 'The Duplicate Revelation of Portia's Death', in *Shakespeare Quarterly*, IV (1953). An interesting examination of a famous, minor crux.

R. W. Zandvoort, 'Brutus's Forum Speech in *Julius Caesar*', in *Review of English Studies*, XVI (1940) 62–6. A technical study.

NOTES ON CONTRIBUTORS

JOHN ANSON is an Assistant Professor of English in the University of California at Berkeley.

GEOFFREY BULLOUGH has just retired from the Chair of English at King's College, London, and was formerly Professor at Sheffield. He is the author of *Narrative and Dramatic Sources of Shakespeare*, of which six volumes have so far appeared, and has edited the works of Henry More and of Fulke Greville, besides publishing several critical books.

HARLEY GRANVILLE-BARKER (1877–1946). His main work on Shakespeare is the series of *Prefaces* (1927–47). His management of the Court Theatre, London, from 1904, made him famous as a theatre-director. His best-known plays are *The Voysey Inheritance* (1905) and *Waste* (1907).

SIR MARK HUNTER, who died in 1932, was in the Indian Education Service and later Director of Public Instruction in Burma. He had previously been Professor of English at Madras. He was the author of many articles on education and was knighted in 1923.

LEO KIRSCHBAUM was, at the time of his death, Professor of English at Wayne State University. He edited *The Plays of Marlowe* (1962); and his books on Shakespeare were *The True Text of King Lear* (1945), *Shakespeare and the Stationers* (1955) and *Character and Characterisation in Shakespeare* (1962).

G. WILSON KNIGHT recently retired from a Chair of English Literature at Leeds University. His many writings on Shakespeare include *The Wheel of Fire* (1930), *The Imperial Theme* (1931) and *The Shakespearian Tempest* (1932) – all since published in new editions.

L. C. KNIGHTS is King Edward VII Professor of English Literature at Cambridge and was formerly Professor at Sheffield and at Bristol. His writings on Shakespeare include *Some Shakespearian Themes* (1959) and *An Approach to Hamlet* (1960).

JOHN PALMER, who died in 1944, worked as a dramatic critic in London before the First World War, and was later a member of the permanent secretariat of the League of Nations. His many books include *The Comedy of Manners* (1913), *Ben Jonson* (1934) and *The Comic Characters of Shakespeare* (1946).

NORMAN RABKIN teaches at the University of California at Berkeley, and is the author of *Shakespeare and the Common Understanding* (1967).

ERNEST SCHANZER has taught English Literature at Toronto and Liverpool Universities, and is now at the University of Munich. He is the author of *Shakespeare's Appian* (1956) and *The Problem Plays of Shakespeare* (1963).

J. I. M. STEWART, Student of Christ Church, Oxford, is the author of *Character and Motive in Shakespeare* (1949) and *Eight Modern Writers* (1962). He is also a novelist and detective-story writer.

BRENTS STIRLING, Professor of English at the University of Washington, Seattle, is the author of *The Populace in Shakespeare* (1949) and *Unity in Shakespearian Tragedy* (1956).

VIRGIL K. WHITAKER, Professor of English at Stanford University, California, is the author of *Shakespeare's Use of Learning* (1953) and *The Mirror up to Nature* (1965).

J. DOVER WILSON, formerly Professor of Rhetoric and English Literature at Edinburgh, edited the New Cambridge Shakespeare and is the author of *What Happens in Hamlet* (3rd edition, 1951), *The Fortunes of Falstaff* (1944) and much else of the first importance on Shakespeare.

INDEX

Characters in the play are distinguished from their historical counterparts, who are indexed separately, by being printed in capital letters.